Literature, Money and the Market

Literature, Money and the Market

From Trollope to Amis

Paul Delany
Professor of English
Simon Fraser University
British Columbia

palgrave

First published 2002 by
PALGRAVE
Houndmills, Basingstoke, Hampshire RG21 6XS and
175 Fifth Avenue, New York, N. Y. 10010
Companies and representatives throughout the world

PALGRAVE is the new global academic imprint of
St. Martin's Press LLC Scholarly and Reference Division and
Palgrave Publishers Ltd (formerly Macmillan Press Ltd).

ISBN 0–333–97135–3

This book is printed on paper suitable for recycling and made from fully managed and sustained forest sources.

A catalogue record for this book is available from the British Library.

Library of Congress Cataloging-in-Publication Data
Delany, Paul.
    Literature. money, and the market: from Trollope to Amis / Paul Delany
        p. cm.
    Includes bibliographical references (p.) and index.
    ISBN 0–333–97135–3 (cloth)
        1. English fiction—20th century—History and criticism. 2. Money in literature. 3. Economics and literature—Great Britain—History--20th century. 4. Economics and literature—Great Britain—History--19th century. 5. Literature publishing—Great Britain—History--20th century. 6. Literature publishing—Great Britain—History--19th century. 7. English fiction—19th century—History and criticism. 8. Authorship—Marketing—Great Britain—History. 9. Authorship—Economic aspects—Great Britain. I. Title.

PR888.M65 D45 2002
823'.809355—dc21
                                                    2001050807

10   9   8   7   6   5   4   3   2   1
11   10   09   08   07   06   05   04   03   02

Printed and bound in Great Britain by
Antony Rowe Ltd, Chippenham, Wiltshire

Contents

1
Introduction:
The Peculiarities of the English

Dear Cleinias, the class of men is small...who, when
compelled by wants and desires of every sort, are able to
hold out and observe moderation, and when they might
make a great deal of money are sober in their wishes, and
prefer a moderate to a large gain. But the mass of
mankind are the very opposite: their desires are
unbounded, and when they might gain in moderation they
prefer gains without limit; wherefore all that relates to
retail trade and merchandise, and keeping of taverns, is
denounced and numbered among dishonorable things.
—Plato, *The Laws*

Economic Criticism Today

In *The Passions and the Interests* Albert Hirschman has traced the development, from the seventeenth century onwards, of a radically new idea:
that the best policy for a country should be to give "free rein and encour-
agement to private acquisitive pursuits."[1] We can call this belief
economism: the idea that economic motives should come first for individuals and governments since, as Adam Smith puts it, "An augmentation of
fortune is the means by which the greater part of men propose and wish
to better their condition."[2] Yet even Smith, the great founder of
economism as an ideology, goes on to say that such self-improvement is
"the most vulgar and the most obvious" of human ambitions. A major
theme of this book will be the persistence, in the most varied forms, of
Plato's originary contempt for commerce and the vulgar and obvious desires people have to enrich themselves. In particular, this contempt is
still pervasive among literary scholars, regardless of the global hegemony
of capitalism since the collapse of its communist alternative in 1989. In
the course of a sweeping attack on neo-liberal economics and the "Anglo-Saxon model" of capitalism, Pierre Bourdieu writes: "To this we may
now add the destruction of the economic and social foundations of humanity's rarest cultural achievements. The autonomy enjoyed by the
universes of cultural production in relation to the market, which has

increased continuously through the struggles of writers, artists and scientists, is under increasing threat. The dominion of 'commerce' and 'the commercial' increases daily over literature."[3]

Should literature and its affiliated critical institutions be centers of resistance to the market? Can they be? In addressing these questions, I will be looking both at the representation of economic interests in English literature since 1875 and at the economics of authorship. When Anthony Trollope wrote that "Buying and selling...cannot be the noblest work of man," he expressed an entirely orthodox English disdain for "trade," and support for the "prestige values" of the aristocracy and its allies.[4] Before the nineteenth century, the critique of commercial society was largely articulated from the right, in the "blood and soil" values of the landowning nobility. Beginning with Plato's admiration for Sparta as a foil to mercantile, cosmopolitan and relativist Athens, this theme is persistent in Western culture and is mirrored, to the East, in the exclusion of Japanese merchants from political power by the Samurai. The liberalism of Adam Smith and Richard Cobden (built on Lockean foundations) provided the first systematic vindication of economism and of commercial interests. Radicals (as they were then also called) denounced the regime of aristocratic "old corruption," and looked to the market as the best solvent of the absolutist pretensions of a state controlled by the landowning class.

When Marx challenged that liberalism, his critique was curiously divided between nostalgic and modernizing impulses. One voice in *The Communist Manifesto* denounced the destructiveness of bourgeois economism, and lamented the relative humaneness of the traditional "face-to-face" societies threatened by the market system.[5] The other voice proposed Marxism-as-science: that only a vanguard party of the proletariat could fully mobilize the potential of modern forces of production. The two voices were to be harmonized in a classless utopia that would crown the transitional phase of revolution; but in many ways they remained divided between the actual economist Marxism of the Eastern bloc, after 1917, and the ideal humanist Marxism of western intellectuals.[6]

Adam Smith's gospel of efficiency, and the Soviet Marxism of steel mills and electrification, share common ground as forms of economic universalism, where the impersonal laws of productivity steadily destroy the feudal particularities of the old order. Both systems, confined within a rigorously economist calculus of human motives, leave little room for the autonomy of cultural pursuits. This is one reason why even leftist literary scholars have tended, in recent years, to move from economic to cultural concerns, such as ethnicity, gender, and Foucauldian domination rather than Marxist exploitation. The shift is also from economic universalism to cultural particularism; in Jonathan Dewald's formulation, from Adam Smith to Max Weber:

> For Smith, the cultural and psychological costs of market behavior are feeble; experience of the market is mainly liberating, closely associated with release from age-old experiences of violence and inequality. Weber stresses instead the psychological shock of the market's arrival and the range of mental habits that had to be changed to accommodate it.[7]

Weber's particularist cultures or bureaucracies have non-economic hierarchies, and are oriented towards stability; Smith's universalist economies are structured only by individual drives to maximize utility and are oriented towards development. In today's humanities faculties the prevailing ethos is Weberian: hostile to capitalism, the market and globalization, sympathetic to the politics of recognition and identity, and to ways of life that are threatened by the market.

Yet it is worth recalling that for Smith, recognition and identity are among the market's great benefits. In the market, our innate disposition to *persuade* is harnessed to the cause of individual and collective prosperity:

> The offering of a shilling, which to us appears to have so plain and simple a meaning, is in reality offering an argument to persuade one to do so and so as it is for his interest. Men always endeavour to persuade others to be of their opinion even when the matter is of no consequence to them. If one advances anything concerning China or the more distant moon which contradicts what you imagine to be true, you immediately try to persuade him to alter his opinion. And in this manner everyone is practising oratory on others thro the whole of his life. You are uneasy whenever one differs from you, and you endeavour to persuade him of your mind; or if you do not it is a certain degree of self command, and to this everyone is breeding thro their whole lives.[8]

In a market exchange, each party hopes to increase their welfare; but to realize that gain each must appeal to the interest of the other. The alternatives are begging – which Smith dislikes because it is "servile and fawning" – or just taking what you want, because the other party cannot refuse.[9] For Smith, this last way of satisfying one's needs is a common, but dangerous vice: "The love of domination and authority over others . . . I am afraid is naturall to mankind, a certain desire of having others below one."[10] It goes without saying that Smith associates love of domination with aristocratic regimes, whereas commercial society is founded on the more genial principle of persuasion. In a market transaction, persuasion achieves mutual satisfaction with the bargain struck. But there is more to the exchange than just shared advantage: each party affirms the other's autonomy and dignity. As Thomas Lewis puts it, "Successful persuasion generates recognition and approval by others."[11] In aristocratic dealings, conversely, only the stronger party enjoys recognition: the one in a position to satisfy "that tyrannic disposition which may almost be said to be natural to mankind."[12]

Smith's views on markets and human nature will inform much of the discussion in the first part of this book. British society in the time of Trollope was divided between an aristocratic sector based on domination and a commercial sector whose guiding principle was free exchange between social (if not economic) equals. At the level of psychology, these opposing principles lead to a division of motives between the passions and the interests. Much of my dissatisfaction with the Foucauldian model (which is taken for granted in so much contemporary criticism) is that it recognizes only domination as the glue holding societies together. This may reflect the wider and more intrusive power of the state in modern France, compared to the Anglo-Saxon countries. But whatever its source, the premise of domination seems particularly inadequate when applied to the literary marketplace, where authors understand themselves as having to *persuade* publishers and readers to accept their works.

Much of the economic literary criticism in today's academy takes its stand, paradoxically, in opposition to economism, whether of the right (neo-liberalism) or the left (determinist Marxism). It first began to move beyond Marxism with structuralist critics, notably Marc Shell and Jean-Joseph Goux, who focused on the analogy between the linguistic and the monetary systems as the two great determinants of social values. For each system, they noted the progression from a validation by *correspondence* (between word and object, between value and a precious substance), to validation by *relations* within a self-determining system. This analogy between language and money can be a fruitful one, especially for such early modernists as Mallarmé and Gide, but it threatens to reduce economic activity to an ephemeral circulation of signifiers, subordinated to a totalizing symbolic system – economics as a special case of the linguistic model.[13]

The eclipse of structuralism, with its grand theories of representation, led to a more situated and particularist approach to cultural phenomena that came to be known as "new historicism" in North America and "cultural materialism" in Britain.[14] The main stream of economic criticism since, say, Kurt Heinzelman's *The Economics of the Imagination*, has been broadly new historicist in tendency.[15] Brilliant and challenging as much of this work is, I need both to acknowledge my debt to it and register my disagreement with several of its foundational beliefs. New historicism arose from those of the generation of 1968 who became academics wanting to preserve their oppositional stance, but also to move beyond the economic determinism of traditional Marxism. Instead of the old base/superstructure model, we now find, for example, Stephen Greenblatt's claim that "Society's dominant currencies, money and prestige, are invariably involved."[16] Aram Veeser defines the critic's role as "to dismantle the dichotomy of the economic and the non-economic, to show that the most purportedly disinterested and self-sacrificing practices, including art, aim to maximize material or symbolic profit."[17] Dettmar and Watt, for example, argue that modernist cultural productions "reveal their inevitable incorporation within an exchange system to which many modernists were staunchly opposed."[18] The final, and most controversial move of the new historicists is then to extend the concept of "involvement" to an inescapable complicity between their own work as critics and the cultural practices that they take as their objects. In Veeser's words: "a critical method and a language adequate to describe culture under capitalism participate in the object they describe."[19]

Here one might deploy the *ad hominem* argument that new historicist critics both oppose capitalism and succumb to its academic manifestations, in the form of the star system and the translation of intellectual prestige into economic reward.[20] More important, though, is the danger that new historicism, by harping on its tropes of "complicity" and "commodification" might be caught up in an ultimately sterile re-tracing of the endless circulation of power through culture. Catherine Gallagher, for example, speaks of:

> The new historicist's tendency to identify precisely the things in texts that had been named subversive, destabilizing, and self-distantiating, as inscriptions of the formative moments, not the disruptions, of the liberal subject . . . . Such a representation seems in itself quietistic to some critics because it apparently presents culture as achieving, through its very fracturing, an inescapable totalizing control.[21]

Gallagher's invocation of "totalizing control" points to the predominant influence of Foucault on new historicism, which Richard Terdiman places within "a whole tradition of historically-sensitive reflection on language, ideology, and power."[22] My misgivings about this tradition include its *lack* of sensitivity to the historical specificity of English cultural economics. England and France have such fundamental differences in, for example, revolutionary traditions, cultural institutions, and the role of the state, as to make it implausible that the Foucauldian model could have equal explanatory power on both sides of the Channel. I am concerned, also, with Veeser's proposed dismantling of "the dichotomy of the economic and the non-economic." The existence of complicities between prestige and market sectors does not make them merely interchangeable. In England one formation emerged centuries before the other; from the seventeenth century on, their distinctiveness was marked by an immensely complex mixture of interaction and opposition between aristocratic and commercial interests. The dichotomy between these two systems of value should not just be dissolved into a totalizing system of social control; individuals are conscious of playing a double hand, as they manoeuvre for position in the hierarchies of status and class.[23]

A criticism that takes as its starting-point the saturation of the social field with "language, ideology, and power" will not be wrong – how could it be, in those terms? – but can easily be caught in a monologism that overlooks the particularities of individual authorial projects, or national literary institutions. Sean Burke has mounted, against Foucault's "What is an Author?" and kindred texts, a rousing defense of authorial subjectivity as an indispensable given of literary criticism.[24] One of my aims in this book is to extend Burke's critique by focusing on the author as one whose drive for *economic* self-assertion has to engage with the external constraints of the literary marketplace. That is, the Foucauldian model of literary culture as a dominating and relatively impersonal discursive field devalues not only the ontological subjectivity of authors, but also their economic subjectivity as it engages with the systems of literary production. Gissing's *New Grub Street*, for example, recognizes the blind forces of market and genre, but also shows the impact of these forces on the aspirations of individual authors.

A third kind of current economic criticism suffers from its lack of dialogue with the new historicism prevailing in literary studies. This criticism approaches culture from a base within the academic discipline of economics; much of it has been associated with *The Journal of Cultural Economics*. Typically adopting a neo-liberal economic stance, it addresses such topics as the costs and benefits of cultural activities, the effectiveness of state intervention in the arts, and the workings of the cultural marketplace.[25] Tyler Cowen's *In Praise of Commercial Culture* accuses literary critics of chronic cultural pessimism and unreasoned dislike of market forces; it argues strenuously for the ability of the market to foster both popular culture and other, more refined interests. Cowen claims, for example, that Florentine art flourished in the Renaissance because Florence had a more commercial and artisanal culture than other Italian city-states.

Though I share the cultural economists' respect for neo-classical economic principles, I am less inclined to find in the extension of modern markets grounds for cultural optimism. Even the most vigorous supporters of Thatcherism would concede, surely, that England's cultural products from 1979 to 1997 were not specially glorious or distinctive; nor is there likely to be any fundamental change under New Labour. The most prominent changes in English cultural life of the past decade have been driven by funding from the National Lottery: in effect, a great revival of state patronage. As I discuss in Chapter 11 below, this kind of funding works much better at cultural reproduction than in stimulating new creative work. The more general point is that art is not produced by design; as Whistler said, "Art Happens." Many of the supreme modes of cultural expression – religious painting and architecture, grand opera, epic poetry – flourished under regimes of feudalism, patronage or private inheritance, and withered when exposed to pure market forces. The market is both a theoretically efficient formal system, and a social institution embedded in particular historical circumstances; that is, there are many different markets. In seventeenth-century Amsterdam, anyone with money could order a Rembrandt. One reason why not even Bill Gates can order one now is that it's not just a question of buying a painter's services, but of buying what made Rembrandt: the whole culture of seventeenth-century Amsterdam. Since 1989, the "market model" has become the only credible economic strategy, as it rapidly extends and consolidates itself under the rubric of globalization. But there is no necessary connection between a general increase in living standards – which market societies have delivered – and the arrival of a new golden age of art or literature.[26] Rather, as I argue in my chapter on "The New Literary Marketplace," ever-increasing *segmentation* in the market makes individual genres – otherwise known as "market niches" – more distinct and dispersed, while undermining the kind of unitary cultural authorities that made possible the masterpieces of earlier traditional societies.

Even a grudging respect for the operations of the market is unacceptable to many literary intellectuals, who still resist the imperatives of the post-1989 world economic order. François Furet's *The Passing of an Illusion* writes a magisterial epitaph for communism, yet also denounces commercial society in essentially Platonic terms:

Rather than make an inventory of this hodgepodge of dead ideas [i.e. communism], we should take as our starting-point the passions that fuelled it. Of all those passions – spawned by modern democracy and bent on destroying the hand that fed them – the oldest, the most constant, the most powerful is hatred of the bourgeoisie.... Bourgeois society is thus animated by a corpuscular agitation, constantly driving it forward. Yet this agitation tends to deepen the contradictions inherent in that society's very existence; for not only does the bourgeoisie consist of associates who care little for the public interest, but the idea of the universality and equality of man, which it claims as its foundation and is its primary innovation, is constantly negated by the inequality of property and wealth produced by the competition of its members.[27]

To this one might respond that the bourgeoisie is the only class that is critical of itself, so that bourgeois intellectuals have devoted vast amounts of political and cultural energy to repudiating their origins, and attempting to pull down Adam Smith's *homo economicus* from his throne. Even Furet, at the end of his dismal chronicle of communism's follies and crimes, reaffirms that same project: "Democracy, by virtue of its existence, creates the need for a world beyond the bourgeoisie and beyond Capital, a world in which a genuine human community can flourish."[28]

Despite Furet's testament, I want in this book to give commercial culture its due, and to respect the Cobdenite agenda that so closely anticipated the globalism of today. Against the messianic or destructive projects of both the right and the left, J.M. Keynes' apologia for liberalism, tepid as it is, may still be a salutary rejoinder:

The advantage to efficiency of the decentralization of decisions and of individual responsibility is even greater, perhaps, than the nineteenth century supposed; and the reaction against the appeal to self-interest may have gone too far. But, above all, individualism, if it can be purged of its defects and its abuses, is the best safeguard of the variety of life, which emerges precisely from this extended field of personal choice, and the loss of which is the greatest of all the losses of the homogeneous or totalitarian state.[29]

English Cultural Economics

English economic liberalism has always co-existed with the "feudal remnants" (Marx's phrase) of the prestige order, such as the monarchy, the House of Lords, the public schools, Oxbridge, the Church of England, shabby gentility, and the concentration of landownership in a few hands. These are what E.P. Thompson called "the peculiarities of the English," reliable and persistent features of the English economic and literary cultures.[30] Until at least the third Reform Bill of 1884, political power in England was still the prerogative of the landed aristocracy and gentry. They upheld prestige values based on hierarchy rather than wealth, and were disdainful of those engaged in "trade." This was why Cobden called England an aristocratic country, America a commercial one. Really, though, England was both aristocratic *and* commercial. The rise of the City of London in the later seventeenth century made commerce a power in the land, yet without any sweeping demotion of the older feudal and aristocratic powers; a prestige order and a monetary order co-existed in an uneasy mixture of rivalry and mutual dependence. Aristocrats needed means to uphold their status, and merchants aspired to gain recognition from the aristocracy by imitating their manners and by acquiring prestige goods (above all, a country estate).

The Englishness of English society rests on this dialectic between prestige and market values, caste and class. The United States lacks England's parallel hierarchy of gentility, that creates such complex contradictions between, say, the shabby genteel and the *nouveau-riche*. As Lord Beaverbrook put it, "in the new world, unlike the old, the only difference between the rich and the poor is that the rich have more money."[31] Everyone in England has traditionally held two kinds of rank, and they may be completely disparate for characters like Mrs Bates (the Vicar's impoverished widow in *Emma*) or Sir Roger Scatcherd (the plebeian railway contractor in Trollope's *Dr Thorne*). Innumerable English novels have explored the rival claims of brute financial power on the one side, traditional or genteel morality on the other. Yet the two value systems are closely intertwined, even when they come into opposition in such novels as *Clarissa, North and South,* or *The Way We Live Now.* Melmotte's crime in *The Way We Live Now* is to try to buy social prestige, something that should never be simply "for sale." Walter Michaels, discussing Hawthorne's differentiation between American and European society, observes that "The capitalist who loses everything loses everything, whereas the nobleman, losing everything material, retains his nobility, which has a 'spiritual existence.'"[32] When Melmotte loses his money he kills himself, because money is the only identity he has.

The English prestige culture is like a Mandelbrot set where homologies replicate themselves at every level of detail. Values are not generated by labor, but accumulate through sheer length of tenure: status comes from a classical education at an ancient university, living in a period house, drinking old wine, hanging game, possessing an old family name with land attached to it, appreciating the patination of antique furniture and the slow growth of timber on an estate. Aristocrats and rentiers (those who have withdrawn from business and live off their capital) both assume that things need only to persist in order to improve, to be refined, and to become desirable. Their consumption and display of such properly seasoned goods establishes their claim to caste superiority. New things may be more functional, but are viewed with suspicion because anyone with money can acquire them. The entire domain of English high culture can be seen as a patination that is gradually laid down on the surface of possessions. Huge amounts of new wealth were generated in the Victorian era, and it was hugely concentrated, but the wealthy in England could not be blatant plutocrats, as in the American Gilded Age; they wanted to disguise, or to adorn, the massive workings of the accumulative process.[33] Culture presented itself as a way of refining, spiritualizing, even transcending the economic base of society; yet culture also became steadily more implicated with money power, and drawn more comprehensively into the marketplace.

The culture of the English upper class could be reduced to a single economic determinism: the receipt of unearned income from land or other accumulated capital. But in the circles where prestige goods are enjoyed, they are also mystified as being "priceless" and thus unavailable to just crude purchasing power. Money is the ticket to a world where the show of money is vulgar and it is other things that "really matter"; to put it another way, money alone is not enough, it must be "old money" that is in some way connected to land. Trollope's Duke of Omnium (in the Palliser novels), George Gissing's "Henry Ryecroft," and Mr Wemmick in *Great Expectations* largely agree on the desirable way of life, even though they live that life on very different scales. Ryecroft's country retreat, where he lives with one servant and reads the classics, is a smaller copy of the Duke's life in his stately mansion; Wemmick's villa in Walworth, with its moat and battlements, is smaller yet – "the smallest house I ever saw" says Pip – but still a faithful model of a real castle.[34]

The replication of prestige culture values throughout the social hierarchy also works to disrupt historical narratives that put the Industrial Revolution at the center of English development. From the late seventeenth century, England made itself a distinctive niche in the world economy, as the City of London had an astonishing burst of financial creativity. The developments of around 1690 included deposit banking, banknotes, a central bank, insurance, double entry book-keeping, government debt management, and the stock exchange. Many of these had already existed in other places, such as Amsterdam, Genoa or Venice; but it was in London that they were combined into an interlocking structure, and placed at the center of a new system of colonial trade extending around the globe.

London remained a more complex city than Amsterdam, its great rival (until the Napoleonic Wars) as a mercantile center and source of finance for international trade. Adam Smith observed that Dutch society had a unitary basis, rather than a dual one as in Britain. "The republican form of government seems to be the principal support of the present grandeur of Holland," he wrote, "The owners of great capitals, the great mercantile families, have generally either some direct share, or some indirect influence, in the administration of that government."[35] Smith saw Amsterdam as a "trading city," the opposite of "court cities" like Paris, Madrid, or Vienna. But London was home both to trade *and* the court. In England, the owners of great capitals and the owners of great lands shared power; they may have been rivals, but they were not distinct and hostile castes. Part of the aristocracy, the "landed interest," remained faithful to the old organic order; but part, the "moneyed interest," became alert to new economic opportunities. Among the Whig magnates, great capital and great lands might easily be found in the same family. From the seventeenth century onwards, such families formed alliances in the City, lived several months of the year in London, and invested much of their agricultural profits in trade, industry, and finance.

England's Industrial Revolution, a century or more later than the financial revolution, now seems like a less sweeping and more uncertain social transformation. It was an article of faith for Marxist historians that industrial capitalists had installed themselves as a ruling class by the middle of the nineteenth century, and that the central contradiction in English society then opposed this class to the organized proletariat. The prestige order was dismissed as a jumble of picturesque relics, that did not even need to be swept away because there was no real power behind them. Alternatively, the "declinist" historians argued that England was a special case amongst advanced countries because of its inability to throw off its feudal remnants and become economically efficient.[36] Germany, the United States and Japan, when their time came to industrialize, did so in a much clearer field than England. Their ruling classes were more ready to accept the imperatives of industrial development, so that banks became eager partners in industrial projects, educational systems were adapted to provide technological leadership, and captains of industry claimed the heights of social prestige and political power. In England it was not so. The established culture looked down on the factory owner or businessman; the landed elite retained control of Parliament (as late as 1867, they held over 500 of the 658 seats); and the City went its own way, with little sense of responsibility for England's industrial future.

My own perspective here is neither Marxist (industrial capitalists took control of the state) nor declinist (England failed industrially and technologically in the twentieth century). England is simply *different* from Germany, France, the U.S., Japan. In England, the aristocracy and the City co-operated to limit the social pretensions of the industrialists, and to maintain their hold both on the machinery of state and on cultural institutions. Geoffrey Ingham has argued convincingly that England has two rival centers of capitalism, the industrial and the financial, but financial capital has never lost its pre-eminence.[37]

Martin Wiener posited a decline in England's "industrial spirit," in the face of the challenge from newly-industrialized rivals.[38] The English imagination retreated to the cathedral close and the village green, reluctant to modernize its factories or embrace technical education. However, the "Wiener thesis" is a fable of national decline that neglects the success and the autonomy of English finance capitalism. Against Wiener and other declinists, I would argue that the financial sector represents the highest and indeed the hegemonic form of English capitalism. The grand narrative of English economic development since the early modern period might then be re-written in terms of a continuous movement, at all levels of the economy, towards a commercial rather than a material economy, and symbolic rather than "real" exchanges. Agricultural societies produce material commodities, industrial societies process them, and tertiary societies process *representations* of commodities. Since World War II, this drift has been evident in the rise of knowledge industries and the role played by dematerializing technologies in computers, the media, and telecommunications. A much longer monetary evolution is now being consummated in entirely abstract or virtual forms like lines of credit, futures, derivatives or electronic funds transfer. The financial culture is thus severed from any material base, yet functions more powerfully and pervasively than ever: not as ancillary to production, but as a system of representation that is productive in its own right.

England's leadership in tertiary or symbolic activities, deriving from the financial revolution of the 1690s, can be seen as carrying over into its achievements in literary and theatrical representation. For the nineteenth century John Vernon, in *Money and Fiction*, has already made the analogy between banks and novels as great repositories of social values and images.[39] The density and specificity of English culture derives from the economic exceptionalism of its financially-oriented capitalism. England had a long tradition of mobile personal capital, and was unwilling to reform its educational system or to displace its prestige-culture hierarchies. It opted for a strategy of external development, directing most of its surplus capital into overseas portfolio investment. The City channeled old wealth into foreign ventures, while inflicting a relative backwardness on domestic industry; and the return flow of income on those investments supported a growing rentier class with its own distinctive culture. England thus became a rentier country where, at the peak before World War I, nine percent of national income was being invested abroad, and Britain held forty-one percent of all international debt.[40] In the same period, it also became the first consumer society, where consciousness was more determined by mass consumption than by a relatively occluded process of production.[41] It may also be true that English industry was handicapped by imperial ambitions that were economically irrational; in two later chapters on Conrad I discuss the conflict between prestige and market values in the imperial sphere. But at the center of England's strategic choices was the pre-eminence of the City as a financial power, first domestically and then globally after the decline of Amsterdam from the end of the eighteenth century.

The Writer in the Marketplace

Since at least the sixteenth century, English literature – especially drama and the novel – has been shaped by market forces. Writers had to be interested in money, both as a force in society and as the reward for their enterprises, no matter how strict a line the genteel tradition tried to draw between literature and "trade." Respect for this line has persisted in literary studies, in the distinction between the novel as a picture of social life, and as a commodity that is produced for sale. Studies of authorship as a profession, and of the literary marketplace in general, have not been well integrated with criticism of what is inside the covers of the books that are bought and sold – except for the inadequate idea that books simply reflect class interests. A focus on money brings together both sides of the literary transaction: what authors hope to get by writing books, and what they hope to show about the market society in which they live.[42]

The paradox of marketing books is that each one has value by virtue of being unique and yet, as a consumer product, it can be measured on a common monetary scale. Money reduces even the most complex artifacts to the crude question: "how much is it worth?"; but this power of abstraction does not simplify the critic's task. A monetary theory of literature must consider how books are priced, in the sense of providing income to authors and articles of consumption to readers. The literary marketplace, as mediated by publishers and reviewers, probably has more influence on the evolution of culture than writers and critics are willing to credit. But we have to look beyond the production and sale of literature as a market commodity. Literature is the most complete and complex record of a society's system of values: not just the money prices of articles of commerce, but also the subtle social valuations that shape market supply and demand. "The market" (like natural selection, its Darwinian equivalent) can indeed be applied to everything people do: the marriage-market, the marketplace of ideas, and so on. But each market has its particular ecology; in England, local circumstances created a special relationship between literature and money which this book seeks to explain.

Since English literature has been largely hostile to commerce and industry, it might be taken for a nostalgic enterprise that resists all aspects of modernity. Yet authorship, printing and publishing, considered as economic enterprises, are not examples of backwardness. The financial revolution of the 1690s was based on sophisticated modes (for their time) of information and communication: coffeehouses, newspapers, networks of correspondence. This was the beginning of those tertiary information industries in which England took a lead that it has never lost. The ideological content of English literature, largely expressing a nostalgic organicism, is in contrast with its place in the global vanguard as a "cultural industry." The paradox is not really so unusual: we could point to the international success of English television programs that trade on an imaginary idyllic past, or Hollywood's rise to pre-eminence through the Western, which romanticized a vanishing America. However, critics should perhaps be more alert to the long-standing *construction* of nostalgia in English literature – that is, to question its authenticity as utterance by bringing into play its status as a marketable product.

In recent years, the search for a vital organicism has shifted its focus from historical myths to feminism, "queer" sexuality, identity politics, or similar domains. Fredric Jameson has argued that every stratum of high culture, every kind of content or traditional genre is now so deeply "commodified" that redemption must come from the margins of artistic production that are not yet corrupted by the market:

> The only authentic cultural production today has seemed to be that which can draw on the collective experience of marginal pockets of the social life of the world system: black literature and blues, British working-class rock, women's literature, gay literature, the *roman québecois*, the literature of the Third World; and this production is

possible only to the degree to which these forms of collective solidarity have not yet been fully penetrated by the market and by the commodity system.[43]

One could make the debating point that these "authentic cultural products" all come to our attention through the marketing channels of global media; and one could ask Jameson for the exact date when culture was vitiated by the market (what were Shakespeare and Rembrandt producing for?). But the real problem with Jameson's argument is that one cannot usefully read the past two centuries of English literature, or understand its present condition, by invoking the touchstone of a virtuously primitive or pre-commercial margin.

Literary critics have a history of sympathy for the organicist hostility to commerce – the fantasy expressed in the Schlegels' frolicking in their hay-field at the conclusion of Forster's *Howards End*. The pastoral and rentier fringe of the prestige culture necessarily had its material base (as Margaret Schlegel, to her credit, recognized), and this must have its presence both in English fiction and in the concerns of those who produced it. Yet it has always, it seems, been a veiled and devalued presence; so that England could never have a purely bourgeois culture like that of seventeenth-century Holland, and Cobden was disappointed of his hopes that English merchants and manufacturers should have "more *mind* [and] become the De Medicis, and Fuggers, and De Witts of England, instead of glorying in being the toadies of a cloddish aristocracy, only less enlightened than themselves."[44] Arnold's view of the businessman as philistine by definition became the received idea: the market as the enemy of culture, rather than the maker of it. Yet money takes its sinuous path all through that culture: from Yeats's "greasy till" to the private incomes of authors and the sanctified endowments of the established church and the ancient universities, and from the writer's haunted study to the bloody crossroads of the literary marketplace.

Part One considers the representation of monetary motives in English fiction, mainly by Trollope, Gissing, James and Conrad. These authors, like many others, cherished the prestige order, and feared its disruption by "market forces." Such emotions were typical of the status groups with which authors identified. Yet their alignment also made them specially attentive to the economization of culture, and the rise of a consumer society where money could literally purchase identity. Part Two looks at writers from the other side of the counter: as producers whose livelihood depended on the market reception of their goods. I make this the second part of my study in order to avoid any determinism of the literary work by the conditions of its production: rather how writers were able to live was largely determined by the reception of their works.[45] Although success may have been unpredictable for the individual, literary production and distribution was a system governed by economic laws, and included within the broader evolution of Western economies. Rail as they might against the market, authors belonged to it; and their natures were subdued to what they worked in.

Part One
Representing Money

2
Who's Who: Land, Money and Identity in Trollope

I hold the paper money men say truly, when they say
They ought to pay their promises, with promises to pay;
And he is an unrighteous judge, who says they shall or may,
Be made to keep their promises in any other way
　　　　　—T.L. Peacock, "A Mood Of My Own Mind"

The Landed and the Monied Interests

The Way We Live Now begins with an impoverished aristocrat, Lady Carbury, having to go into the literary marketplace to restore her fortunes. But she seeks more than fortune in becoming an author; she hopes also for what Trollope calls, in his *Autobiography*, "the charms of reputation." "Over and above the money view of the question," Trollope writes, "I wished from the beginning to be something more than a clerk in the Post Office. To be known as somebody, – to be Anthony Trollope if it be no more, – is to me much."[1]

Trollope goes on to say that money, rather than reputation, was still his "first object" in becoming a writer: "I wished to make an income on which I and those belonging to me might live in comfort."[2] As one reads his *Autobiography*, it becomes clear that his literary success can hardly be separated from his ability to earn an average of £2,000 a year from his work. In that sense, identity and reputation are products of the market: who you are is determined by what you have offered for sale, and how the market has valued it. Yet *The Way We Live Now* is an elegiac novel, a lament for the passing away of the old prestige order where identity depends on one's rank, lineage, and connection with the land. The market, and especially the financial system that is its purest expression, is a house built on paper; how, Trollope asks, can a nation and a community stand on such insubstantial footings? Only the landowning classes, he needs to believe, have the stability and continuity of tenure to provide a moral center for the English way of life. Yet the greatness of *The Way We Live Now* (and of the novels that followed it, like *The Prime Minister* and *The Duke's Children*) lies in its recognition of the profound contradictions within the aristocratic myth.

One of these contradictions arises from the conflict between the anthropological and the economic status of the aristocracy. Victorian Britain may be viewed as a culture, whose health depends on the proper performance of rituals by its ruling caste. A traditional rural society provides recognition and sense of belonging; even the subordinated classes value stability and look to their traditional leaders to provide it. The great country house is its secular temple, with a time-honored cycle of hunting and hospitality. But if one shifts to an economic perspective, aristocrats appear as a largely parasitic class who scorn economic rationality, defend privilege, and exclude those who have gained fortunes through their own efforts.

A century and a half before *The Way We Live Now*, Swift had argued that "the possessors of the soil are the best judges of what is for the advantage of the kingdom."[3] Trollope still had a deep loyalty to this metaphor of England as a garden or estate, to be looked after by the great landowners. In his novels, those happy few who own land do enjoy a kind of immortality. The continuity of landed property is the foundation of his "myth of the land," which sets out his ideal for the condition of England. This myth has three elements – identity, trusteeship, and duty – that bind together the fate of the individual landowner with that of the commonwealth.[4]

Identity proposes that people are most real and knowable through a name marking their ancestral possession of a tract of land. Landowners therefore deserve to be the very soul or essence of the English nation; their opposites are the Jews, a people without land, country, or stability of name. Yet those who hold land are also held by it, since the principle of trusteeship reduces their identities to mere links in a mystical and eternal chain. In *The Way We Live Now*, Trollope tells us that Roger Carbury "did not presume himself to have more than a life interest in the estate. It was his duty to see that it went from Carbury to Carbury as long as there was a Carbury to hold it, and especially his duty to see that it should go from his hands, at his death, unimpaired in extent or value."[5] The legal expression of this continuity of tenure is entailment which, in binding one generation to the next, limits the rights of both. Although he is on bad terms with his father, Lord Chiltern (in *Phineas Finn*) is secure in the knowledge that his father "can't leave an acre away from [him]."[6] In turn, Chiltern will not be able to escape obligation to his own heir. Another rich landowner, Mr Scarborough, chafes against the bondage (as he sees it) of entailment. "If a man has a property," he complains to Harry Annesley, "he should be able to leave it as he pleases; or, – or else he doesn't have it." "That is what the law intends, I suppose," replies Harry; he means that the owner doesn't "have" his property except as a link in an eternal chain of familial, rather than personal, ownership.[7]

Duty, finally, requires the owner to hold the land in a way that preserves the interlocking customs and values of country life. In the great foxhunting dispute between Lord Chiltern and his neighbor, the Duke of Omnium, the latter has allowed his steward to trap young foxes in one of his woods. "A man's property is his own in one sense," argues Lord Chiltern, "but isn't his own in another. A man can't do what he likes with his coverts. . . . If he's in a hunting county he is bound to preserve foxes."[8] The landowning individual must subordinate himself to the institution he personifies, and to the nation that it is his hereditary mission to rule.

In principle, then, landowners put the collective good before their self-interest; and Trollope admired them for this, though not blindly. In 1873, just before he began writing *The Way We Live Now*, the "new Domesday" survey revealed that a tiny group of fewer than seven thousand aristocracy and gentry held eighty percent of all English land.[9] The myth of a nation of yeomen, sturdily independent on their freehold plots, had to yield to the reality of a nation of tenants, holding their land at the pleasure of a handful of magnates. Trollope presents this traditional class of guardians, ranging from Roger Carbury to the immensely rich Plantagenet Palliser, Prime Minister and Duke of Omnium, as archaic and largely ineffectual types. Palliser fritters away his Prime Ministerial mandate by carrying his rigid code of personal honor into the opportunistic world of politics. Neither Palliser nor Carbury has any sense of enterprise: Palliser uses his surplus rents to buy more land, Carbury just tries to keep his estate intact. Trollope saw that the myth of the land was being threatened not just by the dynamism of commerce, but also by the internal weakness of the landed classes. The passing of this myth becomes the predominant social and moral concern of his later novels.

If estates are to remain perpetually intact and in the same hands, land is the supreme social value yet outside the market. The proper way to transfer land is by marriage settlement or inheritance, not by sale.[10] To make land available to anyone with ready cash would debase it into a mere article of commerce, and would undermine the claim of the landed aristocracy to be a hereditary and continuous ruling caste. In practice, however, landed proprietors became closely involved, after the Restoration, with the emergent financial economy of the City of London. Those who sought opportunity in the City or in industrial ventures became known as the "Monied Interest," as opposed to the "Landed Interest" who lived only on agricultural rent and spent most of the year on their estates.[11] In the later Victorian period, landowners still commanded majorities in both the Lords and the Commons; but those who were *only* landowners were in relative decline.[12] The Secret Ballot Act of 1872 (which Trollope opposed) made it more difficult for landlords to influence their tenants' votes.[13] Trollope's discontent in *The Way We Live Now* reflects his sense that Land is everywhere yielding to Money.

The estates held by the traditional gentry, like Roger Carbury or Sir Alured Wharton in *The Prime Minister*, are no longer either morally or economically adequate to the society that encompasses them. Sir Alured's estate, "delightful as it was in many respects . . . was hardly sufficient to maintain his position with that plentiful hospitality which he would have loved; – and other property he had none."[14] Outside of his domain, and of his imaginative grasp also, is the reality of an imperial nation whose power derives from commerce and industry more than from agriculture. The center of that nation is not the country house, but London. Rising landowners benefit from investments in finance or industry; reciprocally, successful City men are drawn to invest their profits in land and claim the accompanying political and social privilege.[15] The plot of *The Way We Live Now* is driven by Melmotte's eagerness to consolidate his position in Britain by buying an estate, which Trollope deplores. He can accept the commercial classes so long as they remain "in their place," deferring politically and socially to the landed aristocracy. What dismays him is the apparent capitulation of the aristocracy to the new men of speculative wealth, the swallowing up of the traditional values of peers and gentry by universal covetousness.

John Vernon has argued for an intimate connection between the rise of paper money and the form of the nineteenth-century novel. Each is a comprehensive symbolic system: "a fiction with its roots in the actual – but a fiction nonetheless." Novels are like banks, in being "great fictional storehouses of representation . . . in which all our desires reside." "The nineteenth century is characterized," Vernon argues, "not so much by the conquest of paper money as by the long-drawn-out transition, extending back to the previous century, from older forms of wealth to paper. Many still thought of gold as the only real money and land as the only stable and secure form of wealth. . . . The point is that *both* gold and paper were social forces in the nineteenth century."[16] Carlyle and Marx, in the 1840s, denounced the corrosive effect of the "cash-nexus" on a feudal society based on barter and personal loyalty; like Cobbett and Trollope, they extolled the disappearing *gemeinschaft* based on agricultural production, barter, and paternalism, while denouncing its replacement, a heartless and insubstantial financial capitalism. Just as true personal identity had to be based on something fixed and tangible – a continuously held parcel of land – so did true economic value require linkage to useful objects and ultimately to a sacred object, a piece of gold. To define identities and values as merely relative or differential was to cast over the whole human enterprise the specter of arbitrariness.

Yet money also stands out as a massive and material expression of human will. Nineteenth-century novelists are peculiarly obsessed with money, Vernon argues, because they find in the rise of paper money a parallel with their own project of mastering the "real" world of objects and desires. We may add that novelists, like bankers, hope to convince everyone that their tokens can be cashed out on demand – in other words, that they have endowed the conventional with all the functional attributes of the essential.[17] Trollope is specially concerned to establish his credit in this regard; both by the sober verisimilitude of his novels, and by his obsessiveness about the material process of inscribing words onto the blank page. It is as if he can make his own trade more "real" by denouncing the new wealth that is invisible, intangible and, worst of all, ontologically unreliable: shares in unbuilt railways, IOUs circulating at the Beargarden Club, claims on coffee and guano that may never arrive in port. Unable to understand the mysteries of finance, but greedy for riches, England's traditional rulers have abased themselves before those who claim to know how money breeds. In fact, Trollope insists, these promoters are made up from the same baseless appearances that are their stock in trade.

Mr Wharton of *The Prime Minister* is not himself landed gentry – he is a commercial lawyer – but he is allied to them by birth and temperament; and, like them, he has slowly accumulated wealth by spending less than his income. The plot turns on the contrast between Wharton and the speculator Ferdinand Lopez, for whom a "natural" rate of increase is not enough. Wharton rejects Ferdinand Lopez's request to marry his daughter on the grounds that "No One Knows Anything About Him." He sees Lopez as a mere adventurer, "certainly a man not standing on the solid basis of land, or of Three per Cents."[18] But Lopez explains that quick profits can only be made on that which is *not* solid:

> in such a trade as this they were following there was no need at all of real coffee and real guano, ... "If I buy a ton of coffee and keep it six weeks, why do I buy it and keep it, and why does the seller sell it instead of keeping it? The seller sells it because he thinks he can do best by parting with it now at a certain price. I buy it because I think I can make money by keeping it. It is just the same as though we were to back our opinions. He backs the fall. I back the rise. You needn't have

coffee and you needn't have guano to do this. Indeed the possession
of the coffee or the guano is only a very clumsy addition to the trouble
of your profession. I make it my study to watch the markets; – but I
needn't buy everything I see in order to make money by my labour
and intelligence."[19]

This is Lopez's "great doctrine" – which to Trollope is no more than "speculating in money without capital."[20] His trade also offends Trollope by its
dependence on invisibility, secrecy, or, at a pinch, outright lies. Lopez re-
bukes his partner Sexty Parker for wanting to "see the money" that they
have made by trading in commodities. "What's the use of money you can
see?" he protests. "How are you to make money out of money by looking
at it? I like to know that my money is fructifying."[21] Speculation, like sexual reproduction, is a mystery that should be celebrated in the dark. Augustus Melmotte, similarly, whets the greed of his aristocratic investors by
refusing to tell them where he comes from, or what machinations he is
preparing in the City. When the "Evening Pulpit" publishes an article
about Melmotte's projected railway from California to Mexico, no one can
tell if the article praises or ridicules the scheme; but most choose to read it
as praise, so that shares in the railway go up. Lady Carbury, whose son is a
director of the company, is delighted. "If a thing can be made great and be-
neficent," she argues, "a boon to humanity, simply by creating a belief in
it, does not a man become a benefactor to his race by creating that belief?"
Her claim is plausible, provided that the railway does get built and achieve
its mission of "civilizing Mexico by joining it to California."[22] But the railway is not built; worse, there is reason to suspect that Melmotte never
cared whether it was built or not.

Critics have noted how Trollope equates Melmotte's railway bubble with
the circulation of IOUs among the young aristocrats who gamble at the
Beargarden Club.[23] The lack of inherent discipline in the financial sector of
the economy is fatally attractive to the young aristocrats who consume
rents and do nothing but amuse themselves. Those who are drawn into the
whirlpool of gambling, speculation, and debt – like Sir Felix Carbury – face
inevitable ruin. Those who entice them, the Melmottes and Lopezes, are ruined too, of course; for Trollope insists that finance capital is a bubble that
must burst, by the principle of its own inflation. Yet he is also a realist who
depicts an upper class obsessed with the power of money, and with their
own need for it. The formally stable world of the landed aristocracy is now
driven by restless ambitions to prevail over rivals, and money is what one
must have for this: to get a seat in Parliament, a beautiful spouse, a coveted
piece of land to round out an estate. Characters like Roger Carbury stand for

the traditional virtues of the landed gentry, but also for the obsolescence and ineffectuality of those virtues: Roger longs for his cousin Hetta to grace his estate, but loses her to Paul Montague – who dabbles in Melmotte's schemes, and gets out in the nick of time with a profit. Roger Carbury settles for living vicariously, relishing the good things to be enjoyed by his heir (who is also the rival who defeats him in love). Despite the contrived ruin of his exemplary financiers, Trollope must grudgingly concede the superior vitality of the "Monied Interest." *The Way We Live Now*, one of the most grandly inclusive of titles, also means "Who We Are Now."

Jews and Gentlemen

> The importance of money as a means, independent of all specific ends, results in the fact that money becomes the center of interest and the proper domain of individuals and classes who, because of their social position, are excluded from many kinds of personal and specific goals. . . . There is no need to emphasize that the Jews are the best example of the correlation between the central role of money interests and social deprivation. . . . The basic trait of Jewish mentality to be much more interested in logical-formal combinations than in substantive creative production must be understood in the light of their economic condition. The fact that the Jew was a stranger who was not organically connected with his economic group directed him to trade and its sublimation in pure monetary transactions.[24]

Georg Simmel, in analyzing the affinity with money of marginal groups, could draw on his own experience of exclusion (as a Jew) from the mainstream of German academic life. Money, he observed, had a "metaphysical quality . . . a form of being whose qualities are generality and lack of content"; it was the most powerful of symbols, but also supremely impersonal and dissociated from the immediate utility of the sensual world.[25] Troubled by this paradox, the average person has tended to be suspicious of those who seem familiar with the mysteries of money; and criticism of new or esoteric monetary phenomena often has been intertwined with anti-semitism.

Early in the nineteenth century, Cobbett stigmatized finance – and its agents, the Jews and the Quakers – as the enemy of the virtuous primary producer:

> the Quaker gets rich, and the poor devil of a farmer is squeezed into a gaol. The Quakers . . . . are, as to the products of the earth, what the

Jews are as to gold and silver. How they profit, or, rather, the degree in which they profit, at the expense of those who own and those who till the land, may be guessed at if we look at their immense worth, and if we, at the same time, reflect that they never work. . . . Here is a sect of buyers and sellers. They make nothing; they cause nothing to come; . . . if all the other sects were to act like them, *the community must perish.*[26]

For Cobbett, parasitism is measured by distance from the primary source of increase, the land. England's decay is hastened by the cancerous growth of London, called by Cobbett "the Wen" (that is, a fatty tumor), the natural home of "Jews, loan-jobbers, stock-jobbers, placemen, pensioners, sinecure people, and people of the 'dead weight.'"[27]

Trollope follows Cobbett in suspecting the association between Jews and finance capital, that fluid and pervasive money power which allows the new classes to claim so much, and obliges the old ones to concede it. The Jews are unrestrained by land, national loyalty, or custom; their wealth derives from invisible sources and is peculiarly ephemeral, rising or dissipating with the winds of fortune, and shifting suddenly from one place to another.[28] Nonetheless, critics have assumed too easily that Trollope always stigmatizes the Jews.[29] Cobbett's anti-semitism is comprehensive, directed against an entire group that he defines as alien to the "real" England. But Trollope extends to Jewish manners and aspirations a certain novelistic sympathy; and he has an acutely dialectical sense of how Jews are assigned an identity by the host society, even as they play a crucial role in transforming it into something else.

Trollope's treatment of Melmotte in *The Way We Live Now* shows how Jewishness may be more metaphor than fixed racial or religious identity.[30] Various originals have been proposed for Melmotte, from the financier Albert Grant (born Gottheimer) to Dickens's Mr Merdle in *Little Dorrit*. But the most likely model for Melmotte's plutocratic style of life is Trollope's friend Baron Meyer Rothschild. Rothschild had lived as a country gentleman for some thirty years, taking no direct part in the family bank. In January, February, and March of 1873, Trollope regularly hunted with him at his lavish Berkshire estate, Mentmore (an assonant for Melmotte?). Once hunting was over, Trollope moved house and then started writing *The Way We Live Now*, on the first of May.[31] Given Trollope's intimacy with the Rothschilds, it is significant that he so studiously refuses, in *The Way We Live Now*, to identify Melmotte as unambiguously either a Jew or a gentile.

The vagueness of Melmotte's identity is precisely the point: it corresponds to the opacity of his speculations and the slippery anonymity of finance capital itself. His name suggests kinship with Charles Maturin's "Melmoth the Wanderer," a hero who derives from the archetype of the wandering Jew but is not Jewish himself.[32] Trollope's notes for the novel describe Melmotte's wife as a "Fat Jewess"; but the origins of Melmotte himself, and his daughter Marie, are left obscure.[33] So far as we can reconstruct the story, Marie was born to Melmotte's German mistress in New York; she has "no trace of the Jewess in her countenance."[34] Her mother died or disappeared; Melmotte then moved to Frankfurt (the financial center of Germany and home of the Rothschild family), married Madame Melmotte and converted to Judaism in order to ingratiate himself with his new wife's co-religionists. Soon after, the family moved to Paris and passed themselves as Christians.[35] Melmotte's unknowable identity is contrasted with his openly Jewish associates Cohenlupe and Brehgert – the former a predatory financier, the latter a virtuous banker who is cheated by Melmotte out of a substantial part of his fortune.

Trollope's visits to Mentmore coincided with a family crisis that anticipates the prominence of mixed marriages in *The Way We Live Now* and *The Prime Minister*. In February, Meyer Rothschild's niece Annie married (in a Registry Office, and then in a church) a gentile from the landed aristocracy, Henry Yorke. Rothschild was bitterly opposed to this match.[36] In *The Prime Minister* it is the gentile Emily Wharton who upsets her father by proposing to marry a Jew, Mr Lopez. Trollope distances himself from Mr Wharton's blunt prejudice, and shows considerable sympathy for Lopez. He wants simply to rise in the world, from obscure origins as the son of a Jewish peddler to at least the level of Mr Wharton; and English society resists such ambitions, regardless of justice or equality of opportunity. Trollope first condemns Lopez's plan of campaign, and then goes far to condone the methods that Lopez was forced to employ:

Ferdinand Lopez was not an honest man or a good man. He was a self-seeking, intriguing adventurer, who did not know honesty from dishonesty when he saw them together. But he had at any rate this good about him, that he did love the girl whom he was about to marry. . . . It was his ambition now to carry her up with him, and he thought how he might best teach her to assist him in doing so, – how he might win her to help him in his cheating, especially in regard to her own father. For to himself, to his own thinking, that which we call cheating was not dishonesty. To his thinking there was something bold, grand, picturesque, and almost beautiful in the battle which such a one as himself must wage with the world before he could make his way up in it. He would not pick a pocket, or turn a false card, or, as he thought, forge a name. That which he did, and desired to do, took with him the name of speculation.[37]

This passage hinges on the authorial "we" in "that which we call cheating." In one sense, it implies a racial judgment: that from which we gentiles refrain, the Jews will do as a matter of course (though they do it because they are more loyal to their families than to an impersonal and prejudiced society – not an altogether bad motive). But the "we" also defines the established class, in which both author and readers are honorifically included. Those who have already arrived at a place of comfort – often by the efforts of their ancestors rather than themselves – are free to proclaim an honesty that costs them little, for they have long put the struggle for a place in the world behind them.

Trollope's vision of the late Victorian establishment is thus not so narrowly ethnocentric as it may appear at first. His theme is miscegenation in the widest sense: not just the entry of new races or types into the traditional ruling class, but the calling into question of the whole basis of social differentiation within a known hierarchy. In some crucial respects Trollope is an evident enemy of the emerging "Open Society" founded on individual talent and money power; yet he knows only too well the irresistible forces that are making for still more openness rather than less. He has already conceded the great public issues: extension of suffrage, the secret ballot, emancipation of Catholics and Jews, a measure of Home Rule for Ireland. Now he broods on the implications for private life when the principles underlying emancipation are extended to their logical conclusion. But he has to admit that there is now no consensus about how classes are constituted, or where the boundaries between them should be fixed. Lopez *did*, after all, succeed in making himself a gentleman in the eyes of the world:

> It was not generally believed that Ferdinand Lopez was well born; – but he was a gentleman. And this most precious rank was acceded to him although he was employed, – or at least had been employed, – on business which does not of itself give such a warrant of position as is supposed to be afforded by the bar and the church, by the military services and by physic. He had been on the Stock Exchange, and still in some manner, not clearly understood by his friends, did business in the City.[38]

The rise of Lopez is itself proof that social position has become conventional rather than essential – outside the ranks of the landed gentry, at least. There may still be a taint to money made in the City but money, once made, can buy protective coloration for its possessor. Status can now be gained by the general consent to recognize it; and that consent goes by such appearances as clothing, looks, manners, church attendance, and visible signs of wealth.[39] The social and financial systems resemble each other in having uncoupled their exchange function from any ultimate standard of value. Reputation in the one realm, credit in the other, create values out of thin air. At the same time, one may recognize that this situation, so disturbing to Trollope, is only the limit case of the general conditions required for the writing of novels: that social mobility be possible, and social status itself be subject to the play of opinion.

Trollope is therefore well aware of how hard it is to find solid ground on which to make a stand against this late Victorian inflation of appearances. "I ain't sure," says Mr Wharton, "that I wish to marry my daughter in the City. Of course it's all prejudice."[40] Prejudice, as he admits, is an arbitrary belief that one race or class has fixed and intrinsic qualities; and in calling his faith in marrying "like to like" by that name he has already conceded that his preferences conflict with the normal operation of the social system. For prejudice in these novels is a stubborn assertion of bias against people who, in appearance, have conformed to upper-class English norms. That, indeed, is the problem: Lopez's complete assimilation fuels Wharton's distrust, rather than disarming it. In due course, his suspicions are confirmed: Lopez turns out to be the son of a Jew who had been "little better than a travelling pedlar."[41] The father had made enough money by trading in jewelry to send Ferdinand to a Public School, where he acquired his protective coloration, his Anglicanism, and his aspiration to marry into the gentry.[42] These were the attributes of Trollope's *bête noire*, Disraeli. Yet Trollope clearly respects those Jews – like Mr Brehgert in *The Way We Live Now* – who are true to their faith and their traditional role.

When Georgiana Longestaffe sets out to make a financially attractive match with Mr Brehgert, she can point to many in her class who are acting similarly. But she demands too much, and Brehgert breaks the engagement; she comes to regret the lost match, and to deplore the relentless anti-semitism of her mother. Georgiana's only escape from a wretched family life is to run off with a penniless curate, Mr Batherbolt. Since Felix Carbury's "keeper" in Prussia is also a clergyman, it is surely not accidental that two of the greediest characters in *The Way We Live Now* should be left at the end of the novel in the hands of the Established Church. Yet it is a measure of Trollope's skepticism that Christian orthodoxy is given no effectual role in the novel until after the financial bubble has burst, and then only to restrain, rather than reform, Felix and Georgiana. Melmotte himself commits suicide in the honorable style of an antique Roman. Trollope condemns all who compromise their established identities for the sake of money; but his sharpest animus is directed against a Christian landed elite who have forgotten their duties, rather than against the financiers, whether Jew or gentile, who never had a duty to forget.

When Mr Wharton in *The Prime Minister* finally decides to let his daughter's match go ahead, it is because he knows that social opportunism has become too powerful a force for him to resist single-handed:

> The man was distasteful to him as being unlike his idea of an English gentleman, and as being without those far-reaching fibres and roots by which he thought that the solidity and stability of a human tree should be assured. But the world was changing around him every day. Royalty was marrying out of its degree. Peers' sons were looking only for money. And, more than that, peers' daughters were bestowing themselves on Jews and shopkeepers. Had he not better make the usual inquiry about the man's means, and, if satisfied on that head, let the girl do as she would? Added to all this there was growing on him a feeling that ultimately youth would as usual triumph over age, and that he would be beaten.[43]

Wharton does inquire, but not carefully enough. Lopez's "solidity and stability" turn out to be a mere fleeting appearance, and when all his schemes have failed he commits suicide, like Melmotte before him. But what is Trollope trying to claim as the moral of these conspicuous failures? In the world of speculative finance, whether there is gold or dross at the bottom of things is as irrelevant as whether there is real coffee or guano. For each Melmotte or Lopez who fail, a hundred interlopers will succeed in worming their way into the ruling class, discarding or disguising their origins along the way. Before long, the distinction between parasite and host will cease to have any meaning. Trollope looks forward – even if grudgingly – to modernity; to a world of wall-to-wall relativism and of identity cast adrift.

Trollope's Passage to Elysium

Trollope's professed allegiance to the myth of the land, which assumes the moral excellence and social centrality of the country gentry, is completely at odds with his personal history. As a boy at Harrow he was tortured and ostracized by "the sons of peers and big tradesmen"; but he was also too much *self*-tortured to adopt any Shelleyan stance of contemptuous revolt. Rather, he confesses, "It seemed to me that there would be an Elysium in the intimacy of those very boys whom I was bound to hate because they hated me."[44] Beginning as a complete outcast, he made himself accepted – that is, achieved a viable identity as a "gentleman" – through one of the most relentless efforts of ambition in literary history. That ambition expressed itself in the market – the only place open to him, as it was for Melmotte and Lopez. Trollope eventually was able to keep hunters, to rub shoulders with the gentry, and to pass for an established member of the upper-middle class. Yet he remained profoundly ambivalent even in his success: he had no mixed feelings about having risen, but could not forget that those who now made him welcome were of the same sort as those who, in his youth, had so brutally suppressed and excluded him.

When Trollope was a child his father Thomas Trollope, a London lawyer, had leased a farm at Harrow on the strength of his expectations from his rich landowning uncle, Adolphus Meetkerke. But Meetkerke then re-married and sired a male heir, thus cutting out the Trollopes. Thomas never got over this disappointment; and when Anthony was nineteen his family's country estate – modest as it actually was – was ignominiously bankrupted and sold up. The Trollopes were thus a family whose pretensions to a "county" status proved hollow, and who were cast down into an abyss of poverty, sickness, and struggle. They climbed back to comfort by heroic feats of verbal productivity: his mother Fanny Trollope's hundred and fourteen volumes, then Anthony's own tens of thousands of pages – more than any other English author living, he boasted.[45] Driven by his "pervading sense of inferiority," Trollope set out to master the world of appearance and pretension; we might say, by issuing notes on his own bank and getting that world to accept them. Trollope's myth of stability – the ideal of something, whether gold or land, that transcends convention and mere appearance – grows out of his fear that he is living in an age of impostors; moreover, that he himself is as much an impostor – a paper money man – as any of them. The great irony of the *Autobiography* is that Trollope only allowed it to be published after his death, when it revealed his secret life of industry, in the hours between 5.30 and breakfast. The book is a heroic narrative of success in the marketplace, where Trollope began without capital or reputation, and viewed himself as a tradesman sedulously catering to his customers. The myth of the land was what these customers enjoyed; but it was under conditions far removed from the life of a country gentleman that Trollope labored to create the happy land of Barsetshire – by way of creating his own name.

3
The Market for Women

He never yet had set his daughter forth
Here in the woman-markets of the west,
Where our Caucasians let themselves be sold.
                    —Tennyson, "Aylmer's Field."

Sex and Money in Trollope

The English prestige culture tried to exclude land from the system of monetary exchange, by making it into something "beyond price."[1] In the nineteenth century, however, money was steadily making inroads and making landed estates into marketable items.[2] The position of women was in important ways homologous with that of land, and was subject to similar forces. Within a pure prestige culture, women were the instruments for the exchange of land between aristocratic families through marriage, and for the production of male heirs to provide continuity of tenure and name. In this system of homosocial barter, all that was required of a woman was to be chaste and a bearer of sons.[3] As the market economy imposed on aristocrats an increasing need for money, beyond the agricultural produce of their estates, a prospective wife also came to be assessed as a source of cash. The disquieting implication was that a woman now could be priced, or "chalk-marked for the auction" as Kate Croy puts it in *The Wings of the Dove*.[4] Even more disquieting is the idea that she might choose to price herself, through a conscious exploitation of her own desirability.

Richardson inaugurates, and Trollope concludes, the high era of the "marriage novel" that takes as its matter the interaction between love, family and economic interest, within the constraints set by the marriage system of upper-class English society. Richardson shows the system leading to tragedy; Thackeray sees in it "the grim workings of marital capitalism"; Austen and Trollope are more inclined to grant, for their heroes and heroines at least, a happier balance between self-expression and the observance of social and economic norms. Trollope, especially, examines the tension between two different modes of marital exchange. The more archaic one is entirely homosocial, and rooted in the aristocratic system of land tenure: land should only be transmitted by a claim based on "blood," rather than through money purchase (which would threaten the exclusivity of the landowning

32

caste). Under the regime of "strict settlement" that prevailed from the sixteenth century to 1882 – the year of the Married Women's Property Act – land could be made inalienable from one generation to the next. This made a father a "life tenant" rather than full owner of his estate.[5] Ownership of landed estates was exclusively male, passing either to the oldest son on the proprietor's death or to some more distant male relative. The wife's role was to cement an alliance between two landed families, to bear a son, and to provide her husband with a "portion," normally of cash, to help with the upkeep of his estate. Her status was defined by the legal doctrine of coverture, whereby "when a woman married, her legal personality was subsumed in that of her husband."[6] The wife's very identity, along with any assets she owned at the time of her marriage, came under her husband's absolute control.

The aristocratic marriage system rests on the contradiction that a woman is a person, with whom one can fall in love, but she is also an exchangeable asset, priced by her degree of wealth, beauty, and gentility. Aristocratic young men exercise their monetary power in the sexual underworld of prostitution, but in the marriage market they expect "pure" women who rise above both mercenary sexuality. The reality, of course, is that the sexual will be implicated with the financial at all social levels, and that female purity and availability both have a market value. Even the most sanctified and legitimate of sexual unions will be haunted by its mercenary shadow. The wife's economic status will always conflict with her position as the "angel in the house," because money connects her to the material world of commodities, and the sensual world of intercourse and reproduction. As Byron put it: "Money is the magnet; as to Women, one is as well as another."[7] If a marriageable woman is deficient in money, other assets – especially beauty or aristocratic blood – have to be brought in to make up the count. In Trollope's *Dr Thorne*, Mary Thorne is rejected by her beloved's mother, who wants her son to marry money. The son remains faithful, though, and when Mary inherits a fortune out of the blue their marriage can take place to universal applause. "I often think that you are the happiest woman of whom I ever heard," comments her friend Miss Dunstable, "to have it all to give [i.e. her wealth], when you were so sure that you were loved while you yet had nothing." Miss Dunstable herself is a wealthy woman who suffers from being plain and the daughter of a self-made businessman; she has plenty of suitors, but no sincere lovers:

> how is it possible that any disinterested person should learn to like me? How could such a man set about it? If a sheep have two heads, is

not the fact of the two heads the first and, indeed, only thing which the world regards in that sheep? Must it not be so as a matter of course? I am a sheep with two heads.[8]

Miss Dunstable's second head is the several million pounds she is thought to possess, and which no one in society is capable of forgetting. The only escape from this pricing mechanism might be found by matching a man and a woman of exactly equal monetary resources; yet such symmetry rarely occurs in novels of the period. There must be some imbalance of worth between the suitors: to motivate the plot, to provide a focus of interest, and to demonstrate how the sexual and monetary systems engage each other.

Beauty and status are supposed to be "priceless"; but the marriage market makes all qualities fungible, able to be quantified and traded one for the other. Someone who is supremely beautiful, wealthy and noble belongs in a fairy-tale rather than in the contingent world of the novel. Trollope still uses repeatedly the standard comic plot in which a true lover is favored over a socially more eligible rival; once fidelity has been tested, the lover's deficiency can be remedied by some final twist of the plot. Since beauty and status are relatively constant values, the usual reversal is for a poor lover to acquire money, though delivered as a gift or legacy rather than as the reward for effort.

The challenges to this scheme in Trollope and Henry James come from the sheer weight of industrial and financial capital that has accumulated in Britain by the later nineteenth century. New wealth necessarily destabilizes the reference points of social hierarchy. No longer can the novel be restricted to a preoccupation with using marriage to achieve a stable and comfortable gentility. Money now counts for more in claiming status, and landownership or "good breeding" count for less. As Habakkuk notes, newly rich landowners in the eighteenth and nineteenth centuries were less likely to tie up the ownership of estates for generations ahead in a "strict settlement," and more willing to provide for daughters or younger sons with parcels of land or cash endowments.[9] In such a milieu it becomes a consuming interest to price the wealth and prospects of everyone one meets; and characters of obscure origins, like Madame Goesler or Miss Dunstable, can be promptly accepted by the highest in the land, if only their wealth be sufficient.[10] The money-marriage system becomes a bridge between the worlds of commerce and of the landed gentry, with a profitable traffic in both directions.

Still, such trade and profit are not unproblematically available to all comers. It might seem straightforward enough to take a young man who is poor, but handsome and of good family, and match him with a rich wife who can bring to him what his birth deserves: leisure, an estate, and a seat in the House of Commons. Harry Clavering is such a young man, in Trollope's *The Claverings*. But if men can go to the marriage market to buy, they should not be carried there to be sold. Harry's cousin, Julia Brabazon, tells him: "You are very handsome, Harry, and you, too, should go into the market and make the best of yourself. Why should you not learn to love some nice girl that has money to assist you?"[11] Julia agrees with Bulwer-Lytton's maxim that "in good society the heart is remarkably prudent, and seldom falls violently in love without a sufficient settlement," and claims to have no misgivings about selling herself high.[12] But Harry believes that marriage to a rich wife would require him to play a woman's part. He would no longer have to fight his way to worldly success; his wife might control him through her power of the purse; and he would have traded his physical charms for domestic comfort. When his cousin Hermione suggests that "A girl is not the worse because she can bring some help," Harry retorts "I think it best when the money comes from the husband."[13]

Trollope recognizes that there is a market for beauty, but feels that its reward should be either love, or an equal beauty in the chosen partner. Material interests should not be valid currencies in the exchange. Harry's modest fiancée, Florence Burton, calls Julia Brabazon "a bold, bad woman who could forget her sex, and sell her beauty and her womanhood for money."[14] Prostitutes sell their womanhood on set terms; they are paid immediately, and in cash, for each act of intercourse; they have no love for the man who buys them; and they will go with any man who pays their price. Julia believes that she can avoid the stigma of meretriciousness by selling herself for a longer term, on an exclusive basis, and to a husband who has £60,000 a year. As she leaves the church where she has married Lord Ongar:

> she told herself that she had done right. She had chosen her profession, as Harry Clavering had chosen his; and having so far succeeded, she would do her best to make her success perfect. Mercenary! Of course she had been mercenary. Were not all men and women mercenary upon whom devolved the necessity of earning their bread?[15]

Perhaps one can learn to love the person one marries for money, Julia argues; in any case, Lord Ongar is sick, and after a short term of servitude she will be both rich and free to marry her true love, Harry. Against his reproaches, she can justly claim that "Everybody compliments [her] on [her] marriage." Such compliments illustrate Simmel's cynical rule:

> The abhorrence that modern 'good' society entertains towards the prostitute is more pronounced the more miserable and the poorer she is, and it declines with the increase in the price for her services, to the point at which even the actress whom everybody knows is kept by a millionaire is considered presentable in their salons, although she may be much more extortionate, fraudulent and depraved than many a streetwalker.[16]

Florence Burton stands for the view that female sexuality must stay out of the marketplace entirely, and the plot of *The Claverings* seems to endorse her side of the argument. Once Lord Ongar has duly expired – of alcohol poisoning, perhaps combined with venereal disease – Julia still has her beauty, and has added to it riches and a title. She expects to reclaim Harry and make him a present of her late husband's wealth. Julia nearly seduces Harry out of his commitment to Florence, but he finally holds firm and, via his cousin's timely death in a fishing accident, is rewarded with Clavering Park. This is a legitimate way for him to enter the class of landed proprietors, and everyone approves of his good fortune. Julia, on the other hand, is shunned by society for her tainted marriage: "When women hear how wretched I have been," she tells her sister, "they will be unwilling to sell themselves as I did." In a desperate attempt to purge herself of guilt, she even gives away almost all the money she inherited from Lord Ongar. Yet her sister wonders if Julia has gone mad, with "this idea of abandoning money, the possession of which was questioned by no one."[17]

Julia's moral collapse is caused by her inability to reconcile Christian and secular marriage values. She marries Lord Ongar purely for money, but after his death she is ashamed of the sexual bargain she made, disappointed by Harry's rejection of her, and humiliated by the social ostracism she encounters. She becomes one of Trollope's fanatics: people who cannot accept the contingent nature of everyday life, and who succeed only in making themselves and everyone around them miserable. All such fanaticism is an over-valuation of the self (as Trollope represents it); morality is a collective and conventional system, and a wise person will not aspire to be morally autonomous. Julia handled both phases of her life badly: she was wrong to scorn the modesty and romanticism appropriate to a young woman of her class when seeking a mate, and wrong again in her failure to enjoy her advantages as a rich and beautiful young widow. Marriage and the established church must both find a place for monetary interests; to have too sharp a nose for prostitution or simony is to deny the mixed nature of the common business of life.

Yet Trollope's account of Julia suffers from moral incoherence. He can take a sentimental and absolutist view of female virtue, equating Julia's ill-earned wealth with Judas's thirty pieces of silver; but he can also recognize the inevitability of money-marriage in a society where capital and land must circulate between families and be passed on across generations. Such wealth makes possible the "good things" that Trollope invokes so insistently in his novels: things that are always good in a worldly and materialist sense rather than a moral one. His uncritical devotion to these good things makes us sceptical about how far his moral range extends. And why should female virtue be an exception, when elsewhere – with political or religious virtue, notably – Trollope always spies out the worldly motives of those who profess it? The Victorian double standard requires women to remain naieve and virtuous, yet subjects them to a homosocial system that commodifies their bodies and makes them mere vehicles for the transfer of wealth.

Within the money-marriage system, spontaneity of feeling seems impossible, except by a negative test: if you love someone with no money then the love must be true (or, if you are poor and in love, you will renounce your beloved rather than damage their worldly prospects). To reward emotional altruism with a legacy in the last pages of a novel can scarcely be a general solution to the conflict between love and interest. Trollope's constant recourse to Providence for a happy conclusion to his marriage novels expresses a wish to escape a conundrum that, in the secular world, he feels unable to solve.

In or About 1882: The End of the Marriage Novel

The subjection of women in prestige society was moderated by the law of equity, whereby a married woman could retain some control over the property she brought into the marriage.[18] But equity often meant little more than the desire of the wife's male relatives to conserve wealth in their own family line:

> both the old landed aristocracy and the new aristocracy of the business world felt acutely the special need to protect the property of their daughters from the common-law rights of husbands, and to ensure that if there were no children of a marriage the property would not pass to their daughters' husbands but would return to their own families.[19]

If a prospective husband was poorer than his fiancée, her male relatives would try to limit his control over his wife's property through the marriage settlement (pre-nuptial contract); if the woman was poorer, her husband's family would try to claim his property if he predeceased her. In Trollope's *The Eustace Diamonds*, the widowed Lady Eustace clings tenaciously to the diamonds her husband gave her, but which his family are determined to recover. Sir Hugh Clavering, in *The Claverings*, drives a hard bargain over his sister-in-law Julia's marriage settlement, and she gets control of all Lord Ongar's wealth after he dies – to the fury of *his* relatives. Both situations are anomalous in that neither woman produced a son before her husband died; if they had, everything would have been held in trust for him, and the widows would have got only a life income (jointure) from the estate.[20] Because women play only an intermediary role in the inheritance system, their rights are easily contestable; but the right of the oldest son must be universally acknowledged, as the keystone of all property-holding.

The law of equity gave upper-class English women a modicum of economic independence, as against their complete subservience under the law of coverture. From the 1850s onward, English feminists struggled to gain, for all married women, full control over their own incomes and property; this campaign culminated in the Married Women's Property Act of 1882. The principle underlying this Act was equal treatment of individuals regardless of gender; whereas equity had assumed that women were separate, weaker beings who needed the protection of the law against their husbands (protection that would normally be supplied by their male relatives). Equity was consistent with homosociality and its correlative, the "double standard"; but the 1882 Act assumed the individuality of women. As one anxious male saw it, if the husband "is no longer the head of the wife (and, as far as property goes he is no longer), there seems no reason why wives should not have independent views, and independent profession, independent society, and independent interests."[21] Of course, this independence would only be enjoyed by a minority of women, those who had property of their own to begin with.

Female autonomy and money-marriage can still co-exist, but it is probably no accident that money-marriage is a less popular motif in novels written after 1882 (also the year of Trollope's death). Novelists still engaged by the subject – notably George Gissing and Henry James – had to change their angle of approach. The Married Women's Property Act helped to make money power more universal in its extent, less a specifically male preserve. Once a wife had become financially independent of her husband, money-marriage lost its titillating association with prostitution. Under the old system, sexual services were much more directly linked to economic obligation, and there was even the assumption that the male could make any demand he wanted on the woman whom he had acquired as "property." Separate property constrained homosocial exchange, and encouraged the liberation of female sexuality.

The Settlement Act, also of 1882, recognized the desire of landowners (like women) to be autonomous actors in the marketplace rather than mere trustees or intermediaries. Under strict settlement, husband and wife were not just restricted by the interests of their immediate relatives; they had also to respect what their families had been in the past, and the desire of future generations to remain landed proprietors. But as money extended its sway, marriage became more simply a matter of quantification, less a conflict between religious and material systems of value. Marie Melmotte, in *The Way We Live Now*, is pursued by a pack of worthless young aristocrats simply for her raw wealth; they have no disinterested class ideal that they might need money to uphold. In the later novels of Trollope, suitors focus on little more than the price tag attached to the one they desire. Julia Brabazon at least suffers a moral crisis (if delayed) over her mercenary marriage; but Georgiana Longestaffe in *The Way We Live Now* cold-bloodedly sets out to her fiancé the terms on which she can be bought, and she does her own bargaining rather than letting her father bargain for her. She has no internal conflict because her femininity has been completely secularized: there is no quality in her that a man might revere, or whose loss she might regret.

In his typology of married woman and prostitute, Simmel argues that "The significance and the consequences that society attaches to the sexual relations between man and woman are . . . based on the presupposition that the woman gives her total self, with all its worth, whereas the man gives only a part of his personality in the exchange . . . . Only a monetary transaction corresponds to the character of a completely fleeting inconsequential relationship as is the case with prostitution."[22] This is why, in the transaction between prostitute and client, it is only the woman who is degraded: a man's status can be separated from his sexuality, a woman's can not. But Georgiana Longestaffe's calculation of prospective gains shows that her woman's "total self" of which Simmel speaks is no longer total, but easily divisible. Another term for her self-management is "commodification": the separation of use-value from exchange-value that, according to Marx, first became predominant in the mercantile capitalism of the Renaissance. But there is a long evolution from that period to the characteristically modern situation in which the very self or personhood of an individual becomes "a commodity, a subject in the market."[23] Marx's theories of alienation and commodification are variants of organicism: as goods have an intrinsic value that is directly related to their materiality, so do people have a true worth that precedes social exchange, and which can only be distorted by "marketing." "Let us assume *man* to be *man*," Marx observes, "and his relation to the world to be a human one. Then love can only be exchanged for love, trust for trust." Then comes money, with its power "to confuse and invert all human and natural qualities into their opposites. . . . It is the alienated *power* of *humanity*."[24]

Julia Brabazon's decision to sell herself (more specifically, her beauty) in the marriage market is a cultural milestone of sorts. By Marx's logic, she should only have exchanged her beauty for a similarly organic male quality: the beauty of Harry Clavering. But he lacks money, and Julia decides to enter a circuit of exchange: her beauty for Ongar's money, Ongar's money for Harry's beauty. She is doubly punished for thus commodifying herself; she fails to get Harry for a second husband, and finds that she takes no pleasure in the money she got from her first (also a way for Trollope to hint at the sexual frigidity that was supposed to be the prostitute's "punishment" for accepting money).[25]

The commodification of the female self leads naturally, towards the end of the nineteenth century, to her asserting her self by the acquisition of commodities. For Trollope, though, woman tends to be commodified passively, as an object of male consumption: "a handsome woman at the head of your table, who knows how to dress, and how to sit, and how to get in and out of her carriage . . . how beautiful a thing it is!"[26] Sceptical as Trollope may be about such commodification, he suggests no way of resisting it, except for a retreat into the convention of fairy-tale marriage. Once the lovers have been united, he shows little interest in their future of shared consumption, and to consider that future too closely is the sign – in a woman – of a suspect disposition. Bargaining with their husbands over consumer goods comes too close to marketing their sexual services, even if only to a single and legitimate buyer.[27]

Independent female consumption seems also to arouse Trollope's suspicion in *Phineas Finn*. There are two set-piece descriptions of the possessions of Madame Goesler, the banker's widow: one of her dress and jewellery, the other of the drawing-room of her cottage on Park Lane.[28] Exquisite as her appurtenances are, they are unequivocally a bait, designed to tempt Phineas away from the simple, true-hearted Irish girl to whom he is betrothed. Female consumption is thus metonymic for sexual aggression and the exotic pleasures of the boudoir. It is true that Phineas eventually yields to temptation, but only after the death of his first wife. Having proved his fidelity, and enjoyed success in his political career without Madame Goesler's help, he can now accept her offer of "an even partnership" in spending her riches.[29] In all, Trollope does not develop the theme of the bourgeois marriage as a theater of consumption, where the partners jointly strive to acquire commodities and where the wife, especially, makes herself into an object of consumption for her husband. It is enough for Trollope that an eligible woman be desired, whether for beauty or wealth; he does not show how these qualities might be consumed – consciously, at length, and to the discomfiture of rivals. For such concerns we look to the elaboration of consumer society after Trollope's death, and to the handling of money marriage by such successors as Henry James and George Gissing.

Commodity Marriage: *The Wings of the Dove*

In a posthumous tribute, Henry James pronounces Trollope a good novelist, but not good enough:

> The American girl was destined sooner or later to make her entrance into British fiction, and Trollope's treatment of this complicated being is full of good humour and of that fatherly indulgence, that almost motherly sympathy, which characterizes his attitude throughout toward the youthful feminine. He has not mastered all the springs of her delicate organism nor sounded all the mysteries of her conversation.[30]

Almost all of James's novels sound out the mysteries of the "American girl"; the example I choose is Milly Theale in *The Wings of the Dove*, because the plot of this novel is a kind of mirror-image of *The Claverings*. Merton Densher embarks on the same course as Julia Brabazon: he will marry Milly, knowing her to be mortally ill, to get her money – and then be free to marry the woman he truly loves, Kate Croy. In Trollope, though, the object of Julia's love – Harry Clavering – disowns her scheme; whereas in James, Kate both instigates Densher's opportunistic marriage and fornicates with him to keep him up to the mark. Sexual degradation in *The Wings of the Dove* is thus outside marriage, instead of within it, as in *The Claverings*; and Densher never consummates any relation with Milly, the virginal dove. Yet the two novels are alike in that, when their mercenary relationships are ended by death, the surviving couples are unable to wipe their slates clean and marry for love. The reason is similar in both cases:

women who have once commodified their sexuality have made themselves permanently unfit for a true marriage. Both, accordingly, seem to be left discredited and desolate when their novels end.

Behind Kate's fall is her aunt Maud, who stands for greed and ambition entirely undiluted by sentiment. Maud offers Kate a bargain: if she will cut herself off from her disreputable father, and marry a man of Maud's choosing, Maud will take Kate into her luxurious home and (it is implied) provide her with a dowry. But Kate must marry either a rich man or an aristocrat, and Merton Densher is neither. Kate hopes to escape her aunt's veto of Densher; but she is soon seduced by her aunt's values, and decides that the way out of her dilemma is to make Densher rich, by whatever means. Maud's house embodies Maud's will; once ensconced in it, Kate "saw as she had never seen before how material things spoke to her. . . . She had a dire accessibility to pleasure from such sources."[31] Densher, too, finds himself overwhelmed by the "material things" of Maud's drawing-room:

> Yet the great thing, really the dark thing, was that, even while he thought of the quick column he might add up, he felt it less easy to laugh at the heavy horrors than to quail before them. . . . He had never dreamed of anything so fringed and scalloped, so buttoned and corded, drawn everywhere so tight, and curled everywhere so thick. He had never dreamed of so much gilt and glass, so much satin and plush, so much rosewood and marble and malachite. But it was, above all, the solid forms, the wasted finish, the misguided cost, the general attestation of morality and money, a good conscience and a big balance. These things finally represented for him a portentous negation of his own world of thought – [32]

Densher's "quick column" first enters his consciousness as the journalistic column he might write about the room. But that belongs to his own "world of thought," and his mind is drawn by the room to another kind of column, the list of prices adding up to a "big balance" – which is what he lacks. The heaviness, the solidity, even the waste shown forth by Maud's furniture attest to qualities in its owner that make Densher feel small and slight by comparison. James says of Densher that he "looked vague without looking weak – idle without looking empty. . . . He suggested above all, however, that wondrous state of youth in which the elements, the metals more or less precious, are so in fusion and fermentation that the question of the final stamp, the pressure that fixes the value, must wait for comparative coolness."[33]

The younger characters of the novel therefore await being formed by money and even, in the daring metaphor of this passage, being formed *into* money.

Into this world where everyone seems "to think tremendously of money" enters Milly Theale. She is a spiritual dove floating above the material world of London, and an orphan whose parents have left her rich:

> it was, all the same, the truth of truths that the girl couldn't get away from her wealth. . . . She couldn't dress it away, nor walk it away, nor read it away, nor think it away; she could neither smile it away in any dreamy absence nor blow it away in any softened sigh. She couldn't have lost it if she had tried – that was what it was to be really rich. It had to be *the* thing you were.[34]

Milly's wealth, like Bathsheba Everdene's beauty in *Far From the Madding Crowd*, is a standing provocation to the predators of a fallen world. Mrs Stringham, Milly's American chaperone, tries to separate Milly's gift for life from her wealth: "The mine but needed working and would certainly yield a treasure. She was not thinking, either, of Milly's gold." But in London gold is what people always *are* thinking of. Kate Croy later explains to Milly that Lord Mark, a hanger-on at Maud's, "was working Lancaster Gate for all it was worth: just as it was, no doubt, working *him*, and just as the working and the worked were in London, as one might explain, the parties to every relation." Lord Mark's own sense of it is that "Nobody here, you know, does anything for nothing."[35]

In Trollope, beauty and money are typically alternative (and mutually exclusive) forms of female value, at least in the starting situation of the plot: Julia Brabazon is beautiful and poor, Marie Melmotte homely and rich. In *The Wings of the Dove*, however, Kate Croy's beauty and charm – and human qualities generally in the novel – are constantly expressed in the vocabulary of finance. Speaking of the value she places on Kate's companionship, aunt Maud observes that "I've been keeping it for the comfort of my declining years. . . . I've been saving it up and letting it, as you say of investments, appreciate, and you may judge whether, now it has begun to pay so, I'm likely to consent to treat for it with any but a high bidder." Maud is warning Densher that he is not sufficiently impressive as a suitor to give her what she wants and expects from any prospective match for her niece. Kate's marriage will be a three-party transaction from which, everyone agrees, aunt Maud deserves her profit. As Kate explains to Milly, "I *am* – you're so far right as that – on the counter, when I'm not in the shop-window; in and out of which I'm thus conveniently, commercially whisked: the essence, all of it, of my position, and the price, as properly, of my aunt's protection."[36]

The Wings of the Dove registers the pervasive commercialization of sentiments in its milieu; and even, behind a veil of propriety, of sexuality itself. No corner of social life now remains immune from market imperatives. Milly's purity and freshness are greatly in demand in the marketplace of society, instantly seized on and "worked" for the benefit of more hardened participants. Aunt Maud and Kate Croy consider this system entirely proper, and have no interest in shielding or excluding female virtue from the market. Indeed, Kate's description of being put "in and out of" the window, in exchange for the "protection" of her aunt, corresponds exactly to the relation between prostitute and pimp. It is natural, then, for her to promote a mercenary sexual relationship between Densher and Milly Theale, in the hope of getting her share of the proceeds of Densher's masculine charms. Densher speaks of his agreement to woo Milly "as a service for which the price named by him had been magnificently paid": Kate wanted him to get Milly's money by marrying her, Densher agreed so long as Kate would immediately become his mistress.[37] But how can one pay a price "magnificently"? Did Kate try to make her commercial bargain with Densher less sordid by throwing in things usually regarded as "priceless": her authentic sexual ardor and spontaneity (perhaps her virginity, too)? In using so insistently the discourse of finance to represent the "higher" emotions, James registers the saturation of London society by materialism; this discourse has spread out from the marketplace to occupy those realms of feeling traditionally thought to be most distant from commerce.

Granted all this, in what way should James be held accountable for the mercenary world of his late novels? Jean-Christophe Agnew seeks to implicate the author in his creation, to "trace through his sensibility a route of access to the very culture of consumption from which it is assumed to have recoiled in dismay."[38] Agnew argues that James's sensibility was captured by the spirit of his age, and by the discourse of commercialism, regardless of his fastidious desire to hold himself aloof. James is thus "placed" by Agnew as an equivalent to Adam Verver in *The Golden Bowl*:

> Adam's authority comes not from his wealth alone – the creature comforts and security it affords – but from the power of that wealth to fulfil the appropriative habits of mind that collectively form the second nature, the social medium within which the characters have for so long operated. The world of Portland Place and Eaton Square cannot be more distantly removed from the crude and callous transactions of

the marketplace (the place where Adam made his millions), yet it is nonetheless a world saturated with the imagery of the market, a world constructed and deconstructed by the appreciative vision.[39]

Agnew posits a functional continuity between the crude appropriation of the marketplace, the secondary appropriation of the social world (in which people "consume" each other aesthetically), and the "appreciative vision" that James himself casts on his characters. In this account, James's writerly nature is entirely subdued to what it works in: the mercenary world of the *fin de siècle*. Yet such readings (typical of New Historicism) assume too readily that authors can only transmit – over and over – the capitalist structures and vocabularies of their time. Agnew leaves James no standpoint from which he might make a disinterested moral assessment of his characters. It is not just that James, as a rentier artist, is complicit with the privileges of the kind of people he represents; it is further assumed that in affecting a commercial vocabulary James has no voice left with which to express an ironic as much as an appreciative vision, and to discriminate morally between one character and another.

Milly Theale's role in *The Wings of the Dove* is precisely to define the limits of Agnew's "world saturated with the imagery of the market." Two things do exist, James intimates, that escape the dominion of the market: death, and love. Sir Luke Strett's medical attendance on Milly may show "proof of a huge interest as well as of a huge fee," and the huge fee may make it impossible for the huge interest to be anything but material; but no concern of Sir Luke's can ward off Milly's death by so much as a day. Once Milly learns that Densher's attentions, too, are "interested" she bars her door to him and thus affirms her belief in another kind of love, one uncontaminated by interest. By leaving a fortune to Densher in her will Milly shows her contemptuous belief that money is the only thing he *is* capable of appreciating. Ironically, her gesture convinces Densher that it is possible to transcend the world in which everyone is "working and being worked." He refuses to carry through his marriage to the all-too-interested Kate Croy unless she agrees that they will jointly renounce Milly's legacy.

Kate's answer is to "turn to the door," unable to do what Densher asks – and knowing, also, that if they don't marry Densher will give *her* the money he refuses to accept. So James leaves Densher in love with Milly's memory and a convert to Milly's dream – it may be no more than a dream – of disinterestedness. To say that James necessarily recommends what he represents – the mercenary society of London – is to ignore the agonistic design of his novels. He first places Kate and

Densher in the enjoyment of their "young immunities": "each had the beauty, the physical felicity, the personal virtue, love and desire of the other."[40] These are precisely the goods that should be immune from the market; only the "great genial good" of wealth is lacking from the list, but Kate and Densher should have found the goods they *did* possess sufficient for their happiness. If no moral judgement can be made on their attempt to get wealth at the risk of the other goods, the entire novel is trivialized. James was still American enough to pursue the exposure of a European leisure class that scorns the everyday transactions of the market as vulgar, while happily dealing in such "higher" commodities as beauty, charm or prestige. He may have been assimilated into that class, but he was not captured by it.

James's *agon* also opposes passive and conscience-ridden men – Densher and Lord Mark – to women who are more potent, whether for vice (Maud and Kate) or virtue (Milly). Victorian convention had assumed a division of labor between the competitive male, oriented to the struggle in the marketplace, and the ornamental female who practiced the gentler arts of consumption. But Kate and Maud are both buyers and consumers in a marketplace that now trades in people and sensations, not just commodities. Their effectiveness in this realm reflects the weakening of homosocial money-marriage after the Married Women's Property Act. James has also made all of his young protagonists – Kate, Densher, Milly – free of parental authority; their emancipation from a conventional or patriarchal family structure can be seen as homologous with the economic emancipation of the class to which they belong. None are so needy as to have to work for their bread; as Agnew puts it, "The only things Jamesian characters actually produce are effects."[41] In such a society, women are at least as "productive" as men, and enjoy much more autonomy than their counterparts in Trollope.

James certainly recognizes the social forces that condition individual wills, but a belief in moral autonomy remains necessary both for how his characters understand themselves, and how he chooses to represent them. This is articulated in his critique of Zola (which we can also read as a critique of interpretive strategies, like New Historicism, that tend to bracket out personal agency). James suggests that Zola approached the task of literary art from the wrong direction:

It is not of course that multiplication and accumulation, the extraordinary pair of legs on which [Zola] walks, are easily or directly consistent with his projecting himself morally; this immense diffusion, with its appropriation of everything it meets, affects us on the contrary as perpetually delaying access to what we may call the private world, the world of the individual. . . . It is in the great lusty game he plays with the shallow and the simple that Zola's mastery resides, and we see of course that when values are small it takes innumerable items and combinations to make up the sum.[42]

It is a corollary, then, of Zola's accumulative approach that "The individual life is, if not wholly absent, reflected in coarse and common, in generalised terms." James views Zola himself as one whose life was virtually crushed out of him by the labors that his method imposed, so that he could not match the achievement of his predecessor, Balzac:

The mystic process of the crucible, the transformation of the material under aesthetic heat, is, in the *Comédie Humaine*, thanks to an intenser and more submissive fusion, completer, and also finer; and the individual case it is that permits of supreme fineness.[43]

James's greater indirection and, in every sense, refinement in comparison with Trollope, reflects his attunement to the great shift away from the material in the emergent consumer society and finance capitalism of his time. The difference is between an external and an internal understanding; on a personal level, the difference between one proud to be a self-made literary producer, and one who had always lived in the world of inherited capital.[44] James represents from within the values of a rentier class that has insulated itself from the crude workings of either the productive or the speculative activities of nineteenth century capitalism. At the same time, there is a fine line between inwardness and simple complicity – a line across which James's sensibility constantly goes back and forth, elusive of any determinate system of interpretation.

One even could go further, and argue for a determinacy on the side of worldliness. Leftist critics assume that the "commodity form" is necessarily decadent, a falling away from the more immediate social relations of earlier periods. Agnew speaks of "the most denatured of experiences: our own"; consumer society, it is assumed, effects our alienation from a better nature that might, otherwise, still be within our grasp.[45] But Milly Theale, in refusing the choice of "working or being worked," does not restore herself to any such state of innocence; she turns her face to the wall and dies. We might consider the possibility that acquisitiveness, in its most refined form, is something that James appreciates as a kind of heroic vitalism: that Kate Croy is not a figure of decadence and corruption, but one who shows a commendable devotion to the world's business. Instead of opposing mercenary sexuality to organicist purity of instinct, James may be saying that the pursuit of sexual or financial success belongs to the side of life – even, or especially, when they are pursued in tandem. By this reckoning Milly, or Densher in his final renunciation, are withdrawing into an asceticism that is literally deadly; though a critical stance that assumes the market is always wrong could scarcely appreciate any such reading of *The Wings of the Dove*.

4
Money, Marriage, and the Writer's Life: Gissing and Woolf

fiction is like a spider's web, attached ever so lightly perhaps, but
still attached to life at all four corners. Often the attachment is
scarcely perceptible; Shakespeare's plays, for instance, seem
to hang there complete by themselves. But when the web is pulled
askew, hooked up at the edge, torn in the middle, one remembers
that these webs are not spun in mid-air by incorporeal creatures,
but are the work of suffering human beings, and are attached to grossly
material things, like health and money and the houses we live in.
—Virginia Woolf, *A Room of One's Own*

George Gissing: The Price of Marriage

Gissing's *New Grub Street* (1891) and Woolf's *A Room of One's Own* (1929) are the two most renowned examinations of the modern literary marketplace. Yet the one outcome that neither book takes seriously is market success; rather, the writer's problem is presented as how to escape from the market before it spiritually, and even literally, kills you. For both writers, also, the market's power to do harm derives from society's sexual arrangements. Gissing sees the male writer as trapped between his longing for female solace, and the economic demands that a wife makes of him. For Woolf, it is domesticity that holds women back from literary success, and the room of her own has a lock that keeps both masculine and market exactions at a distance. Where they agree, however, is in finding the writer's only hope of salvation in a private income of some five hundred pounds a year.[1]

George Orwell, in a late essay, seizes on Gissing's obsession with the economics of sex:

Money was a nuisance not merely because without it you starved; what was more important was that unless you had quite a lot of it – £300 a year, say – society would not allow you to live gracefully or even peacefully. Women were a nuisance because even more than men they were the believers in taboos, still enslaved to respectability even when they had offended against it. Money and women were

and into writing; but they become alienated as they realize that what they think of as their own creations are really accountable to external forces. Books and marriages then become enemies of the writer's self-realization, and are no longer of his own "writing." What he originally invested his self in turns back on that self as a destroyer.

What dooms both Reardon's marriage and his literary career is more than just his failure to write successful novels. He is a genteel snob who, like so many British intellectuals, disdains the market. But if he had remained firm in that disdain, he might have pulled through. Unfortunately, he also holds the Social Darwinist belief that the market is a modern expression of biological law. Failure in the market is proof of unfitness to be included in a social group, to breed, ultimately even to survive. Reardon loathes Grub Street, but also loathes himself for being defeated by it. In a Darwinian view, Amy is acting naturally in transferring her affections from Reardon, the weaker male, to Jasper Mylvain, the stronger:

> Sexual selection depends on the success of certain individuals over others of the same sex in relation to the propagation of the species . . . . The sexual struggle is of two kinds; in the one it is between the individuals of the same sex, generally the male sex, in order to drive away or kill their rivals, the females remaining passive; whilst in the other, the struggle is likewise between the individuals of the same sex, in order to excite or charm those of the opposite sex, generally the females, which no longer remain passive, but select the more agreeable partners. . . .
>
> The more attractive males succeed in leaving a larger number of offspring to inherit their superiority in ornaments or other charms than the less attractive males; . . . I have shewn that this would probably follow from the females, – especially the more vigorous females which would be the first to breed, preferring not only the more attractive but at the same time the more vigorous and victorious males.[9]

Adam Smith's market may create wealth or facilitate exchange, but Gissing sees Darwin's market: not so much a place of incentive as one of struggle. Its most important function, in the great scheme of things, is to discipline the weaker males and limit their chances to reproduce. Reardon cannot help feeling, therefore, that there is no appeal from its verdict. Amy is justified in leaving him, and break-down followed by death is his biologically appropriate fate.

Gissing's alternatives to such market-driven doom are fantasies rather than credible escapes, such as the dream of cosy bachelorhood with a simple country woman to keep house in *The Private Papers of Henry Ryecroft*. Of course, solitude is no solution either. Harold Biffen lives in a garret while writing his Zolaesque novel, *Mr Bailey, Grocer*. His aim is to master the society he lives in by documenting the great impersonal forces of the market system; but for his own psychic survival he depends on worshipping Amy Reardon from afar:

> seldom in his life had he enjoyed female society, and when he first met Amy it was years since he had spoken with any woman above the rank of a lodging-house keeper or a needle-plier. Her beauty seemed to him of a very high order, and her mental endowments filled him with an exquisite delight, not to be appreciated by men who have never been in his position.[10]

Biffen keeps to the back streets of London to avoid being tormented by the beauty of fashionable women:

> Yet even here he was too often reminded that the poverty-stricken of the class to which poverty was natural were not condemned to endure in solitude. Only he who belonged to no class, who was rejected alike by his fellows in privation and by his equals in intellect, must die without having known the touch of a loving woman's hand.[11]

When his novel finds a publisher, Biffen goes to call on Amy, by now a widow; but he realizes that he is too shabby to be in her company, and ends by poisoning himself on Hampstead Heath. Biffen is killed by wanting Amy; before, Reardon was killed by having her. Both are victims of their middle-class tastes, and of the sensitivity that made them writers in the first place: they make Amy into their pearl of great price, then find the price to be beyond their means.

Independent Women

In *The Odd Women*, Everard Barfoot and Rhoda Nunn come close to a loving marriage of equals, but turn back because they are both too "proud and independent."[12] For Gissing, independence means the power to live comfortably on one's own resources. *The Odd Women* is remarkably sympathetic to the emergent feminism of the 1880s, and recognizes that women, as much as men, need self-reliance if they are to have self-respect. Rhoda Nunn teaches in a secretarial school, where she gives middle-class young women skills that will help them to avoid lives of dependency as governesses. She considers marriage an equivalent kind of dependence, and discourages her students from thoughts of romance. Gissing brings out Rhoda's forbidding qualities, but he also identifies with her determination to evade the trap of parasitism on a male, to assert herself boldly as a personality, and to nip off any shoots of emotional tenderness that she espies in herself. She is presented as less vulnerable to sexual desire in its crude form than a man would be; but Rhoda is like Gissing – and many of his male protagonists – in trying to live by a doctrine of self-denial. This doctrine is shown to be firmly grounded in reality, yet she is tempted to give it up for the sake of having a lover. Marriage to Everard Barfoot would compromise Rhoda's feminist vocation, just as surely as Gissing's male writers end up being compromised by their domestic responsibilities.

We can sympathize with Rhoda's refusal to give up her principles and freedom to the institution of marriage. But neither will she accept Barfoot's offer of a "free union"; she fears social ostracism if people learn they are living in sin, and is jealous of Barfoot's masculine promiscuous instincts. Since Barfoot sternly refuses to give guarantees on either point, they cannot be together on any terms.[13] Rhoda will be a celibate feminist, Barfoot a man-about-town on his £1500 a year, before settling down with a wife who also has independent means. This marriage, to Agnes Brissenden, promises to be one of equality, mutual respect and shared intellectual interests; but the social agenda of feminism must be discarded, as it would interfere with the couple's pursuit of pleasure.

Nancy Tarrant, of *In the Year of Jubilee*, is another example of the incompatibility of marriage with the wife's self-expression. When her husband Lionel absconds to America in search of fortune, Nancy lives with independence and dignity as a single mother. She even finds time to write a novel, in the hope of supporting herself through literature. Lionel comes back to her, takes up the same career, and tells her she must not submit her novel to a publisher, though he knows it is good enough to be accepted:

> "it isn't literature, but a little bit of Nancy's mind and heart, not to be profaned by vulgar handling. To sell it for hard cash would be horrible. Leave that to the poor creatures who have no choice. You are not obliged to go into the market. . . . I am writing, because I must do something to live by, and I know of nothing else open to me except pen-work. Whatever trash I turned out, I should be justified; as a man,

it's my duty to join in the rough-and-tumble for more or less dirty ha'pence. You, as a woman, have no such duty; nay, it's your positive duty to keep out of the beastly scrimmage."[14]

Her duty, in Darwinian terms, is to offer herself as a reward to a successful male; woman's mercenary nature is thus biologically determined. The peculiar domestic arrangements of the Tarrants suggest Gissing's inability to cope either with the old system of money-marriage, or with the aspirations of the "new woman" of the 1890s. By taking lodgings in London, Lionel will be able to compete unencumbered in the literary marketplace (or battleground); Nancy will live on her modest inheritance in the suburbs and devote herself solely to raising their son. Lionel will invite her out from time to time, thus proving "that I enjoy your company, which is more than one man in ten thousand can say of his wife."[15] They will live together only when he has made enough money to take an old country house, big enough that they don't get on each other's nerves from living in too close contact.

Gissing's male writers are almost all sexually beleaguered. There are no women left like Nancy Tarrant's grandmother, "one of the old-world women whose thoughts found abundant occupation in the cares and pleasures of home."[16] The Married Women's Property Act has allowed women to control their own property and pursue separate economic interests. The Education Act of 1871 has led to the production and marketing of literature for the masses, putting the social status of writers in doubt and commodifying their work. Finally, consumerism has given women a new and problematic role in marriage. Charlotte Perkins Gilman's analysis might have been written as a commentary on Gissing's Darwinian view of sexual selection:

While [women's] power of production is checked, [their] power of consumption is inordinately increased by the showering upon [them] of the "unearned increment" of masculine gifts. For the woman there is, first, no free production allowed; and, second, no relation maintained between what she does produce and what she consumes. She is forbidden to make, but encouraged to take. Her industry is not the natural output of creative energy, not the work she does because she has the inner power and strength to do it; nor is her industry even the measure of her gain. She has, of course, the natural desire to consume; and to that is set no bar save the capacity or the will of her husband . . . . Between the brutal ferocity of excessive male energy struggling in the market-place as in a battlefield and the unnatural greed generated by the perverted condition of female energy, it is not remarkable that the industrial evolution of humanity has shown peculiar symptoms.[17]

Olive Schreiner made a similar critique of middle-class female "parasit-ism," in *Women and Labour*. In spite of Gissing's disbelief in any creative role for women within marriage, the only exit from the *cul de sac* of gen-der conventions in his novels had to be through feminism. But the eco-nomic element in this feminism implied a greater power of market forces over men and women alike, and over both the public and private spheres of life.

In the "Married Woman's Property" chapter of *New Grub Street*, Amy inherits £10,000 from her uncle, enough for her to live comfortably apart from her husband. She is tempted to "play the part of a generous wife" by returning to Edwin: if she took care of his health, he could revive his flag-ging literary career. But her years of poverty have taught her emotional prudence:

> On the other hand, was it not more likely that he would lapse into a life of scholarly self-indulgence, such as he had often told her was his ideal? In that event, what tedium and regret lay before her! Ten thou-sand pounds sounded well, but what did it represent in reality? A poor four hundred a year, perhaps; mere decency of obscure existence, un-less her husband could glorify it by winning fame. If he did nothing, she would be the wife of a man who had failed in literature. She would not be able to take a place in society. Life would be supported without struggle; nothing more to be hoped.[18]

Before the Act, Amy's inheritance would have become her husband's property, despite their living apart; now, she can do with it as she likes. Almost her last words in the novel are that "independence [is] the root of happiness."[19] Once Reardon has conveniently died – effectively of emo-tional frustration and overwork – Amy marries the facile journalist Jasper Mylvain, using her legacy to "trade up" in the marriage market. Mylvain becomes editor of an influential magazine, *The Current*: the title contrasts with Edwin Reardon's devotion to the classical past – part of his unfitness for success – and also suggests Mylvain's ability to "swim with the current." The current of Gissing's world is a double stream, where the power of money combines with a Darwinian imperative for each person to assert themselves at everyone else's expense. Reardon might have been happy as a reclusive scholar, but Amy would not accept his with-drawal from the literary marketplace: she craves the reflected glory of his success. Money and collective selfishness are too strong to be resisted; and women, in Gissing's view, are less likely than men to have the courage even to try.

Yet Gissing does not seem to begrudge Amy her financial good fortune. If lack of money narrows the mind, wealth can be expected to open it (as it does for the circle of women around Mrs Brissenden that Everard Barfoot joins himself to). Gissing gives the Married Women's Property Act credit for the "new woman" of the 1890s, since it enables a few fortunate women to develop their minds in true independence:

> Since the parting from her husband, there had proceeded in Amy a notable maturing of intellect. Probably the one thing was a consequence of the other. . . . When she fell in love with Edwin Reardon her mind had still to undergo the culture of circumstances; though a woman in years she had seen nothing of life but a few phases of artificial society, and her education had not progressed beyond the final school-girl stage. Submitting herself to Reardon's influence, she passed through what was a highly useful training of the intellect; but with the result that she became clearly conscious of the divergence between herself and her husband. . . .
>
> When she found herself alone and independent, her mind acted like a spring when pressure is removed.[20]

Amy reads Herbert Spencer, Darwin, and "Anything that savoured of newness and boldness in philosophic thought." So far, Gissing seems to anticipate Woolf's argument in *A Room of One's Own*, that woman's intellectual potential can only begin to develop when she enjoys the same economic advantages that men have benefited from over the centuries. But then he adds his characteristic sting: "[Amy] was becoming a typical woman of the new time, the woman who has developed concurrently with journalistic enterprise."[21] As usual, Gissing is of two minds about intellectual women (and one who, in this case, enjoys the financial independence he longed for himself). There is a masculinist scepticism about women's capacity for original thought, and a belief that they are specially vulnerable to the contemporary menaces of popular journalism, advertising, fashion, and hire-purchase.[22] Amy is no worse than her second husband, the opportunist man of letters Jasper Mylvain; and Gissing accepts the principle of a woman's need for independence to develop her capacities, whatever the results. Yet neither men nor women can find salvation in the market: anyone who goes there loses their self, whether it be alienated by success, or crushed by failure.

Five Hundred Pounds a Year

Virginia Woolf grew up as a sheltered and secure member of the upper middle class, but her father saw fit to oppress her with lamentations about imminent financial ruin. Reading Gissing, she was confirmed in her understanding of poverty as a stripping away of what one needed to be human at all:

> what Gissing proves is the terrible importance of money, and, if you slip, how you fall and fall and fall. With learning, sensitive feelings, a love of beauty both in art and in human nature - all the qualities that generally (one hopes) keep their possessor somehow afloat - he descended to the depths where men and women live in vast shoals without light or freedom. What a strange place it is - this Nether World! There are women as brutal as savages, men who are half animals, women still preserving some ghost of love and pity, men turning a stunted brain upon the problems of their lot. All the things that grow fine and large up here are starved and twisted down there; just as the squares and parks, and the houses standing separate with rooms measured off for different occupations, are shrivelled into black alleys, sooty patches of green, and sordid lodging houses, where there is shelter, but only the shelter that pigs or cows have, not room for the soul. Without money you cannot have space or leisure; worse than that, the chances are very much against your having either love or intelligence.[23]

Woolf's vision here is not just one of upper and lower, but of different species in different elements – a biological perspective that accepts Gissing's Social Darwinism, rather than any more optimistic view of the proletariat and their capacities. Alex Zwerdling speaks of Woolf's characteristic "combination of sympathy, guilt, and helplessness."[24] Like Gissing, Woolf sees the market (including the literary market) as part of the world "down there," a world of struggle where all higher qualities such as leisure or sympathy are trampled into the mud.

A Room of One's Own begins with a view of the very tip of the world "up there," the privileged halls and courts of Oxbridge. Again, it is with Darwinian eyes that Woolf observes the dons assembling for Chapel:

> Many were in cap and gown; some had tufts of fur on their shoulders; others were wheeled in bath-chairs; others, though not past middle age, seemed creased and crushed into shapes so singular that one was

reminded of those giant crabs and crayfish who heave with difficulty across the sand of an aquarium. As I leant against the wall the University indeed seemed a sanctuary in which are preserved rare types which would soon be obsolete if left to fight for existence on the pavement of the Strand.[25]

The fight for existence goes on in the marketplace, where "merchants and manufacturers . . . made, say, a fortune from industry, and returned, in their wills, a bounteous share of it to endow more chairs, more lectureships, more fellowships in the university where they had learnt their craft." "Urbanity, geniality, dignity" in one place were derived from death-struggles in another.[26] The industry of women, meanwhile, went into housekeeping and childrearing; any money they had, until 1882, was not theirs to give to their own causes, since their husbands had control of it.[27]

Before inheriting her five hundred pounds a year, Woolf's imaginary woman novelist lived "by cadging odd jobs from newspapers, by reporting a donkey show here or a wedding there; I had earned a few pounds by addressing envelopes, reading to old ladies, making artificial flowers, teaching the alphabet to small children in a kindergarten. Such were the chief occupations that were open to women before 1918."[28] Woolf herself began her literary career, after her breakdown in 1904, by writing articles for a religious journal, *The Guardian*:

it would be a great relief to know that I could make a few pence easily in this way – as our passbooks came last night, and they are greatly overdrawn. It is all the result of this idiotic illness, and I should be glad to write something which would pay for small extras. I honestly think I can write better stuff than that wretched article you sent me. . . . But there is a knack of writing for newspapers which has to be learnt, and is quite independent of literary merits.[29]

In *A Room of One's Own* Mary Carmichael is saved from a life of such hack work by a legacy from her aunt. Woolf had been a journalist for three years when she started her first novel in 1907 – *Melymbrosia*, later *The Voyage Out*. In 1909 she inherited £2,500 from her aunt Caroline, and she already had about £6,500 in capital from the deaths of her father and her brother Thoby. But Woolf always left the capital intact and drew only the income of about £350 a year.

Since Leonard Woolf had only a few hundred pounds when they married in 1912, he and Virginia earned most of their income on "Grub Street" until Virginia started to earn large royalties in the mid-1920s.

Lionel Tarrant speaks of the "beastly scrimmage" of the literary market-place; *A Room of One's Own* finds it just as beastly, with the narrator complaining of the "hardness" of the work and the "difficulty" of living on the proceeds:

> But what still remains with me as a worse infliction than either was the poison of fear and bitterness which those days bred in me. To begin with, always to be doing work that one did not wish to do, and to do it like a slave, flattering and fawning, not always necessarily perhaps, but it seemed necessary. . . . and then the thought of that one gift which it was death to hide – a small one but dear to the possessor – perishing and with it myself, my soul – all this became like a rust eating away the bloom of the spring, destroying the tree at its heart.[30]

These were the feelings of the narrator *before* she inherited her £500 a year, and with it an instant end to her bitterness. Woolf herself had capital behind her from the beginning of her journalistic career; and her relation with Bruce Richmond of the *Times Literary Supplement* (her most important outlet) does not seem to have required "flattering and fawning." Richmond was "the admiring editor of my works," she noted in her diary, "a kindly and very unambitious man, who has been quite pleased to spend his time in doing kindnesses to poverty stricken young men."[31] Three years later, though, she was upset when Richmond made her change "lewd" to "obscene" in a review of Henry James. "No more reviewing for me," she vowed, "now that Richmond re-writes my sentences to suit the mealy mouths of Belgravia (an exaggeration, I admit) and it is odd how stiffly one sets pen to paper when one is uncertain of editorial approval."[32]

Woolf makes the narrator of *A Room of One's Own* a Gissingesque slave to "pen-work," all the worse off for being female. Her own anxieties about journalism had less to do with economics, and more with her loss of creative freedom and her insecurity about any writing that had to pass the scrutiny of an outsider. The establishment of the Hogarth Press, which published all of Woolf's novels from *Jacob's Room* (1922) on, was at least as important to her sense of creative independence as her private income. One could say that the press only moderated the power of the literary marketplace, since Woolf was still subject to reviewers and to the response of the book-buying public; but control over the production and distribution of her books was psychologically crucial to her, and may even have prolonged her life.

Outsiders might take a more hostile view of Woolf's literary situation.

A Room of One's Own offers a fairy-tale narrative: an unexpected legacy saves the heroine from the attentions of a predatory and philistine Grub Street. But Woolf herself was never so powerless; and by 1929 (when *A Room of One's Own* was published), she and her friends were widely resented for their influence on the literary marketplace. One response to *A Room of One's Own* was Wyndham Lewis's acerbic *The Apes of God* (1930), which complained that to succeed in the literary racket "you had to be allied with somebody or something affluent" – which Lewis wasn't.[33] Feeling sorry for aspiring writers who lacked £500 a year might also be seen as a way of justifying one's own enjoyment of such a sum, and of claiming a special civility and literary quality for those whose cabins were above the £500 a year watermark.

Woolf also seemed to be saying that writers who had less than £500 could not be as good as those who had more, and that few who had less could manage to be serious writers at all. Her argument in *A Room of One's Own* was as much a self-justification as a plea for the economic emancipation of writers. She was well aware – even jealously so – of major modernist works produced by writers like Joyce and D.H. Lawrence on much less than £500 a year; but she espied in them faults – of narrowness and "underbreeding" – that her theory said *must* be there. Even when free of snobbish rivalry, Woolf's standards required her to find unrealized potential in masterworks like *Jane Eyre*:

> the woman who wrote those pages had more genius in her than Jane Austen; but if one reads them over and marks that jerk in them, that indignation, one sees that she will never get her genius expressed whole and entire. Her books will be deformed and twisted. She will write in a rage where she should write calmly. She will write foolishly where she should write wisely. She will write of herself where she should write of her characters. She is at war with her lot. How could she help but die young, cramped and thwarted?
>
> One could not but play for a moment with the thought of what might have happened if Charlotte Brontë had possessed say three hundred a year – [34]

To look for a more philosophic mind in the Brontës seems no more relevant than to want more indignation in Jane Austen. Woolf's argument takes for granted the opposition between genteel values and "trade," and she transfers it, more or less intact, from the drawing room to the literary scene. It is true that Gissing makes a similar case for writerly leisure; yet his fantasies of rural or classical retirement are much less vital than his tirades against Grub Street and London slums. Woolf assumes that the "beastly scrimmage" of literary subsistence can only lead to cramped and deformed writing, and that people only start to live when they have enough wealth to be polite and contemplative.

Woolf's insistence that writers need to be above the struggle runs parallel with her dislike of competition and aggression as intrinsically male practices. But she also admits that participation in literary struggles, at least, could be a way for women to emancipate themselves. "There has been no battle of Grub Street," she observes in *Three Guineas*. "That profession has never been shut to the daughters of educated men. This was due of course to the extreme cheapness of its professional requirements."[35] Yet a woman who succeeded in Grub Street – Woolf takes Mrs Oliphant as her example – would have to be one who "sold her brain, her very admirable brain, prostituted her culture and enslaved her intellectual liberty in order that she might earn her living and educate her children." What Woolf does not say is that writing for the market was just about the only way for Mrs Oliphant, like Frances Trollope before her, to maintain her family. Liberty to compete on equal terms is much less important to Woolf than intellectual liberty, and this remains the preserve of "those daughters of educated men who have enough to live on."[36]

Grub Street – like all the cultural institutions of Woolf's time – was still controlled by men and an expression of their values. Woolf remained strongly drawn to the potential of a "separate sphere" where women might preserve their intellectual chastity:

> "Just as for many centuries, Madam," we might plead, "it was thought vile for a woman to sell her body without love, but right to give it to the husband whom she loved, so it is wrong, you will agree, to sell your mind without love, but right to give to the art which you love." "But what," she may ask, "is meant by 'selling your mind without love'?" "Briefly," we might reply, "to write at the command of another person what you do not want to write for the sake of money."[37]

Female writing and female sexuality both need to be sacralized and defended from the marketplace. When Mrs Lyttleton, the editor of *The Guardian*, edited her articles, Woolf complained that "she sticks her broad thumb into the middle of my delicate sentences and improves the moral tone."[38] The image is one of violation, to which one must submit once one has offered oneself for sale.

In the realms of art, economics and sexuality alike there is an underworld – implicitly male – of struggle and aggression; from this the artist needs to escape, to the "view of the open sky."[39] Yet in leaving behind struggle one can discard passion too, and arrive at the quietism of Clarissa Dalloway on her narrow and solitary bed. In The *Wings of the Dove*, James makes Milly Theale's choice for purity also a choice for death. Novels are traditionally concerned with immanence rather than transcendence, and with the pursuit of those worldly "good things" so near to Trollope's heart. These things usually come from the two great forms of secular commerce, monetary or sexual exchange; and to want something more than such good things often makes a character a misfit in the novelistic universe. Death, or death-in-life, is the probable fate of such characters: Clarissa Dalloway, the married nun; Septimus Smith, rejecting his wife's embrace and jumping to his death; Milly Theale, dying a virgin and leaving her fortune to the man who betrayed her; Lady Julia Ongar, renouncing her wealth and living in celibacy to atone for her mercenary marriage; Clarissa Harlowe, choosing to die rather than submit to either Solmes or Lovelace.

Both Gissing and James show their characters having to become conscious of their own marketability. Woolf is well enough aware of such commodification; yet, in "Mr Bennett and Mrs Brown," she strives to define modernism as separate from it. Arnold Bennett, she says, "would notice the advertisements" in Mrs Brown's railway carriage; but most of the time, he notices the wrong things.[40] What a novelist should notice is:

> something permanently interesting in character in itself. When all the practical business of life has been discharged, there is something about people which continues to seem to them of overwhelming importance, in spite of the fact that it has no bearing whatever upon their happiness, comfort, or income.[41]

What is "permanent" in Mrs Brown can be separated from the system of exchange that she inhabits. As in *A Room of One's Own*, material interests need to be bracketed out from the domain of essential humanness.

It would not be hard to show that Woolf's perceptions of Mrs Brown are themselves conditioned by assumptions about her subject's financial worries, subservience to the patriarchal order, and the like. We cannot disregard the dependence of Woolf's own perspective on social and economic privilege. Mrs Brown is not directly subordinated to her observer across the carriage, as a servant might be; yet there is a hierarchy of seer and seen, just as surely as between Mrs Brown and the man who, in some unspecified way, oppresses her. The gradations of that hierarchy are precisely measurable, whether in terms of money or of relative gentility.

Woolf argues that five hundred a year liberates the mind; Margaret Schlegel in *Howards End* argues the contrary: "all our thoughts are the thoughts of six-hundred-pounders, and all our speeches."[42] For Woolf, disinterestedness is an automatic result of financial independence; for Margaret, it is a balance between her own (determined) interests and those of her opposites, the Wilcoxes above and Leonard Bast below. Woolf and Forster come together, though, on the effects of the gendered division of labor: women are more disinterested than men because they are further removed from direct engagement with market forces. This moral sensitivity would diminish if they assumed their share of the world's work on equal terms. James and Gissing take a more cynical view: their women may still display the traditional proprieties, but at heart they are often mercenary, and able to manipulate men who cling to chivalric values. Though neither James nor Gissing are feminists in a programmatic sense, their novels abound with women who escape conventional roles and patriarchal sanctions. Kate Croy's father in *The Wings of the Dove*, or Nancy Tarrant's in *In the Year of Jubilee*, give up or lose control over their newly assertive daughters. Woolf's female protagonists, such as Clarissa Dalloway or Mrs Ramsay, seem more likely to withdraw into a self-delighting female sphere and leave patriarchy in its place – the market place.

5
Conrad and the Economics of Imperialism: *Heart of Darkness*

> Take up the White Man's burden –
> In patience to abide,
> To veil the threat of terror
> And check the show of pride;
> By open speech and simple,
> An hundred times made plain.
> To seek another's profit,
> And work another's gain.
> —Kipling, "The White Man's Burden"

Mixed Motives

The current fascination of imperialism for Western literary critics lies in its exemplary status as a Foucauldian system of discipline and domination. Edward Said proposed the grand narrative of Orientalism in 1978; and since the later 1980s, post-colonialism has made even stronger claims to represent relations between "the West and its Others" as a struggle for control over discourses and identities.[1] Kipling's poem fits in with these themes, by denying to the White Man his own profit – in the material sense – while assigning to the subjugated peoples profit of an opposite kind, that is, moral improvement. To foreground the economics of imperialism is to go against the current of Orientalist readings, and still more so if one gives weight to neo-liberal assumptions about the mutual gains from international trade, or the economic incentives that cause migrants from the Third World to prefer life the West. In these two chapters on *Heart of Darkness* and *Nostromo* I will examine Western imperialism as an economic enterprise, while recognizing its coexistence with the "prestige" imperialism that sought domination for its own sake, rather than within a calculus of profit.

As the imperialists moved outwards from Europe, they had a variety of aims: to convert the heathen to Christianity, to gain a military advantage, to acquire glory in extending their nation's rule, to find an outlet for surplus populations, or simply to enrich themselves. Imperialism was a system founded on mixed motives, and it should not be reduced to a single cause, whether power or profit. Rather, we should look at how different motives generate their own discourses and social formations (leading, in turn, to different readings of the literature of imperialism). With English imperialism, especially, the country's pre-existing division between prestige and market cultures was replicated overseas. In Kipling's verse, the "White Man's burden" is a discursive task, the constant enunciation of the principles of justice by the "service class" of colonial administrators, who hold themselves aloof from the "profit" or "gain" of their merchant compatriots. For Kipling, the civilizing mission of imperialism would be discredited if economic gain were its underlying purpose.

For Adam Smith, conversely, the lack of a rational economic motive is imperialism's fatal flaw. Capital, he argues, will always be employed more efficiently in open markets than in closed ones. Britain should renounce its monopoly on trade with its North American colonies, and save the huge military cost of keeping rivals out of American markets by force. Yet, in a magisterial passage, Smith explains why economic rationality is unlikely to prevail:

> No nation ever voluntarily gave up the dominion of any province, how troublesome soever it might be to govern it, and how small soever the revenue which it afforded might be in proportion to the expence which it occasioned. Such sacrifices, though they might frequently be agreeable to the interest, are always mortifying to the pride of every nation, and what is perhaps of still greater consequence, they are always contrary to the private interest of the governing part of it, who would thereby be deprived of the disposal of many places of trust and profit, of many opportunities of acquiring wealth and distinction, which the possession of the most turbulent, and, to the great body of the people, the most unprofitable province seldom fails to afford.[2]

By coupling terms like "interest" and "pride," "wealth and distinction," Smith shows his awareness of how prestige and market values coexist within imperialism. Each has its own dynamic; for prestige imperialism this is summed up in Cecil Rhodes' maxim, "Expansion is everything" – often, expansion beyond any rational economic interest. Smith recognizes that nations are psychologically unwilling to give up imperial possessions, whether or not it makes economic sense to keep them.

By Conrad's time, imperialism as an outlet for the love of dominion had been reinforced by the ideology of Social Darwinism. The main

European powers hardly needed any internal motive for expansion; each nation found motive enough in the need to respond to its rivals:

> de nos jours, l'expansion d'une race hors de ses frontières est la condi-tion de sa durée, la forme moderne de la lutte pour la vie . . . dans ce temps de concurrence universelle, qui n'avance pas recule, et qui recule est submergé par le flot.[3]

Lord Salisbury, similarly, predicted in 1898 that "From the necessities of politics or under the pretence of philanthropy – the living nations will gradually encroach on the territory of the dying."[4]

Leonard Woolf argued that the Darwinian imperative must be eco-nomic, rather than any desire for prestige or adventure. Just as a species needs food and territory in order to survive, so does a nation need raw materials and markets; any invocation of "higher" motives can only be humbug. Leftist critics of imperialism, like Woolf, assume that imperial-ism must have been profitable, or it could not have happened.[5] They ar-gue that all motives can be reduced to material interest (to use Conrad's recurrent phrase), and that capitalism is a logical system driven by quan-tifiable aims such as prices, wages or profits. But if this were true, nations would only expand where there was a rational expectation of profit, and modern research has shown that this was often not the case (even allow-ing for over-optimism about how much profit a new colony might yield). Evidence is piling up that the British Empire – apart from the "white" Dominions – cannot have been profitable even when it was at its height. Between 1865 and 1914 Britain was a massive exporter of capital, invest-ing more than twice as much overseas as it did in its domestic economy; but only about eleven percent of these funds went to the Empire.[6] Any profits from Empire investments then had to be offset against the costs of administering and defending it. Davis and Huttenback estimate these costs at a quarter of the total English tax burden, and argue that the Em-pire could not have shown a net profit.[7]

Another way of assessing the value of the Empire would be to compare England with countries of more modest imperial ambitions. Its strategy of external investment made England into a different place from the U.S. or Germany, with their dynamic of internal development. Not only did Eng-land have the most significant rentier class by 1914; it was also the most significant rentier country. Its huge transfer of wealth overseas, into mainly passive investments, limited the growth and modernization of British industry; and as industry found it harder to compete in global mar-kets, it became more dependent, after 1918, on the shelter of Imperial preference. Reluctance to give up the Empire was surely a major cause of the relative economic decline of 20th-century Britain.

Joseph Schumpeter, writing just before the First World War, summed up imperialism as an aristocratic reaction against the secular trends of rationalization and modernization:

> Imperialism thus is atavistic in character. It falls into that large group of surviving features from earlier ages that play such an important part in every concrete social situation. In other words, it is an element that stems from the living conditions, not of the present, but of the past – or, put in terms of the economic interpretation of history, from past rather than present relations of production. . . . If our theory is correct, causes of imperialism should decline in intensity the later they occur in the history of a people and of a culture.[8]

In Schumpeter's theory, the industrial revolution creates an "economically oriented leadership" that becomes "democratized, individualized, and rationalized," as economic competition gradually supersedes "the primitive contingencies of physical combat":

> In a purely capitalist world, what was once energy for war becomes simply energy for labor of every kind. Wars of conquest and adventurism in foreign policy in general are bound to be regarded as troublesome distractions, destructive of life's meaning, a diversion from the accustomed and therefore "true" task.
>
> A purely capitalist world therefore can offer no fertile soil to imperialist impulses.[9]

Marxists argued that imperialism was on the rise, as the last resort of a "late" capitalism that needed to conquer new markets to prop up a declining rate of profit.[10] Schumpeter argued the precise opposite: imperialism was a feudal remnant that would wither away as capitalism became a purely rational economic system. Aristocratic values were by definition archaic, and sure to be undermined by the advance of commercial modernity. This meant, in the long run, free trade, the dissolution of special interests in a global economic system, and commercially-motivated pacifism instead of atavistic wars. Britain clung to its role as an imperial nation only because of the political dominance of its aristocratic classes, who loved pomp and circumstance and scorned market values.

Yet to show that British imperialism was unprofitable is not the same as proving that it was an irrational policy, even in strictly financial terms.

Nations are not rational economic entities, but an assembly of interests, which often put their particular concerns before the general good. O'Brien finds the economic basis for imperialism in a group of "gentlemanly capitalists," mainly based in the Home Counties, who expected higher returns from Empire than from domestic investments. For them, the Empire "provided satisfactory outposts for *rentier* capital, defensible and safe even from the emergent threat of trade unionism and the welfare state."[11] Such capitalists mystified their private interest with a rhetoric of national greatness, the White Man's Burden, or whatever else might serve their cause. In O'Brien's scheme, aristocratic imperialists were being manipulated by cunning financiers, whose aim was to socialize the costs of Empire while keeping the profits for themselves. What Smith, Schumpeter and O'Brien all assumed, though, was that imperialism yoked together different kinds of desires, whether for power, or for gain. It is this hybridity of imperial motives that disappears in Foucauldian assumptions of a monolithic deployment of imperial discursive power.

Conrad and the Imperial Idea

Conrad's inquiry into imperialism centers on the "redeeming idea": the ideal purpose that makes imperialism something more than just the pursuit of power or money. Early in his career Conrad was labeled "the Kipling of the sea"; the grain of truth in this identification is that both men were, in their different ways, exceptionalists who believed that English imperialism was more idealistic than that of other European nations. Kipling's "lesser breeds without the law" were not dark-skinned natives, but the citizens of Britain's imperial rivals, especially Germany. Both Conrad and Kipling argued that the redeeming idea could be held by England in good faith, even if for other nations it was only a pretext.[12] In trying to prove the autonomy of "higher" imperial motives, Conrad looked for actions that could be dissociated from material self-interest. At the beginning of the Boer War, he argued that the Boers had "no idea of liberty, which can only be found under the English flag all over the world. . . . Canada and Australia are taking part in this, which could not influence their material interests. Why?"[13] Yet Conrad well knew that even a just war offered arms contracts and promotions for the opportunists, and the smell of blood for the war-lovers, along with the triumph of virtue for the idealists. As a novelist, he found his subject in how easily the higher motives could be contaminated by the lower.

Conrad's acquaintance with the ironies of imperialism began in childhood, when he was raised on the passionate idealism of Polish resistance to Russian domination. But it was also an ideal that ruined his father, Apollo Korzeniowski, and contributed to his early death. His father's mentality was typical of the Polish patriotic nobility, the *szlachta*. After Apollo's death, Conrad was raised by his maternal uncle Tadeusz Bobrowski, a landowner with a much more businesslike outlook. In 1882, when Conrad was twenty-five, Tadeusz explained to him the drawbacks of the *szlachta's* disdain for material interests:

> You have now lived for some years in England and have been taking part in the life there and you will have learned to respect money, and it therefore probably surprises you to hear me calling it 'filthy.' This expression is a survival from the 'romantic period' in which I was born and grew up, and to some extent it reflects our national character, a trait which was supposed to show lack of interest in money matters. I presume the latter to be an apparent rather than a real quality, for it arises rather from a carelessness than from a real contempt for money. This is because we did not work to get it but worked rather to squander it! Now our esteem for it has increased, mine possible more than others, for we have come to realize that it is the 'nervus rerum' and the basis of both the external and inner independence of both an individual and a whole society.[14]

The *szlachta* had to develop more esteem for money after their defeat by Russia in the uprising of 1863. They had failed in their traditional mission, and had to question their viability as a class of knightly warriors with agricultural estates. The only remaining strategy for Poland was modernization and commercial development, since any escape from Russian domination would have to wait on a change in the European balance of power (which came about in 1918, when Poland achieved independence).

Conrad's mature temperament was thus divided between aristocratic pretensions and recognition of the practical necessities of bourgeois modernity. At Kinshasa, he quarreled with the local manager of the Societé Belge du Haut-Congo, Camille Delcommune, whom he described as "un vulgaire marchand d'ivoire a instincts sordides qui s'imagine être un commerçant tandis qu'il n'est qu'une espèce de boutiquier africain."[15] Conrad also had come to the Congo to make money, of course; but he was paid a salary and expected to be in command of a ship (even if it never materialized). His own employment stood on a higher plane than amassing wealth franc by franc, in a grubby series of minor transactions. The merchant has an immediate, daily intimacy with money; the captain or colonial official deals with money only incidentally and can therefore bear himself like a gentleman.

The imperialist enterprise was shared between these two types: the "service class" of officials and the vulgar merchants. In England the division was institutionalized in a dual representation overseas, by the aristocratic "diplomatic service" and the plebeian consular and trade officers.[16] It might be called a factitious distinction, no more than a division of labor within a single project. Nonetheless, the service class held themselves to be separate and superior: they typically had a liberal education, they answered directly to the state, they were paid a fixed salary, and they saw their work as part of Europe's civilizing mission. Benita Parry has defined the service ideology as "the work-ethic, service and action where no ends are specified."[17] Duty can be said to create its own end: you should stand to your post without complaint or speculation about its ultimate purpose. In a storm or a battle, one either does one's duty or runs away; the existential choice is sharpened by the absence of a material or even a rational incentive to "do the right thing."

The characteristic moral atmosphere of Conrad's fiction derives from his habit of interrogating the service code, even as he affirms it as the closest thing he can find to a standard of value. The monetary scale is in principle straightforward, a simple matter of greater or lesser sums; and in traditional societies prestige values are similarly unproblematic, for they are guaranteed by a universal and transcendent signifier: the King, the homeland, the national destiny, the will of God. But Conrad – as exile, outsider, and sceptic – appreciated these values without fully participating in them. His prose mingles a poetics of certitude (the ideal of duty) and a poetics of doubt (the absence of a metaphysical guarantee for fidelity to the service code). Conrad's service, the merchant marine, was in principle a strictly economic enterprise; but its officers also were imbued with the prestige code, and claimed a higher calling than mere shifters of cargo from one market-place to another. In *Heart of Darkness*, Kurtz first places himself within the service mission, then becomes a merchant (of ivory), and at last enters a realm where both the service and mercantile codes have dissolved into nihilism.

Figures of Descent

We may read Kurtz's story as proof that profit-seeking is only a screen for the colonizers' darker purposes: what they do in Africa they would have done in Europe, if it were not for the restraints laid on them by the old-established civilizations. On this view, what J.M. Keynes called "ordinary economic motives" occupy only the middle (and perhaps more benign) realm of human nature. There are aristocratic, ideal standards above them, and below, as Thomas Pynchon has suggested, a whole world of other desires:

> What's a colony without its dusky natives? Where's the fun if they're all going to die off? Just a big hunk of desert, no more maids, no field-hands, no laborers for the construction or the mining – wait, wait a minute there, yes it's Karl Marx, that sly old racist skipping away with his teeth together and his eyebrows up trying to make believe it's nothing but Cheap Labor and Overseas Markets. . . . Oh, no. Colonies are much, much more. Colonies are the outhouses of the European soul, where a fellow can let his pants down and relax, enjoy the smell of his own shit. Where he can fall on his slender prey roaring as loud as he feels like, and guzzle her blood with open joy. Eh? Where he can just wallow and rut and let himself go in a softness, a receptive darkness of limbs, of hair as woolly as the hair on his own forbidden genitals. Where the poppy, and cannabis and coca grow full and green, and not to the colors and style of death, as do ergot and agaric, the blight and fungus native to Europe. Christian Europe was always death, Karl, death and repression. Out and down in the colonies, life can be indulged, life and sensuality in all its forms, with no harm done to the Metropolis, nothing to soil those cathedrals, white marble statues, noble thoughts. . . . No word ever gets back. The silences down here are vast enough to absorb all behavior, no matter how dirty, how animal it gets. . . . [18]

Pynchon places Kurtz's "The horror!" as a discovery of the latent evil in the *European* soul.[19] Colonies transfer wealth to the Metropolis, to help support a high culture of rentier refinement; but they also provide an outlet for another kind of consumption, the indulgence of impulses repressed in Europe – where people possess the currency of their desires but, as it were, no market to spend it in. Africa provides an experience that is the obverse of modernist nostalgia for organicism: a face-to-face society of primary experience, where *anything goes*, and can be bought with a local currency of wire, ivory, if necessary human heads. All this is a sinister parody of the organic idyll. For Pynchon, avarice is not the cause of the worst evils of colonialism; they come from the instinctual release they give their perpetrators, rather than monetary profit.

Conrad begins by making the opposite case: the colonies provide an opportunity to exercise the heroic virtues of renunciation and restraint.[20]

The individual self-control of the colonizer validates the collective political control of Europe over the "savage" impulses of the natives, and the
replacement of those impulses with civic and Christian order. When
Kurtz entered the Congo, he saw trade as no more than a means to this
end: "Each station should be like a beacon on the road towards better
things, a center for trade of course but also for humanising, improving,
instructing." Conrad leaves much unclear about Kurtz's moral degeneration in the Interior, but it is certain that his civilizing mission was first
subverted by trade: "the appetite for more ivory had got the better of the
– what shall I say – less material aspirations."[21] The opposition between
"appetite" and "aspiration" points to the *ascesis* of the colonizer: the
white man in the jungle teaching the natives the lesson of renouncing
their "primitive" desires. Conversely, once the "lower" instinct of acquisitiveness has been released, every other base desire can rush out through
the same gate. Conrad's narrative moves from the redeeming idea, to a
fall into the material, and then a deeper fall, into the abyss of primitivism. There are three orders of being within imperialism: one based on the
ideal, one on trade, one on pillage. The colonial system established by
King Leopold, and the individual servants of the system, pass through
each one in sequence.

Leopold himself seems to have started out with high intentions,
though he also hoped to make money out of Africa, and to rival the imperial possessions of Holland (from which Belgium had seceded in 1830).
He believed that the great advantage of Empire was the return flow of
wealth to the mother country:

> L'armée des Indes néerlandaises, la marine des Indes, l'administration
> des Indes [sont] trois immenses carrières ouvertes à l'activité de la
> jeunesse néerlandaises. Dans l'Inde, toutes les familles anglaises ont un
> ou deux de leurs enfants qui y vivent, y cherchent, et y font fortune.
> Ces fortunes se rapportent à Londres et cette capitale, semblable à une
> ruche d'abeilles où ces insectes, apres avoir sucé les meilleurs fleurs,
> viennent déposer leur miel, est une des plus riches villes du monde.[22]

A Marxist would dismiss Leopold's idealistic schemes for African improvement as mere disguises for his fundamental motive of economic
gain. But such a reductive view excludes the great Conradian theme of
corruption, whether of grandiose national ideals or individual dreams.
Both Leopold and Kurtz saw trade, at first, as an instrument of "eleva-
tion," in the tradition of *doux commerce* defined by Samuel Ricard in
1704:

Commerce attaches [men] one to another through mutual utility. Through commerce the moral and physical passions are superseded by interest. . . Commerce has a special character which distinguishes it from all other professions. It affects the feelings of men so strongly that it makes him who was proud and haughty suddenly turn supple, bending and serviceable. Through commerce, man learns to deliberate, to be honest, to acquire manners, to be prudent and reserved in both talk and action. Sensing the necessity to be wise and honest in order to succeed, he flees vice, or at least his demeanor exhibits decency and seriousness so as not to arouse any adverse judgement on the part of present and future acquaintances; he would not dare make a spectacle of himself for fear of damaging his credit standing and thus society may well avoid a scandal which it might otherwise have to deplore.[23]

Ricard and, later, Montesquieu saw commerce as something that "polishes and softens barbaric ways as we can see every day."[24] However, they were thinking mainly of the encroachment of market culture on the peasant societies of Europe. Economists like David Ricardo took it for granted that the Irish were poor because they were lazy, and that the remedy for their backwardness was "to stimulate exertion, to create new wants, and to implant new tastes."[25] But the conditions for the peaceful development of consumer society scarcely existed in many areas staked out for European expansion; and Cobden argued that Europe should simply leave them alone until they sought trade for their own benefit: "[Parliament] had a great deal to do at home within a stone's throw of where they were before they embarked on a scheme of redeeming from barbarism the whole coast of Africa."[26]

Leopold soon became impatient with the redemptive powers of commerce, and turned to more direct means of achieving his ends – which, meanwhile, had changed for the worse. His original plan for the Congo was to allow free trade to all countries, in the hope that the colony would rapidly become prosperous and give Belgium a large return on its investment.[27] But when profits were less than expected, he abandoned liberal economics in favor of monopolization and the extraction of profit by brute force rather than market incentive. He now traded on his personal account, and his Congo policy became one of mere pillage of the colony's disposable resources.[28] Kurtz, similarly, casts off of the restraints intrinsic to economic exchange and becomes no more than a pirate:

mostly his expeditions had been for ivory. 'But he had no goods to trade with by that time,' [Marlow] objected. 'There's a good lot of cartridges left even yet,' [the Russian] answered, looking away. 'To speak plainly, he raided the country,' [Marlow] said.[29]

To get the ivory, Kurtz has to recruit an army who care nothing for ivory, but are glad of the opportunity to kill and eat their enemies.

By 1890, when Conrad was in the Congo, Leopold had forgotten his promises of long-term investment and cultural development, and sought only to extract from Africa as much rubber and ivory as possible – in effect, stealing it from the natives, who had little interest in participating in a monetary economy. Leopold also moved to drive out the five private trading companies acting in the Congo: they may have brought development to the colony, but to Leopold they were simply unwelcome competition. The Company in *Heart of Darkness* is capitalized because it is the only legitimate agency for extracting profit from the Congo. And there is only one "Manager," who can not only exclude competitors from his territory, he can kill them. As Adam Smith had earlier observed, "The government of an exclusive company of merchants is, perhaps, the worst of all governments for any country whatever."[30]

Six years later, when Conrad was writing "An Outpost of Progress" (a story set in the Congo), he told his publisher that "All the bitterness of those days, all my puzzled wonder as to the meaning of all I saw – all my indignation at masquerading philanthropy – have been with me again, while I wrote."[31] But the term "masquerading" begs the question of *development* that we have been examining. When Kurtz inaugurates his African venture, idealistic aims are foremost in his consciousness; by the time he scrawls "exterminate all the brutes" on the last page of his pamphlet the mask has been ripped off. Yet Kurtz then represses his own fit of misanthropy, and puts the mask back on: "The curious part," Marlow reports, "was that he had apparently forgotten all about that valuable postscription because later on when he in a sense came to himself, he repeatedly entreated me to take good care of 'my pamphlet' (he called it) as it was sure to have in the future a good influence upon his career."[32]

Curious or not, people live with their motives in a complex way, rather than in simple hypocrisy where there is only one real – and base – motive, and only one altruistic motive put forward as a screen. The economic motive in *Heart of Darkness* is exercised in a kind of "zero degree" of everyday, material normality. On either side of this norm lie realms of economic irrationality whose connection is both oppositional and complementary: altruism on the higher side, atavism on the lower. Conrad's great theme is the mysterious way in which higher transforms itself into lower, passing through the neutral ground of economics on the way.

Imperialism and Modernity

Marxist readings of *Heart of Darkness* assume a causal relation between the capitalist expansionism that is the initial motive for colonizing the Congo, and the descent into savagery at the end of the novella. The choice between "socialism or barbarism," first posed in *The Communist Manifesto*, attributes the moral disasters of the twentieth century – war, racism, poverty, genocide – to a principle of evil immanent in the unfolding of modern capitalism. Conversely, human potential can only realize itself completely and benevolently within the "scientific" tradition of socialism. Yet there is a counter-theme in Marxism of nostalgia for unscientific social forms, evident in Jameson's judgment of "the storytelling situation organized around Marlow":

> such literary institutions, once genuine or concrete forms of social relationships, have long since been blasted by the corrosive effects of market relations, and, like so many other traditional, organic, precapitalist institutions, systematically fragmented by the characteristic reorganizational process of capitalism which Weber described under the term *rationalization*.[33]

Jameson proposes a continuity of such reorganization, from the enclosures criticized by Thomas More in the sixteenth century, to the penetration by capitalism of its last frontier – the tribal hinterlands of Africa and Asia – in the latter part of the nineteenth:

> It should be stressed that the destructive effects of capitalism, both irreversible and fatal to the older social forms, are not particularly due to conscious planning on the part of the businessmen, who are neither personally wicked nor, in the earlier stages of this process at least, self-conscious efficiency experts. Rather the process is objective, and is impersonally achieved, or at least set in motion, by the penetration of a money economy and the consequent need to reorganize local institutions on a cash basis . . . [34]

As a general account of the modernizing process this may be plausible enough, but it does not fit Conrad's Congo at all. Personal wickedness is at the center of the European incursion into Africa; "efficiency" is put forward by Marlow as the redeeming imperial virtue; and money penetrates the jungle only in the parodic form of pieces of brass wire.[35] The key word in Jameson's account is "process," a term drawn from the Marxist vision of imperialism as a rational, impersonal and goal-oriented expansion of modernizing capitalism. This may have been Marlow's idea before he went to Africa; but the whole point is that the facts on the ground are nothing like that – whether it be the absence of rivets when needed, or the greater absence of a coherent moral purpose for the whole enterprise. As Conrad shows it, white imperialism in the Congo was not very rational to begin with – the French ship firing into the jungle hints at more senselessness to come – and it is never anything so orderly as to deserve the name of a system or process.

From the very beginning of the novella Conrad teases the reader by intertwining concepts of imperialism as progress or as descent. When the Romans came up the Thames nineteen hundred years before, the site of modern London showed them nothing but "Sandbanks, marshes, forests, savages."[36] That London should now be a great commercial capital implies a narrative of improvement. As the Thames is now, so shall the Congo be: it too will have its pleasure yachts, manned by company directors, lawyers and accountants. Two thousand years ago, the Britons were savages; now they have taken the place of the Romans. In the long run, commerce – with its accompaniment of peace, order and luxury – will replace savagery; and the Africans may in their turn be an imperial, civilizing people.

Yet this comforting prospect can scarcely exhaust the meaning of the tale. The Romans only held Britain for some four hundred years; then they withdrew in despair, and their cities and roads reverted to forest. Kurtz, the apparently virtuous *homo economicus*, went to the Congo to advance the frontiers of civilization; instead, he was swallowed up by the "immense darkness." That darkness has advanced, by the end of the story, to the lower reaches of the Thames itself: the Londoners of today are descended from the savages of Roman times, and their potential for atavism only awaits the right circumstances to declare itself. Schumpeter proposes that commercial rationality is the *telos* of history; Conrad suggests that it can never satisfy more than a fraction of human desires, and can create only local and temporary enclaves of order – which, sooner or later, the jungle will reclaim.

6
Nostromo: Economism and its Discontents

> *War itself, if it is carried on with order and with a sacred*
> *respect for the rights of citizens, has something sublime in*
> *it, and makes the disposition of the people who carry it on*
> *thus only the more sublime, the more numerous are the*
> *dangers to which they are exposed and in respect of which*
> *they behave with courage. On the other hand, a long peace*
> *generally brings about a predominant commercial spirit*
> *and, along with it, low selfishness, cowardice, and*
> *effeminacy, and debases the disposition of the people.*
> —Immanuel Kant, *Critique of Judgement (1790)*

Material Interests

Nostromo begins by establishing two moral registers, and continues to alternate between them. Chapter One tells of the treasure-seekers of Azuera, figures of romance whose ghosts remain to haunt the Golfo Placido. In Chapter Two, the narrative focus changes to the arrival of the "commercial activity" of the Oceanic Steam Navigation Company in the Gulf. This comes as a falling-off from the novel's melodramatic beginning; and a tone of disappointment and denigration will carry on through Conrad's exposition of Costaguana's predominant commercial enterprise, the San Tomé mine. The mingling of these two registers reflects the division of imperialism between imaginative and material projects, adventure and consolidation, violence and consent, power and profit. In *Heart of Darkness*, Conrad shows the division breaking down into brute violence and chaos; *Nostromo* shows a later stage of consolidation, after imperialism has been replaced by a neo-colonialism more characteristic of the twentieth century than of the nineteenth.

The previous chapter examined Conrad's tentative exculpation of imperialism by the "redeeming idea": a higher aim that makes imperialism more than just the pursuit of power or money. In *Nostromo*, Conrad shifts his target, to the long tradition of economic liberalism that opposes the redeeming idea on strictly pragmatic grounds. This tradition decries the love of domination for its own sake, indulged in by the European great powers;

instead, it understands progress as the peaceful extension of modernizing economic rationality. Adam Smith had argued that Britain would be more prosperous as a free trade power than as an imperial one. Jeremy Bentham, in his *Plan for an Universal and Perpetual Peace*, proposed that if the European powers withdrew from their colonies, they would have no further reason to make war on each other. "It is not the interest of Great Britain," said Bentham, "to have any foreign dependencies whatsoever. The truth of this proposition will appear if we consider, first, That distant dependencies increase the chances of war, . . . second, That colonies are seldom, if ever, sources of profit to the mother country."[1] Cobden, similarly, believed that Britain's policy of "trade follows the flag" was misguided. "Cheapness," he said, "and not the cannon or the sword, is the weapon through which alone we possess and can hope to defend or extend our commerce. . . . armies and ships cannot protect or extend commerce; whilst, as is too well known, the expenses of maintaining them oppress and impede our manufacturing industry."[2] He agreed with George Washington's argument, in his farewell address, that: "The great rule of conduct for us in regard to foreign nations is, in extending our commercial relations, to have with them as little political connection as possible." America was a democratic nation, and therefore relied on economic incentives to promote its trade; England was aristocratic, with ruling passions like pride and power.

The ideology of Smith, Bentham and Cobden is economism: that economic values are, in the long run, most peaceful, most productive, and most worthy to prevail over all other social goals. British foreign policy after 1815 was heavily influenced by economist principles. The Reciprocity of Duties Act of 1823 encouraged commercial treaties between England and other countries willing to open their markets, and was followed by Cobden's crowning achievement, the repeal of the Corn Laws in 1846.[3] Throughout the 19th century Britain moved steadily towards Free Trade and, as the world's greatest economic power, presided over huge increases in international trade, global capital movements, and cultural exchange between nations. Even the Empire was run with a frugal administration and without tariff preference.

No critic of Conrad can overlook his disdain for "material interests," which reflects an aristocratic judgement that the pursuit of profit is irredeemably base. But the phrase "material interests" in *Nostromo* is not just a vague label for "business," "greed," or even "capitalism." Rather, it targets a specific ideological and institutional formation: the Cobdenite system of free-trade economism that was espoused by the Liberal Party and that determined British trade policy from 1846 to 1914. Anyone with the slightest interest in politics would be aware of Cobdenite principles; on the personal level, Conrad's first publisher T. Fisher Unwin was married to Cobden's youngest daughter, and drew Conrad's attention to his father-in-law's intellectual legacy.[4] Moreover, Conrad was for twenty years an agent of the free-trade system, in his capacity as an officer of the merchant navy. Yet there was a remarkably sustained exercise of false consciousness in the way he seized on the chivalric code of the sea, while denigrating the economic function to which that code was, after all, ancillary. In his essay on the loss of the *Titanic*, Conrad wrote: "I have seen commerce pretty close. I know what it is worth, and I have no particular regard for commercial magnates."[5] In such remarks, he assumed that an officer on a merchant ship is – by virtue of his code of duty – superior to and morally separate from the trade that he is in fact engaged in.

The Modernization of Sulaco

Nostromo's Sulaco is not an imperial possession. Free of Spanish rule for nearly a century, it has separated from its parent state of Costaguana, which had fallen into a destructive polarization between liberal aristocracy and populist dictatorship. The breaking of this opposition can only come from an external intervention, whose instrument will be the San Tomé mine. The history of the mine recapitulates centuries of Latin American development: from an imperialism of mere plunder, to a failed policy of national autarchy, to incorporation by globalizing capitalism.[6] In its early years, it might as well have been in the Congo as in Latin America: "Worked in the early days mostly by means of lashes on the backs of slaves, its yield had been paid for in its own weight of human bones. Whole tribes of Indians had perished in the exploitation; and then the mine was abandoned, since with this primitive method it had ceased to make a profitable return."[7] The mine is later expropriated by the government and shut down; and its site reverts to jungle. When Charles Gould decides to re-open the mine, it is in the service of a comprehensive project of economizing Sulaco:

> "What is wanted here is law, good faith, order, security. Anyone can declaim about these things, but I pin my faith to material interests. Only let the material interests once get a firm footing, and they are bound to impose the conditions on which alone they can continue to exist. That's how your money-making is justified here in the face of lawlessness and disorder. It is justified because the security which it

demands must be shared with an oppressed people. A better justice will come afterwards. That's your ray of hope."[8]

Before *Nostromo*, Conrad had contrasted the mindless greed of "material interests" to the redeeming idea of paternalist colonialism. But now the material interests have an idea too: a Cobdenite vision of economic liberalism. Mrs Gould doesn't see how "awful materialism" can have any ideals, but in this earlier part of the novel her husband seems to have the best of their argument:

> For the San Tomé mine was to become an institution, a rallying-point for everything in the province that needed order and stability to live. Security seemed to flow upon this land from the mountain-gorge. The authorities of Sulaco had learned that the San Tomé mine could make it worth their while to leave things and people alone. This was the nearest approach to the rule of common sense and justice Charles Gould felt it possible to secure at first. In fact, the mine, with its organization, its population growing fiercely attached to their position of privileged safety, with its armoury, with its Don Pepe, with its armed body of serenos ... was a power in the land.[9]

Earlier, the power exercised in Sulaco by successive *caudillos* was absolute, ruthless, and entirely self-interested. Gould's new power claims only a negative agency, to protect an economic space of liberalism where wealth, civic order and productivity will be able to flourish together.

Yet *Nostromo* ends with a chorus of condemnation against Gould and his American financier Holroyd, the agents of modernizing capitalism. Mrs Gould, Dr Monygham, and Nostromo, who make up the opposing party, are of diverse temperament. For the first, dislike of instrumental economic reason is an expression of her femininity and her genteel origins; the second is an intellectual sceptic; the third is an existential outsider. But the idealist party are all ineffectually detached from the institutions that hold power.

Mrs Gould passes judgement on her husband's work in a characteristically Conradian idiom:

> There was something inherent in the necessities of successful action which carried with it the moral degradation of the idea. She saw the San Tomé mountain hanging over the Campo, over the whole land,

feared, hated, wealthy; more soulless than any tyrant, more pitiless and autocratic than the worst Government; ready to crush innumerable lives in the expansion of its greatness. He did not see it. He could not see it.[10]

Yet if Mrs Gould sees her husband's perspective as impermeable to other views, her own critique is equally self-enclosed. Earlier, the narrator observed that "even the most legitimate touch of materialism was wanting in [her] character." If Gould's disposition does not allow him to see any evil in the mine, his wife's does not allow her to see any good. Further, their disagreement reflects a familiar marital dynamic of jealousy and dissociation: the mine has become, for Mrs Gould, an erotic rival. She and Gould shared the "brief intoxication" of romantic love, a union of soul and sense, but in the long run the mine has displaced her as the object of Gould's passion – "she would never have him to herself." His love of the mine appears to her as "soulless," no more than "hard, determined service of the material interests."[11] Yet Mrs Gould also wants exclusive possession of her husband, in order to subdue him to her own absolutist moral idealism. Her resentment of the mine includes a desire to reclaim her husband from the man's world of economic power and bring him into her own domestic sphere. Nor does she offer any alternative vision of statecraft. Like the Belgian fiancée in *Heart of Darkness*, Mrs Gould's spiritual authority is inseparable from her ignorance and her literal distance from the arenas – the jungle, the mine – of violent conflict or crisis.

No feminine (or feminized) idealist could provide a full articulation of Conrad's world-view, and Mrs Gould's scorn for her husband's enterprise is itself vulnerable to more pragmatic judgements. Her refined and luxurious way of life aligns her with the rentier, one who shuns the contamination of the marketplace even as she allows agents of coarser moral fibre to work her capital. And her idealism carries weight in society because of her proximity to the throne from which economic power is exercised; if she were married to someone ordinary, who would attend to her? Dr Monygham's anti-capitalism is similarly conditioned by his quietist temperament and privileged social position. He complains that "There is no peace and no rest in the development of material interests" – interests that, for him, lack "the continuity and the force that can be found only in a moral principle."[12] Yet the previous rulers of Costaguana have been far more malignant than Gould, so where is Monygham to find an anti-economic regime constant in its virtue, free from the self-corrupting dynamic of idealism?

Nostromo, faithful to his populism, comes to see the mine as "hateful and immense, lording it by its vast wealth over the valour, the toil, the fidelity of the poor."[13] But the immensity is precisely what he must acknowledge, relative to his own present resources. Global capitalism may be without an intrinsic principle of rectitude, but its dynamic is so comprehensive as to render futile any individualist attempt to mount an opposition to it. It is precisely that futility that gives Nostromo the rationalization for keeping his boatload of silver. His vacillation between Giselle and Linda Viola, and his consequent casual death, confirm his post-revolutionary loss of authority. Whether he has the silver or not, he remains a superfluous man in an era of consolidation; his censoriousness is a product of his superfluity, just as much as his dishonesty is.

The Knitting Machine

There is a, – let us say, – a machine. It evolved itself (I am severely scientific) out of a chaos of scraps of iron and behold! – it knits. I am horrified at the horrible work and stand appalled. I feel it ought to embroider, – but it goes on knitting. You come and say; "This is all right: it's only a question of the right kind of oil. Let us use this, – for instance, – celestial oil and the machine will embroider a most beautiful design in purple and gold." Will it? Alas, no. You cannot by any special lubrication make embroidery with a knitting machine. And the most withering thought is that the infamous thing has made itself: made itself without thought, without conscience, without foresight, without eyes, without heart. It is a tragic accident – and it has happened.[14]

Edward Said sees this machine as Conrad's emblem of the mindlessness of human destiny.[15] But the mindlessness may be of a more literal kind, if we place the knitting machine in its historical role as one of the makers of the Industrial Revolution. The first loom able to weave patterns was built by Jacquard in 1801. Such machines epitomize the impersonality of the new economic system, overriding any individual projects and preferences that try to confront it. The machine serves a material interest without any dimension of conscience (the embroidery that it will never produce). It is supremely effective in destroying the traditional world of the artisan, yet entirely without higher purpose.

That effectiveness includes a certain flexibility in the way it may be deployed. Mrs Gould and Nostromo, like other organicists who oppose the machine, typically view it as constant in its operation, a monotonous and cumulative engine of tyranny. But the industrial system of Sulaco, seeking its best chance of profit, develops one space while ignoring another. Antonia Avellanos wants the Sulacans to do something about the "cruel wrongs" suffered by those who remain in Costaguana:

> 'Annex the rest of Costaguana to the order and prosperity of Sulaco,' snapped the doctor. 'There is no other remedy.'
> 'I am convinced, Senor Doctor,' Antonia said, with the earnest calm of invincible resolution, 'that this was from the first poor Martin's intention.'
> 'Yes, but the material interests will not let you jeopardize their development for a mere idea of pity and justice,' the doctor muttered, grumpily. 'And it is just as well perhaps.'[16]

The rulers of Sulaco wish to consolidate their domain as an enclave of economic order, putting off the modernization of Costaguana to a later date. Sulaco will be a proving-ground for the emergent neo-colonialism of the U.S., which operates through finance capital and Protestant missionaries rather than direct political domination. In Costaguana and most other parts of South America, *caudillo* regimes will remain the political norm. Their resistance to the forces of Cobdenite globalization will be given voice by such figures as Gamacho, of the Costaguanan "Nacionalistas," for whom the Great Powers "by introducing railways, mining enterprises, colonization, and such other shallow pretences, aimed at robbing poor people of their lands."[17]

The expansion of capitalism may appear to the peasants as robbery, but the underlying process is a prolonged and patient work of incorporation. Any continent-wide triumph of Cobdenite liberalism remains far beyond the horizon at the end of *Nostromo* (as it still does today, though surely it has come nearer). Yet its critics within the novel view it as an achieved ideal, and one that is already beginning to fester since it rests on nothing more than "covetousness which, in its universal extent, measures the moral misery and the intellectual destitution of mankind."[18] Mrs Gould and Dr Monygham acknowledge that peace, order, and good government have been achieved in Sulaco; what they resent is that these are by-products of industrialization, rather than benefits conferred by a paternalist aristocracy, or a disinterested "service class" like that which ran the British Empire. When Nostromo denounces the regime as merely the latest form of dictatorship, he overlooks the diminution of personal authority in its rule, and the corresponding predominance of an international system of production and exchange. Sulaco is being rapidly and successfully Europeanized, but as a commercial rather than an aristocratic society, through "Material changes swept along in the train of material interests." What is generated by the requirements of industry can scarcely act as an internal restraint on it. Nonetheless, that system is generating its own countervailing forces, as "other changes more subtle, outwardly unmarked, affected the minds and hearts of the workers." These are the stirrings of class-consciousness: instead of fighting for the Goulds, as they did during the war of secession, the workers are girding themselves to fight for their collective economic interest.[19]

The evolution of the miners – from personal loyalty to their master, to self-interested market agents – corresponds to the economizing of the society as a whole. Paternalism yields to laissez-faire individualism, and foreign relations shift from post-imperial nationalism to neo-colonialism. Conrad was all too familiar with the mechanisms of international capital (he lost the major part of his inherited capital by speculating in South African gold mines), and made financiers into centers of interest in *The Inheritors* (1901) and *Chance* (1913).[20] As a novelist, he could be expected to personalize the emergent global economic system, by showing its moral effects on individuals like Gould or Nostromo. Yet even if one reads Conrad as aligning himself with the criticisms of Mrs Gould, Dr Monygham, and Nostromo, nothing in the conclusion of the novel suggests that either revolutionary socialism or the restoration of the agrarian aristocracy can offer a better future. The chief engineer of the Sulaco railway argues that transcendence lies as a potential in any material task: "things seem to be worth nothing by what they are in themselves. I begin to believe that the only solid thing about them is the spiritual value which everyone discovers in his own form of activity."[21] But it is an engineer who speaks, not a captain; and if he were believed, all vocations could lead equally to salvation, and no one need be troubled by the baser interests that their activities served. Populism is certain, on its past record, to spiral downwards into corruption and terror. We are left, it would seem, with a Conrad whose dislike of the Gould/Holroyd regime incorporates a broad cynicism about any alternatives, and a conviction that the forces now prevailing in Sulaco are impregnable.

Indeed, when in debate with a pure idealist like Cunninghame Graham Conrad liked to argue that material interests were universal and irresistible:

You with your ideals of sincerity, courage and truth are strangely out of place in this epoch of material preoccupations. What does it bring? What's the profit? What do we get by it? These questions are at the root of every moral, intellectual or political movement. Into the noblest cause men manage to put something of their baseness; and sometimes when I think of You here, quietly You seem to me tragic with your courage, with your beliefs and your hopes. Every cause is tainted: and you reject this one, espouse that other one as if one were evil and the other good while the same evil you hate is in both, but disguised in different words.[22]

Conrad here reduces the deeper motives of both Right and Left to the pursuit of similarly base ends: money or power desired for their own sakes, once the screen of idealism has been removed. Hence the great Conradian theme of corruption, whether of grandiose national ideals or individual dreams. Yet if this is true, any moral critique of Cobdenism is either quixotic (because human nature cannot be changed) or hypocritical (because if the critics got into power, they would soon discard their "disinterested" principles).[23]

Nostromo and Globalization

Literary accounts of the relation between the West and its periphery have been dominated by the high imperialism of the later nineteenth century, and by the dissolution of the European empires after 1945. The West and its others have been framed in the perspective of nationalism, with the rich cultural possibilities it has made available (whether hegemonic or oppositional): from the literature of "prestige" or "service" imperialism, whose great names are Kipling, Forster, Orwell, and the Conrad of *Heart of Darkness* or *Lord Jim*, to the contemporary postcolonial literature that has arisen from the continuing links between periphery and metropolis.

   Nostromo stands apart from these traditions, as the single major novel in English that engages not imperialism, but the rival formation of internationalist liberalism. Cobden's vision of a peaceful, commercial and multilateral world-system anticipates the current arguments of the "End of History" school.[24] "Free trade! What is it?" Cobden asked. "Why, breaking down the barriers that separate nations; those barriers behind which nestle the feelings of pride, revenge, hatred, and jealousy, which every now and then burst their bounds and deluge whole countries with blood."[25] Whatever Conrad's reservations about Cobdenism, he does not oppose it in the name of protecting any indigenous cultural identity for Sulaco. That country is modernized by metropolitan intervention, just as the later critique of that modernization comes from the same source, as enlightenment humanism or radicalism.[26] Conrad's representation of Sulaco remains rigorously Eurocentric, and he presents the action of *Nostromo* as a heroic narrative of the replacement of indigenous backwardness by a

European modernizing order. The criticisms of that order are no less European than their object: they arise from traditional oppositions between aristocratic and commercial values, between master and slave, and between moral ideals and material interests.

Conrad represents faithfully the logic of transition from the regime of the *caudillos* to that of economic rationality. But Cobden, in his time, was driven by resentment of the prestige culture of the British aristocracy, with its unearned privileges and its anti-economic values. Conrad is not a radical in that sense, and still esteems such romantic projects as Gould's desire to restore his family's honor (a quintessentially aristocratic motive). The industrialization of Sulaco provides the occasion for those with "higher" agendas to make displays of existential heroism that are, it must eventually be recognized, peripheral to the relatively mundane transition that is going to be repeated in many other backward regions as they are incorporated into global neo-liberalism. It is of the essence of such transitions – seen in retrospect, at least – that they are not revolutions, and that they are incompatible with grand narratives of personal leadership, agency or teleology.

After Sulaco's war of secession, Charles Gould is represented as a new kind of *caudillo*, all the more oppressive for the efficient economic rationality on which his power depends. Yet this gives Gould and Holroyd a degree of agency that is at odds with their actual economic function. The personality cult of an old-fashioned *caudillo* could not extend beyond his frontiers, and economic concerns would always be subordinated to his need for absolute personal power. The *caudillo*, by definition, claims an organic relation with his nation; but that which legitimates his rule internally deprives him of any plausible claim to authority in neighboring countries, who will be fearful of any pretensions he may have to regional hegemony. It is inappropriate, then, to equate the rule of the *caudillos* with that of internationally-oriented capitalists like Gould and Holroyd. The development of Sulaco requires its integration with an emergent global system of trade and capital mobility, a system of which Gould and Holroyd are the managers rather than the masters. By opening Sulaco to the international market, they reduce proportionately the sovereignty of whoever rules it.

It is of course true that Holroyd has religious and U.S. nationalist ambitions that are close to megalomania. The issue (as in *Heart of Darkness*) is whether these aims are continuous with his economic aims, or a turning away from them. With his "temperament of a Puritan and an insatiable imagination of conquest," Holroyd carries the torch of a global "Manifest Destiny" for "the greatest country in the whole of God's Universe. . . . We shall be giving the word for everything: industry, trade, law, journalism, art, politics, and religion, from Cape Horn clear over to Smith's Sound, and beyond, too, if anything worth taking hold of turns up at the North Pole."[27] The list ascends from the material interests of industry and trade to the ideal interests of religion at the top; but how are these elements interconnected? Holroyd claims "The introduction of a pure form of Christianity" into South America as his transcendent goal, but Conrad seems to consider him a religious hypocrite, whose true motives are crudely commercial.

Benita Parry places Holroyd in a specific historical moment, of messianic high imperialism:

> Not until the late nineteenth century . . . did imperialist rhetoric invent an exorbitant and anomalous idiom of messianic utilitarianism and bellicose mysticism, where the positivist and aggressive phraseology of compulsory universal modernisation is joined with the anachronistic and chimerical lexicon of chivalry, 'a mandate of destiny', and 'a high and holy mission' serving as ideological pillars of the west's planetary ambitions.[28]

Holroyd's particular strain in this rhetoric is that of American exceptionalism, whereby the U.S. has a sacred destiny in the world, distinct from the base aims of European imperialism. Conrad thought exceptionalism was humbug – except when it came to Britain where, in some moods, he would argue strenuously for the possibility of imperial disinterestedness.[29] But should high imperialism be seen as a single movement, integrating a mixture of economic and ideological aims, or (following Cobden and Schumpeter) should we try to distinguish between its economic and anti-economic motives?

The Cobdenite era began to dissolve with the protectionist policies of Britain's trade rivals in the years leading to World War I, and culminated in Britain's abandonment of Free Trade in 1931. By 1934, total international trade had shrunk to one-third of its level in 1929.[30] The two world wars were indeed the "deluges of blood" that Cobden predicted if countries chose military rivalry over peaceful commerce. The Bretton Woods agreement of 1945 can now be seen as the inauguration of a second Cobdenite era in world history, whose salient features include multilateral tariff reduction and growth of trade, the end of Empire, the economic integration of Europe since 1963 and of North America since 1992, and the collapse of communism in 1989. All of these developments now culminate in a triumphant economism, what Frederick Buell calls "the new global system."[31]

This system was first theorized by Immanuel Wallerstein, Raúl Prebisch, and André Gunder Frank as oppressively neo-colonial, the Western world perpetuating dominance over its periphery by economic fraud rather than imperial force.[32] The critique of globalization in *Nostromo* thus anticipates later denunciations of transnational capitalism as the enemy of local cultures or exploited classes. Recently, however, mainstream economic opinion has become more respectful of the efficacy of the "new international division of labour." To Buell, the rise of countries like Taiwan, South Korea, Hong Kong and Singapore represents "the death knell of the previous era of nationalism: national development under the protective stewardship of the state has come to seem inhibited, rather than advanced, and integration with the global system – in some ways nationalism's precise opposite – has become the hope."[33] Peter Worsley sees in such developments what "earlier generations of theorists on the Left had deemed to be impossible – the industrialization of Third World economies under capitalism."[34]

Conrad's friend Cunninghame Graham saw the economic incorporation of the periphery as a recurrent and deplorable effect of imperialism. In his essay "Bloody Niggers" he denounced "material and bourgeois Rome. . . . conquering the world . . . . and by its sheer dead weight of commonplace, filling the office in the old world that now is occupied so worthily by God's own Englishmen."[35] Conrad shared Graham's fear that European investment in Latin America would create in the New World the same sordid industrial society that had already taken over the Old, and that "Yankee Conquistadores" would repeat the crimes of their Spanish predecessors.[36] But the idea of the American capitalist as a new conquistador blurs the distinction between Cobdenite liberalism, and the kind of imperialism by force and pillage practised in the Congo.[37] The original conquistador was scarcely an "economic man" in the sense of the Protestant thrift and rationality of Weberian capitalism: he preferred domination to market exchange. Yet Conrad typically sees power and profit as two sides of an integral process, each motive being naturally absorbed into the other. In both *Heart of Darkness* and *Nostromo*, material interests begin to work for constructive ends, but soon accommodate themselves to baser instincts. The economic sector cannot maintain its autonomy; it is the instrument of a will to power that precedes the appearance of economic man, and whose dynamic is always a striving for "positional superiority" (in Edward Said's term) of one individual, class, race, or nation over another.

The Cobdenite ideal makes politics superfluous; its opposite is the view that politics determines everything, including the operations of so-called "free" markets. Evidently, great nations have often proved unwilling to follow a pure Cobdenite policy of free trade with peripheral regions. Having political, cultural and military – as well as economic – power, they have always been tempted to deploy it to "capture" or "defend" markets to which they assert a claim. Nonetheless, it is a long step from saying that imperial nations manipulate markets, to saying that markets don't matter and imperialism is only about power. In Orwell's *Burmese Days*, for example, the timber merchant Flory argues that the whole political and ideological face of imperialism is no more than a screen for economic interests:

> "I don't want the Burmans to drive us out of this country. God forbid! I'm here to make money, like everyone else. All I object to is the slimy white man's burden humbug. . . . the lie that we're here to uplift our poor black brothers instead of to rob them. . . .
>
> The official holds the Burman down while the businessman goes through his pockets. . . . The British Empire is simply a device for giving trade monopolies to the English – or rather to gangs of Jews and Scotchmen."[38]

Neither Orwell nor his creation, Flory, consider that business might be a legitimate activity in itself, still less that it could carry out the civilizing mission it professes in *Nostromo*. Nonetheless, *Burmese Days* takes it for granted that business motives are central to imperialism. The striking achievement of Said's *Orientalism* (and of its sequel, *Culture and Imperialism*) does not obviate its equally striking occlusion of the economic motives for European expansion into the East. If it is a truism that there was a mixture of material and spiritual motives for the Crusades, it is hardly likely that this duality of aim ceased to operate after 1291. Yet Orientalism assumes a Western power that reproduces itself regardless of Western economic interest, or that is in excess of any adequate economic justification. Behind Orientalism stands Foucault's obsession with vertical relations of dominance and submission as virtually the only kind of social bond, combined with the post-structuralist privileging of difference as the ground of meaning. In examining the massive Western project of ideological dominance over the East, one should not ignore the economic "will to profit" that accompanies the political "will to power." Thus Benita Parry criticizes in the postcolonial "discourse analysis" of Spivak and Bhabha:

> a shared programme marked by the exorbitation of discourse and a related incuriosity about the enabling socioeconomic and political

institutions and other forms of social praxis. Furthermore, because their theses admit of no point outside discourse from which opposition can be engendered, their project is concerned to place incendiary devices within the dominant structures of representation and not to confront these with another knowledge.[39]

Implicitly, Parry places "discourse analysis" in the mode of utopian socialism derided by Lenin – where ideas systematize themselves spontaneously, free of any material determination. If economics is recognized at all, it is as "just another discourse"; so that neo-liberalism, for example, is no more than a rhetoric to be exploited by power-seeking elites.

Orientalism thus takes its place at the opposite pole from the liberal economic model that posits a formal equality and community of interest between buyers and sellers. Postcolonial focus on difference would seem to make orientalism incurable, since difference determines, without residue, the relations between persons, races and nations – and also, monotonously, serves the ends of domination. Against this, the Cobdenite perspective argues that patterns of dominance in the global system are much less simple or stable than, say, British imperial control over its Eastern possessions in the nineteenth century. A rapidly shifting international division of labor accommodates the rise of newly industrializing countries, and may inflict a relative decline on the established centers of Europe and North America. The nation itself loses much of its coherence under the pressures of globalization, as appears in Sulaco's loss of sovereignty in *Nostromo*.

What verdict, then, may be pronounced on the modernizing capitalism of *Nostromo*? Recent critics have emphasized the narrative, symbolic or moral incoherence of the novel – projecting the nihilism of *Heart of Darkness* forward into the darkness that so often lies over the Golfo Placido. But a more coherent reading emerges when we look forward to the later twentieth-century world system, rather than backwards to Leopold's Congo. Conrad's essay "Autocracy and War" (1905), an important coda to *Nostromo*, both defines his quarrel with Cobdenism, and differentiates his position from contemporary Orientalism.[40] Conrad identifies a moment of optimism in Victorian thought around the time of the Great Exhibition (1851) and the repeal of the Corn Laws (1846):

A swift disenchantment overtook the incredible infatuation which could put its trust in the peaceful nature of industrial and commercial competition.

> Industrialism and commercialism . . . . stand ready, almost eager, to
> appeal to the sword as soon as the globe of the earth has shrunk be-
> neath our growing numbers by another ell or so.[41]

Looking at the past decade of imperial and commercial rivalry, Conrad
observes: "Germany's attitude proves that no peace for the earth can be
found in the expansion of material interests which she seems to have
adopted exclusively as her only aim, ideal, and watchword."[42] His fright-
eningly accurate prediction of the intentions of the great powers seems
to confirm Dr Monygham's diagnosis, that economic motives are intrinsically restless and aggressive.

Yet Conrad fails to inspect the links in his causal chain from 1846 to
1914. Cobden and Schumpeter posited a rational global trading system
that would eventually overcome the bias of prestige societies towards
belligerent expansionism. In a world of free trade, nations would only
handicap themselves by spending on armaments in the hope of "conquering" or "protecting" overseas markets. That a world war followed the
Cobdenite era does not prove that Cobdenism was the cause of it:
Cobden's ideals may have been abandoned or betrayed, like those of any
other revolution.

The opposition between Cobdenism and imperialist war is implicit in
this chapter's epigraph from Kant, a theme taken up again in Werner
Sombart's 1915 polemic, *Merchants and Heroes*:

> [Sombart] welcomed the "German War" as the inevitable conflict be-
> tween the commercial civilization of England and the heroic culture
> of Germany. His contempt for the "commercial" views of the English
> people, who had lost all warlike instincts, is unlimited. Nothing is
> more contemptible in his eyes than the universal striving after the
> happiness of the individual; and what he describes as the leading
> maxim of English morals: be just "that it may be well with thee and
> that thou mayest prolong thy days upon the land" is to him "the most
> infamous maxim which has ever been pronounced by a commercial
> mind." . . . . Claims of the individual are always an outcome of the
> commercial spirit.[43]

Sombart, who began as a socialist and became a Nazi supporter in the
1930s, assumed that capitalism, and especially the English variety, was
synonymous with the rise of pacifist internationalism since the Napoleonic wars.[44] If the individual pursuit of wealth was the final purpose of
social organization, the state would tend to shrink, and the nation would

have no powerful embodiment of its collective will. Yet late-nineteenth century capitalists proved susceptible to messianic appeals to national destiny that made economics the instrument of other national ambitions.

H.G. Wells registered this shift of opinion in his dining club "The Coefficients," which met from 1902 to 1908:

> I was still clinging to the dear belief that the English-speaking community might play the part of leader and mediator towards a world commonweal. It was to be free-trading, free-speaking, liberating flux for mankind. . . . But the shadow of Joseph Chamberlain lay dark across our dinner-table, the Chamberlain who, upon the "illimitable velt" of South Africa had had either a sunstroke or a Pauline conversion to Protection and had returned to clamour influentially for what he called Tariff Reform, but what was in effect national commercial egotism.[45]

Conrad blamed the European arms race, and the turn towards protectionism that led up to the first World War, on the inner dynamic of material interests.[46] Into economic projects – like any others – men will always "manage to put something of their baseness," and turn them to ill ends. To Johnson's quip that "men are seldom so innocently employed as in making money," Conrad implicitly responded that men are without innocence in anything they do – or, at least, are never innocent over the full course of an undertaking. Economism could not be the exception to history's tragic cycle of idealism and corruption, nor could there be an "end" to this history in any utopian era of global enrichment without limit or relapse. The condemnation of Gould's handiwork in Sulaco thus includes the expectation that it will culminate in another and larger war.[47] But the question remains whether Cobdenism ends in war, or whether war is inevitable when man is no longer content to be *homo economicus*.

Part Two
The Author's Share

7
The New Literary Marketplace, 1870-1914

*For a generation the prestige of the great Victorians remained
like the shadow of vast trees in a forest, but now that it was
lifting, every weed and sapling had its chance, provided only
that it was of a different species from its predecessors.*
        —H.G. Wells, *Experiment in Autobiography*

Segmentation

Towards the end of the nineteenth century, a profound re-organization
of the English literary marketplace created new kinds of writers and readers. The market was made by people with many particular trades and
functions: authors, publishers, printers, binders, librarians, booksellers,
and critics. In this period their relations with each other shifted, and a
new role interposed itself between authors and publishers, that of the literary agent. The changing literary marketplace of 1870-1914 needs to be
placed within a wider transformation of capitalism into a "consumer society." The most strategic decisions now concern not production, but
distribution – which becomes the object of the new science of "marketing."

Goods had traditionally been sold along a spectrum of quality that
matched price levels with social class; in the literary realm, this meant
that reading matter would be expensive or cheap, according to the class
of its audience. In the later nineteenth century this vertical organization
of the market began to be flattened out, under the pressure of mass production and wider demand. The language of marketing would describe
this as a transition from product differentiation (or stratification) to market segmentation:

> While successful product differentiation will result in giving the mar-
> keter a horizontal share of a broad and generalized market, equally
> successful application of the strategy of market segmentation tends to
> produce depth of market position in the segments that are effectively
> defined and penetrated. The differentiator seeks to secure a layer of
> the market cake, whereas one who employs market segmentation

strives to secure one or more wedge-shaped pieces. . . . [segmentation is] a *merchandising* strategy . . . [that] consists of viewing a heterogeneous market . . . as a number of smaller homogeneous markets in response to differing product preferences among important market segments.[1]

In the market for reading matter, this meant a move from a vertical structure (a scale from highbrow literature to trash) towards a horizontal one by genres appealing to differentiated but formally equal groups of readers. Buyers would now be classified by their interests, gender, or life-styles, rather than their social rank.

The book trade had been one of the first to recognize the potential of segmentation, in the sense that each book published appealed to a distinct group of readers, and each literary genre constituted a potential market segment. Caxton identified a market niche in England for vernacular books on secular subjects, and became a printer as a business project continuous with his previous career as a textile merchant. The trade then developed through an ever-finer division of labor, separating out the functions that Caxton combined in his own person – author, translator, printer, publisher, and bookseller.[2] Literature that aimed to satisfy the market (rather than an aristocratic patron) always sought to "target" consumers, and writers were always conscious that others were competing with them to provide a specific kind of reader satisfaction. Earlier novelists, as they observed their sales rising or falling, tended to make adjustments to the market by tinkering within the constraints of the form – Trollope, for example, thinking of how a particular character or turn of plot might appeal to his readers.[3] But they still took for granted, in the high Victorian period, a stratification that established a stable division between high and low literary culture. The domination of the literary scene by a compact group of canonical novelists empowered them to represent the social system as a totality, within a critical realist perspective that was sustained by the author's sense of him or herself as standing at some dignified distance from the market.[4]

If Regenia Gagnier is right that "the fracturing of the old, relatively compact reading public made the public appeal of a [George] Eliot or a Tennyson impossible for late-Victorian artists," then authors had to face up to putting themselves on the market as one kind of writer among many – aspiring, at best, to a specific rather than universal mode of success.[5] But the sharper and more systematic segmentation of the literary marketplace after 1870 forced authors to be aware of their dependent and relative status as producers: to think more of how they were situated between readers, publishers, genres and potential rivals, and less of the intrinsic moral or formal possibilities of a given subject matter.[6] Henry James grasped the flattening-out of the market in saying that the "public we somewhat loosely talk of as for literature or for anything else is really as subdivided as a chess-board, with each little square confessing only to its own *kind* of accessibility."[7] Under this new market regime, traditional kinds of cultural authority were forced to re-group in the emergent realms of the aesthetic, the avant-garde and, in due course, modernism: spheres that became defined by their hostility to the marketplace and by their ethic of an "austere, self-regarding art."[8] Peter McDonald speaks of a division between "purists" and "profiteers."[9] Recent economic criticism of late Victorian literature has rightly focused on Oscar Wilde and Henry James, with their indeterminate status between a mandarin aestheticism and a search for market success in one or another niche.[10] Jonathan Freedman has argued that this aestheticism was "wholly complicit" with the materialism for which it claimed to be the remedy, so that the real motive of cultural producers remained economic.[11] Bourdieu, on the other hand, posits the relative autonomy of aestheticism and the avant-garde within their distinct "zone of restricted production."[12] Artists primarily seek "consecration" by those who possess cultural rather than material capital. English literary culture, however, does not fit comfortably into Bourdieu's binary oppositions between restricted production/mass production; avant-garde/bourgeoisie; Left Bank/Right Bank. The English literary marketplace has been more comprehensive than Bourdieu's scheme would permit: Dickens and Tennyson were creatures of the market in ways that Flaubert and Baudelaire were not. The great exception is modernism, whose project was to institute an alternative regime of literary incentives, independent of the market. The scope and success of that project will be assessed in Chapter Nine.

Segmentation is intrinsic to the development of contemporary consumer societies. In the earlier stages of industrialization, it could be assumed that artisanal production would continue to satisfy the taste of the prestige classes for hand-made, patinated goods, while the masses would get their necessities cheaply from the factory or assembly line. But after World War II, globalization and flexible production systems have established a largely horizontal regime of distribution, which targets goods of roughly equal quality to groups identified by life-style, age, gender, ethnicity, or other markers. The English literary marketplace was one of the first sectors to undergo such a transformation; and many traditional intellectuals, as we have seen, understood the process to be one of cultural degeneration.[13]   On the Continent Per Gedin (following Q.D. Leavis) draws a line between "serious" and "popular" fiction, and deplores the erosion of the high bourgeois novel from the 1920s on, as part of the "Americanization" of the European literary marketplace. In America, Gedin argues, "there has never been a bourgeois, culture-sustaining class," and publishing has been purely capitalistic, interested only in the mass distribution of cheap books.[14]

The class system that underlay the stratifications of the Victorian literary market persisted, of course, after 1880. Nonetheless, there was a great increase in the visibility, self-confidence and articulateness of such subordinate groups as women, industrial workers, and the suburban lower-middle class. The newly literate mass readership for penny newspapers and popular fiction dictated the terms on which middle-class writers would produce its reading. Earlier in the century, there was still an effective consensus that the working classes needed to be raised up, and women to be protected, by a regime of indoctrination imposed from above. The first new voices to approach canonical status emerged from the lower-middle class of provincial towns and London suburbs – some celebrating their milieu like Bennett and H.G. Wells, others castigating it like Gissing. Self-educated, or coming up through the new red-brick universities, such writers diverged from the traditional formation of British intellectuals at public schools and Oxbridge. Their authority rested on their being the authentic voices of a marginal class; but also on their success in the market culture defined by volume of sales, advertising, and sensitivity to the popular mood. Those who did succeed achieved their validation independently of accolades bestowed by the traditional intelligentsia – who, in any case, would always be suspicious of the cultural results of market forces.

In the expanding literary sphere of the late nineteenth century, those forces were undermining the regulatory powers and established hierarchies of the prestige culture. A ranking of authors by status was giving way to an ordering by economic criteria, driven by responsiveness to consumer choice. Exclusivity is always easier to maintain in a steady state, where there is little call to accommodate emergent social groups and new modes of expression. To those committed to exclusion, such emergences typically appear as disorder welling up from below, with a flood of vulgarity threatening the citadels of reason and art at the top; as R.W. Buchanan put it, "After the School Board has come the Deluge."[15] But market culture happily catered to new readers, re-structuring its offerings into new genres and categories. A calmer analysis would not understand market segmentation as a cultural collapse, but as the targeting of new kinds of writing to emergent consumers, and a re-positioning of the older genres.

The Reading Public

John Carey has suggested that "The difference between the nine-teenth-century mob and the twentieth-century mass is literacy."[16] In 1841, a third of English men and half the women could not write their own names in the marriage register; by 1900, only three percent of both sexes were unable to do so.[17] This great emancipation into literacy was driven by the Education Acts of 1870-81, which put in place free and compulsory education for all; but also by the personal initiative of millions of ordinary folk wanting to improve their children's chances in life. Because increased literacy was used as an argument for the extension of the suffrage from 1832 on, it is understandable that the privileged classes should be suspicious of the desire for education of those beneath them; what is less forgivable is that so many writers and intellectuals also joined in the chorus of denigration against popular literacy. Even G.M. Trevelyan, a Liberal and a populist historian, denounced compulsory education for having:

> produced a vast population able to read but unable to distinguish what is worth reading, an easy prey to sensations and cheap appeals. Consequently both literature and journalism have been to a large extent debased since 1870, because they now cater for millions of half-educated and quarter-educated people, whose forbears, not being able to read at all, were not the patrons of newspapers or of books.[18]

The widening of the literary marketplace, and its increased efficiency and complexity, were bound to be viewed with a jealous eye by those hostile to the democratization of the printed word. Intellectuals deplored the vulgarity of popular writing; patriarchs disliked the increased prominence of female authors; evangelicals feared that trashy literature and journalism would corrupt morals; utilitarians noted the loss of economic efficiency when workers knew more than they needed to, and were distracted by too much imagination. All such attacks recognized that the newly educated masses wanted reading suited to their tastes, and that popular writers and entrepreneurs were only too happy to meet the demand.

One can look at reading matter as one among many goods contributing to the transformation of England, in the years around 1900, to a society of mass consumption. The increased income and leisure of the working class multiplied demand; meanwhile, improvements in technology and more efficient markets lowered the cost of consumer goods. Intellectuals on both the right and the left viewed the arrival of mass consumption and mass culture with dismay, and even the emergent Labour Party viewed working people's consumption with suspicion: tracts like R.H. Tawney's *The Acquisitive Society* defended traditional ideas of community against the corrosion of possessive individualism. Within the intellectual consensus that the working- and lower-middle classes could not be trusted to choose their own goods and amusements, cultural goods held a special position as indicators of decline. Mass cultural entrepreneurs like Lord Rothermere or Lord Northcliffe thus loomed as figures of particular menace.

As far back as 1712, newspapers had been taxed at a penny per sheet, rising to fourpence in 1815 in order to make radical papers too expensive for workers to buy.[19] Cobden argued that there should be no difference between free trade in goods and in ideas; he led a successful campaign to have the newspaper "tax on knowledge" repealed in 1855. The tax on paper followed, in 1861, accompanied by dramatic reductions in the cost of its production (before 1800, the cost of paper typically amounted to more than half of the total cost of producing a book). The introduction of free public libraries after 1850, of the linotype machine in 1886, and of cheap newspapers in the 1890s, further reduced the cost of reading.[20] The "reading industry" responded with explosive growth: workers in Paper, Printing and Stationery, up from 125,000 in 1871 to 397,000 in 1911; paper production up from 120,000 tons in 1870 to 774,000 tons in 1903; 380 novels published in 1880, 1315 in 1895; secular magazines up from 375 titles in 1870 to 1997 titles in 1903.[21]

Whatever the laments of the English mandarins, improvements in literacy and communication have been intrinsic to economic and political development over the past century and a half. In the earlier part of this span, the literary system was still based on an exclusivity that was homologous with rule by a narrow political elite: the ideals of the literate person and of the "gentleman" overlapped with each other and were mutually reinforcing. The major Victorian novels were bought by about 30,000 people when they appeared; 25,000 subscribed to Mudie's library in 1890; Walter Besant estimated in 1899 that in the high Victorian period about 50,000 people were "interested in literature."[22] This exclusivity was no bar to the production of critical perspectives on British society in the romantic poets, say, or *Hard Times*, or *Middlemarch*. The literary world was sufficiently small and disinterested that it could credibly claim to be the nation's conscience, and even as they produced for the market, writers were also a kind of clerisy. They formed an order whose mentality was that of a profession rather than a trade, to which one gained admission by qualities of knowledge and refinement. The market for books was still quite small, so that there was no class of literary plutocrats claiming pre-eminence through sheer volume of sales. bestselling writers like Bulwer-Lytton, Disraeli, Macaulay or even Mrs Henry Wood were not sharply distinct in status from such now-canonical writers as Tennyson, Dickens, Trollope or George Eliot (and many books produced by this latter group sold as well as those by the first).

This compact group of major Victorian writers, held together by a collective ethic and coherent standards, achieved a hegemony in the literary system that would be eroded by the revolution in the literary marketplace at the end of the century. Once eroded, that hegemony could never be regained by any successor group; it was precluded by the new conditions of literary production, which could be summed up as a shift from cultural authority to material success, from prestige incentives to monetary ones. The broader and more open literary marketplace, driven by popular literacy and consumer choice, necessarily brought with it a decentering of literary authority.

The establishment view of this process was that cultural standards were being eroded by vulgar commercialism. Much of the time, however, the real target was not the literary marketplace itself, but those subordinate groups that the market was willing to cater to, such as "half-educated" clerks or women. Almost all young women were literate by 1900, and they now comprised a larger share of the market for popular fiction. At higher social levels, women also had proportionately more leisure, education and disposable income, enabling the feminization of culture that male modernists would find so disturbing. This increased female presence aroused resentment among male critics; but within the sphere of the market they had little power to resist it. No one could prevent women buying whatever books or magazines they could afford, and publishers were happy to distribute such bestselling female novelists as Mrs Henry Wood, Miss Braddon, Mrs Humphrey Wood, or Marie Corelli.[23] It was symptomatic of the new regime that these writers used their own names, instead of the anonymous or pseudonymous appearance of many female novelists earlier in the century.[24]

The literary marketplace thus absorbed female participation with remarkable smoothness. Today, writing is probably the only economic sector where women have achieved parity: in 1997, of the eight richest authors in the U.K., four were women.[25] J.K. Rowling is now the highest-paid woman in England, with an income around £40 million a year, and also the world's most successful author. Even as women were becoming steadily more prominent in the literary marketplace in the nineteenth century, prestige culture strongholds like the public schools, the old universities, the Anglican church and the London clubs bitterly resisted their entry (some are still resisting). Admission to these precincts was not to be had just for money; it required qualification by status, gender and the approval of one's peers. Much attention was paid to mechanisms of ranking, gatekeeping and exclusion; for some academies or clubs, it could be said that exclusion was the main reason for the group's existence. These institutions were not directly involved in literary production, but they had close and long-standing ties with literary culture. They did much to shape the mentality of writers as a class, and to validate literary success through the provision of prestige culture rewards – memberships, sinecures, knighthoods, the recognition of gentlemanly status, and the like – that were rarely extended to women.

The End of the Three-Decker

Three-decker novels were written to a set length of about 120,000 words in three volumes; a small number of copies were printed, and each was sold at a very high price – usually one and a half guineas, which was about a week's wages for a junior clerk.[26] Each volume of the novel counted as one book issued to the subscribers of Mudie's or W.H. Smith's libraries, so that three people at once might be reading a new novel. The number of books allowed out on loan depended on the annual subscription paid by the reader: the basic one guinea only allowed for the borrowing of one book at a time. If a novel was successful a cheaper edition would appear a year or more after its first publication, but few readers chose to build up a personal library of novels. Novels were therefore written to the taste of library subscribers or even, more narrowly, to the taste of those who ran the libraries. The name "Mudie's Select Library" meant that Mudie himself guaranteed that all his fiction would be decent and moral. The reading public, he claimed, "are evidently willing to have a barrier of some kind between themselves and the lower floods of literature."[27]

John Sutherland has emphasized that "much of the fiction, good and bad, of the [high Victorian] period was written not in response to what the public or critics demanded, but what the publisher would take" – to which we should add, that the publishers would only take what Mudie's would buy. In 1840-70 all the major novels were put out by seven publishers, and

Mudie's might order more than half of a novel's press-run.[28] Under such conditions, the publishers effectively issued a specification which the novelist would try to meet. The three-decker novel had a fixed form, and embodied such dominant social authority as to be heedless of alternatives. It did not occupy one market niche among others, but defined the whole market in conformity with itself. That market was supplied and controlled by Mudie, which made novel-reviewing an exercise in futility, since the opinion of one person determined a book's success, and Mudie made his buying decisions before any reviews had appeared. Novels by established authors were often issued in parts, thus by-passing Mudie's control of distribution; and they were somewhat more affordable when readers could pay in monthly instalments.[29] But serial publication did not break the established form and moral limits of the three-decker. Still, in spite of grumbling about the English novel being more constrained than the French, many good novels were produced within the system and some great ones. The guidelines for success as a novelist were clear to all, and the novelist who did succeed enjoyed the kind of cultural centrality that in our time can only be achieved within the mass media. Mudie's was the television of its time, and had an equivalent grip on the imagination of the middle classes.

Mudie's standards also made female taste in novels the norm, since middle-class women made up the bulk of Mudie's subscribers. Of course, many elements of female experience were excluded from fictional representation; but even more was excluded on the male side. Thackeray was only the most prominent of those complaining that English novels – unlike French ones – could only give a watered-down version of masculine life.[30] When the market fragmented in the 1890s, the expression of gender also became more segregated: into male-oriented genres like science fiction or colonial adventure, or the female particularism of Dorothy Richardson and Virginia Woolf.

The death of the three-decker novel set off second-order effects within the general re-organization of the market for fiction. After 1896, novels would appear in one volume of varying length, the price would be one-third or less of the old guinea-and-a-half, and the cost of publication would be amortized over many single buyers, instead of from bulk purchases by a handful of libraries.[31] Novelists would now depend for their success on thousands of individual buying decisions. This created a more direct relationship between producer and buyer; but the buyers would be seeking books tailored to their specific interests, instead of the one-size-fits-all of the Mudie's system. The overall market for novels was also expanding, so that there were more chances both for new novelists to enter the field, and for them to write different kinds of novels – experimental in form, with greater sexual frankness, appealing to marginal social groups, and so on.

Initially, the breakdown of the three-decker system made the market for fiction more disorderly, but it was soon re-structured into a number of stable genres, replacing the single dominating form of the three-decker. The market now offered a value-free choice between modes of fiction, such as the psychological as opposed to the documentary novel. What has traditionally been explained as the exploitation by novelists of new psychic or social territory can also be seen as a natural result of market segmentation, changing literary forms within a fashion system that values novelty and seeks to capture new groups of readers.

The rapid decline of subscription libraries in the 1890s brought about a shift of power to novel reviewers, especially those who wrote for journals of mass circulation: people like Arnold Bennett at the *Daily Mail*, or Clement Shorter at *The Sphere* and the *Illustrated London News*. Shorter headed the camp of reviewers who sought to claim for themselves the moral authority of Victorian canonical fiction, by explicitly upholding those moral standards that had been silently enforced by Mudie. They mounted regular campaigns against unconventionality in fiction, from Hardy's *Jude the Obscure* (1895) to Lawrence's *The Rainbow* (1915). They found the causes of degeneracy either in infection from across the channel ("Zolaism"), or in a welling-up from below of the primal instincts of the dangerous classes.

Vice had not really become more prevalent, of course; only more visibly represented in literature than had been allowed within the universe of the three-decker. As the Victorian moral consensus broke down, new categories of fiction emerged to test the limits of the acceptable. Peter Keating's useful survey of the "End to Reticence" in *The Haunted Study* tries to separate commercial and artistic motives for liberalization:

> Vizetelly was not a particularly attractive candidate for literary martyrdom, the role usually allotted him by modern commentators. It was ludicrous to say that Vizetelly had published Zola's novels in order to deprave the minds of readers, but it was not so ludicrous to claim that his main motive was commercial: he was certainly not consciously pioneering new artistic standards in fiction.[32]

But to distinguish between idealism and moneymaking is not really the point. Pornography had long circulated surreptitiously; now it merged with the experimental fiction of the avant-garde to occupy a new niche in the literary marketplace. Newspaper critics resisted the incursion of sexual frankness, but a segmented market implied consumer freedom to choose between various offerings, and that freedom implicitly extended to moral choice as well. In a world offering a diversity of consumer goods, there will be an inevitable slide from fixed values to relative preferences; this was formalized in the rise of marginalist economics after 1870.[33] The weakening of religious orthodoxy also played its part; but segmentation and consumer sovereignty were homologous with other emergent relativisms around the turn of the century – in science, anthropology, politics and philosophy. New Historicist critics have proposed an opposing model, wherein late capitalism consolidates itself into a monolithic order, reducing all literary expression to a commodity form. But the new literary marketplace meant a relaxation of generic and moral constraints; and many of those who were most vehemently opposed to new popular forms and modes of expression did so in defense of traditional hierarchies in church and state.

Payment by Royalty

In high Victorian fiction, almost all works by established novelists were bought by publishers for a lump sum, payable on acceptance of the complete manuscript.[34] But by 1877, Trollope was advising Thomas Hardy that "There can be no doubt that the royalty system is the best, if you can get a publisher to give you a royalty, and if you are not in need of immediate money."[35] Twenty years later the standard arrangement had become a part-payment in advance (either on commissioning, or on delivery of the manuscript), followed by a royalty on actual sales. The royalty seems to have first become standard practice in America; it took over quite rapidly in England from the early 1880s, by mutual agreement between publishers, authors and agents. Henry James was a pioneer of the transition: from 1879 he routinely demanded payment by royalty for the American publication of his books, and in 1883 he signed a royalty agreement with Macmillan, London, for the Collective Edition of his works.[36] James may have had several reasons for preferring payment by royalty. Perhaps he was more optimistic about sales of his books than his publishers were; or he may have thought it fairer to be paid on the basis of actual rather than expected results. American publishers also had an unwritten agreement called "courtesy of the house," whereby publishers were not supposed to entice an author away from his current publisher by making a higher offer on a book. This "courtesy" was an obvious restrictive practice favoring publishers against authors; royalty payments offered a better chance of getting full market value.[37] A final reason for James to prefer royalties may have been that in the earlier part of his career he gained most of his income from American serial rights, for which he was paid by the page as installments appeared in *The Atlantic* or *Scribners*.[38] This may have given him a taste for a steady and moderate flow of payments, rather than a large capital sum every two or three years (similarly, he used short stories to smooth out fluctuations in his income).[39] His ambition was to become both a critically established writer, and one who enjoyed an income that was both respectable and reliable.[40]

The royalty system smoothed out the flow of payments for literary work over authors' lives, including periods when they were too old to write or their current books did not sell. However, such security was paid for out of their own pockets. Under payment by results the author assumed most of the risk for a book's failure, since the publisher was no longer speculating on the success of a book by purchasing it outright before it appeared. Publishers therefore had less need for working capital, since authors' advances typically might be only twenty percent of what the publisher would have paid for purchase outright.

The royalty smoothed out profits for publishers, as well as risks. Canon F.W. Farrar's *Life of Christ* (1873) became a *cause célèbre* that probably contributed to the switch to royalties in the years after its publication. Having commissioned the book for the outright sum of £600, Cassell's hit the jackpot with huge sales; Farrar made speeches denouncing "the sweating publishers . . . who, without a blush would toss to the author perhaps a hundredth part of what, by bargains grossly inequitable, they had obtained."[41] Cassell's responded that they had voluntarily paid Farrar another £1405, while others entered the controversy to suggest that the payment was made in the hope of acquiring Farrar's follow-up bestseller, *The Life and Works of St. Paul* (1879).[42]

The royalty system came to prevail for many reasons. It guaranteed full payment by results to the author, and was much more transparent than the earlier system of "shared profits," which gave the publisher an incentive to exaggerate his actual cost of production.[43] It allowed authors to retain an interest in their literary properties until the expiry of copyright, and if they became successful they could benefit from the re-printing of their earlier works.[44] Under the old system, a work once sold was sold forever (like a painting sold by an artist), and future income depended entirely on new work.[45] In theory, authors could invest the proceeds from the sale of their works as capital; but for a modestly successful novelist like Gissing, this was not really practical – a novel sold for £150 would only yield £6 a year if the money was invested in government bonds.

Gissing had no choice but to live on the proceeds of one novel while producing the next.[46] On the royalty system he would have been even poorer in the earlier years of his career, but more comfortably off later on.

About the effects of the royalty system on literary creativity we can only speculate, because we cannot know how English literature might have been different if outright purchase had continued to dominate in the twentieth century. Under purchase, authors may be confident that they can produce another marketable work, but they have no base comparable to the guarantee of future royalty income from past works. That income may diminish, certainly, but past achievements will have some kind of continuing material recognition. Authors who sell outright will see their careers as a series of successful productions; under royalty they will think in terms of accumulation, of building a body of work that will yield an increasing income.

It might be argued that all authors strive to construct an *oeuvre* regardless of how they are paid, writing books that mutually reinforce each other, and often colonizing a fictional territory like Dickens's London, Trollope's Barsetshire, or Hardy's Wessex. But the royalty system should encourage greater variety between an author's individual works. A Victorian publisher who was paying a large capital sum for a novel would expect it to be similar to the author's previous successes, and close to the established taste of the reading public. Authors who were being paid by royalty had more room to experiment, because they themselves would bear a large share of the cost of failure. The English novel in the twentieth century surely has been more varied in form than in the nineteenth. Factors like the decline of the circulating libraries and the segmentation of the market have played their part in the expansion of genres, but the shift to the royalty system must also have made its contribution.

This greater variation in form may also extend to variability in literary quality. Dickens, Thackeray, Trollope and Eliot (as well as lesser novelists) kept up a remarkably consistent standard from one novel to the next. When paid by royalty, novelists are not necessarily influenced to lower their standards, but they will be inclined to vary their offerings – seeking a formula for greater success, or diversifying the literary capital on which they will be living. Henry James was the first major English novelist to depend mainly on royalties, and his career displays a succession of phases that we can explain as adaptations and explorations within a newly diversified fictional marketplace. His attempt to become a commercial playwright during the 1890s would then take its place within a general orientation towards testing the market with varying productions.

One may attribute diversification to the royalty system and market segmentation, or to an intrinsic urge towards formal experimentation and away from the set form of the high Victorian novel. Feltes rightly emphasizes the concentration of capital within Victorian publishing. A compact group of two circulating libraries and seven major publishers assumed, under the purchase system, almost all of the capital risk of novel-publishing. The royalty spread a large share of this risk to the thousands of small producers who supplied the novels; in exchange for assuming the risk, they were no longer so closely policed by a small group of buyers with a common interest and taste.

The Rise of the Agent

The new literary marketplace brought with it a new function, that of the literary agent. As with so many innovations in markets or financial institutions, agents first became prominent in London, and their activity has remained centralized in the two literary capitals of London and New York.[47] A.P. Watt set up as a literary agent around 1881, though agents for drama and for lecture tours had been established long before, and Watt himself began as an advertising agent.[48] The increasing complexity of the literary marketplace contributed to the appearance of this new specialization; but equally important was the re-configuration of the traditional relationship between author and publisher.

It took some time for others to follow A.P. Watt: J.B. Pinker began his business in 1896, Curtis Brown in 1899. By that time, their advertising for clients brought a welcoming response from authors; publishers, conversely, were either sceptical of the value of agents, or bluntly hostile to them. Yet by 1914 most successful authors were represented by agents, a rapid and fundamental shift in the English literary marketplace. Publishing had traditionally been one of the gentlemanly occupations (unlike the impresario who put on plays or lectures). It had little of the stigma of "trade"; publishing companies were convenient places for the investment of private capital (for example, to buy a partnership for a younger son), and success depended on familiarity with the cultural tastes of the upper middle class. Publishers would treat their authors as fellow-gentlemen, and would not expect them to solicit offers from rival houses, or even to bargain over terms.

For authors like Walter Besant or Canon Farrar, all this gentility was merely a cover for exploitation. Besant fulminated about the iniquities of the shared profit system, which allowed publishers to pad their costs; Ferrar about the unfairness of outright sale, which had denied him the

fruits of his success. But these complaints only found an audience because of changes in the social tone of literary publishing. The Society of
Authors (founded in 1884) gave institutional expression to the dissatisfaction of authors with the old system. In claiming to be gentlemen rather
than tradesmen, publishers were inviting authors into a prestige culture
milieu where one should not be pushy about money. Besant argued that it
was having money that gave prestige, not pretending that you didn't need
it. In the eighteenth century, he observed, authorship became stigmatized
as a "beggarly profession"; but now, "The old bugbear – the prejudice formerly so well founded – of poverty has vanished. It is now well known that
a respectable man of letters may command an income and a position quite
equal to those of the average lawyer or doctor."[49]

The three requirements for a "noble profession," Besant said, were independence, distinction, and "great prizes"; but for him, clearly, it was
the prizes that counted for most. He welcomed the new money coming
in from journalism: "It is, indeed, impossible to over-estimate the assistance which journalism has rendered to the profession of letters."[50] If the
status of authors depended solely on the size of their incomes (regardless
of the kind of writing they were paid for), then the "gentlemanly" business practices of publishers were no more than a confidence game. They
paid their authors in deference and social recognition to avoid paying
them the full market price for their work. Besant certainly felt that
publishers took too large a share of the gross proceeds from book sales
(though his proposed remedy, that authors should become self-publishers,
had little practical result). Authors found it difficult to push royalties
higher than the standard ten to fifteen percent; but by the turn of the
century they had become more militant about their economic interests,
and supported efforts by the Society of Authors to improve contract
terms.[51] They seem to have been receptive to Besant's argument that they
would not become genteel by virtue of their calling, but by virtue of their
success in an expanding and more openly commercial literary marketplace.

A major advantage for authors in being represented by an agent was
that they could continue to relate to their publishers as ladies and gentlemen, and to the critics as disinterested artists, while leaving it to the
agent to drive the shrewdest possible bargain for the literary property
they had on offer.[52] The publisher William Heinemann was a great enemy of agents, and especially of A.P. Watt whom he called a "middle-
man" and a "parasite." The agent, Heinemann warned, "fosters in
authors the greed for an immediate money return . . . at the cost of all
dignity and artistic repose. . . . I do not consider it to be in the interests of

literature that books should be put up to auction."[53] It was humbug to claim that literature should not be made into a commodity, when it was precisely the publisher's interest to buy that commodity as cheaply as he could, and make the largest possible profit on it. But Heinemann was right in recognizing that the new literary marketplace was incompatible with the older world of paternal relations and mutual loyalty between authors and publishers.

Before long, publishers too would realize that agents were more than just enforcers of authors' claims. Michael Joseph, director of the Curtis Brown agency from 1926 to 1935, noted that "The market for good literature far exceeds the supply, and publishers regularly make known their wants to the half dozen agents of substantial reputation."[54] Any agent provides a service to both buyer and seller, and must reconcile their interests in the contract for a property. Publishers cannot know what every writer is planning, and writers cannot know the interests of every publisher. To maximize the value of a book, it needs to find – with the agent's help – its best home, which may be a different one for each new work. As authors become more likely to jump from one publisher to another, agents are also needed to conduct complex negotiations between the holders of individual rights, as with Henry James's project of issuing a collected edition of his works in the 1880s.[55]

As neither publishers nor authors came to expect lifelong loyalty from each other, the relationship between author and agent was likely to become more intimate and continuous than between author and publisher. An author's career tended to become, with an agent's help, a series of auctions. Only the agent saw the author's career as a whole, and the commission system gave the agent a common interest in maximizing the author's income. After the U.S. recognized British copyright in 1891, a typical novel might be sold four times: serial and book rights, British and American. The novelist would thus accumulate dozens of agreements with book publishers and magazines on both sides of the Atlantic (plus separate Continental rights, where Tauchnitz dominated). The agent, having negotiated thousands of contracts for different clients, could steer the author through this labyrinth and make the author aware of the requirements of the new literary marketplace. He dealt with authors as members of an economically defined class, while at the same time sheltering them from actual haggling over terms with publishers. J.B. Pinker would even provide advances out of his own funds, using the money he made from his bestselling clients such as H.G. Wells and Arnold Bennett to subsidize writers who were still struggling, such as Conrad and D.H. Lawrence (today, probably no agent would do this).[56] Pinker was thus carrying a long-term risk in the literary marketplace that previously would have been assumed by publishers.

Conrad lamented in 1902 that he was living in "the age of Besants, Authors' Clubs and Literary agents" and said he would prefer to deal directly with William Blackwood for the books he had in hand.[57] But his actual practice was to squeeze both his publisher and Pinker for cash to keep his household going. Conrad the aristocrat wanted to keep his hands out of the greasy till of the literary marketplace; Conrad the businessman wanted every pound of present income, plus anything he could borrow against future earnings. His attitude to Pinker was a mixture of dependence and disdain. On going up to London his first stop would be at Pinker's office, to borrow a sovereign for walking-around money. When he had his pocket picked at Montpellier in 1906, he wrote to Pinker: "Please send me a £10 note instanter, because life without pocket money is not worth living."[58] He originally signed up with Pinker, in September 1900, because his demands for money from his publishers were getting a chilly reception. He later boasted to Edward Garnett "that he had become expert at exploiting agents and editors" – as if both had to contribute their share to the £650 a year he needed to live in appropriate style.[59] Yet when Pinker grew tired of Conrad's demands, and hinted that he had failed as a writer, Conrad returned fire with no hint of self-reproach:

> Pray do not write to me as I were a fool blundering in the dark. There are other virtues than punctuality. Have you the slightest idea of what I am trying for? Of what is my guiding principle which I follow in anxiety, and poverty, and daily and unremitting toil of my very heart. . . . This is the sort of thing one writes to a grub street dipsomaniac to stop him bothering one – not to a man of my value. Am I a confounded boy? I have had to look death in the eye once or twice. It was nothing. . . . I am no sort of airy R.L. Stevenson who considered his art a prostitute and the artist as no better than one. I dare say he was punctual – but I don't envy him.[60]

Pinker, to his credit, accepted Conrad's rebuke. He paid up the immediate £40 that Conrad was asking for, and went on subsidizing Conrad until the popular success of *Chance* in 1913 allowed Conrad to pay off what he had borrowed from Pinker over the years. He did not feel guilt over the money he chronically owed, but rather discomfort with "this struggle with wretched embarras[s]ments, this scheming and planning for which my previous existence has utterly unfitted me."[61] When he was commissioned to write for *Blackwood's Magazine* he found it "an unspeakable relief" to produce to order "instead of for 'the market' – confound *it* and all its snippety works." Conrad even imagined being put on a regular salary by Blackwood the publisher, with his employer then disposing of his output as he saw fit.[62]

Conrad's disposition towards money was idiosyncratic, certainly. His father instilled in him an aristocratic disdain for "trade," and as a sailor he spent long periods when he had no need or opportunity to spend money. On shore he spent like a sailor, got himself into debt, then returned to sea. After he left the Merchant Navy he could never settle down to handle money prudently. As an author, he found it repugnant to produce piecework for an uncertain market; and from the beginning he lived on loans and advances against future work, so that in trying to complete a book he suffered a financial as well as a creative strain. In theory, Pinker should have stood as a buffer between Conrad and the market, providing for his client the artistic repose that William Heinemann said was an author's need. Unfortunately, Pinker's willingness to fund Conrad only encouraged him to plunge further into debt, and to look on his financial prospects with deeper despair.

Ideally, the agent protected the author against an ever more powerful and intrusive literary marketplace; but, paradoxically, it also was part of the agent's role to make the author conscious of the insistency of the market's claims – and not just because the agent's own income depended on the author's success. Given the extremity of Conrad's resistance to the market, one may speculate about the creative consequences of his stance. Just as other kinds of neurosis may both torment artists and be the enabling conditions of their art, so may financial anxiety have a double effect. For Conrad, certainly, the vision of rising above financial worries was no more than a fantasy. His imprisonment within economic necessity, with no real prospect of writing himself into the clear, contributed to his brooding consciousness of irrationality and doom. Like the knitting machine that symbolized for him the indifference of the universe to individual desires, the market also is a monstrous, impersonal system confronting the writer's vulnerable creativity.[63] In assessing Conrad's career, we must note his deep frustration with his status as a market agent, his fantasies of escaping into economic dignity and independence, and the coincidence between his eventual market success and the withering of his creative powers.

Other writers responded differently, of course, to these new constraints and opportunities. Walter Besant spoke for many in celebrating writers' improved chances of becoming rich and respectable; at the other pole, the modernists set out to create a counter-system of support for writers, rather than submit to the market's grip. But Conrad's bitter complaints about the economic trials of the writer's life have an application beyond his personal discomfort. His earlier tastes of security in a prestige status – as Polish aristocrat and as British naval officer – brought home to him with special keenness the utter vulnerability of the writer in the modern marketplace. This sensitivity linked him with the condition of those many people at many times who saw their place in a prestige order threatened by the advance of market rationality. Part of Conrad's appeal lay in his transposing anxieties about a diminished self from the economic sphere to an exoticized imperial realm. Just as the Darwinian struggle for existence allegorized tensions within Victorian society (rather than in nature), so can Conrad be read as an allegorizer of vulnerability to the market economy. His personal sense of doom, moreover, owed much to his fear of market forces – "material interests" in his terms – that he experienced as both ignoble and beyond his power to resist.

American Copyright and the Single Market

Copyright protection for English books published on the Continent began to be assured in 1846, with the signing of a reciprocal agreement between Britain and Prussia.[64] The Leipzig firm of Tauchnitz paid for rights to its English authors, and refrained from selling its editions in England.[65] In 1887 most of the world's publishing nations signed the Berne copyright convention, but the United States refused. British authors therefore still had no protection against the pirating of their works in the U.S., by far the largest market for their works outside the U.K. Famous authors like Dickens or Thackeray could make large amounts of money for American lecture tours, but only small amounts of literary income moved from the U.S. to Britain.[66]

In 1891 Congress voted to recognize the Berne Convention, though with the proviso that any book seeking copyright in the U.S. had to be printed there.[67] The most important result of the Copyright Act was simply that both British and American authors received substantially more money. Exactly how much is hard to say: the increase would be less than a hundred percent, because authors would normally earn more in their native country (where they already enjoyed copyright protection) than across the Atlantic. We can assume, also, that British authors gained more new income from the larger U.S. market than American ones did from England.

Henry James is a special and instructive case. As an American resident in England he enjoyed, throughout his career, copyright protection in both countries. From 1905 to 1915, seventy-four percent of his total literary earnings of $50,077 came from the U.S. [68] He had more appeal to American readers, and by 1900 the population of the U.S. was twice that of Britain. Most of his income thus derived from his literary representation of Europe to the American market, by someone whose American origins gave him a special authority as an informant. Though James was not directly affected by the 1891 Copyright Act, his career suggests that the merging of the American and British literary markets promoted a new and more complex division of labor.

After 1891, authors had a stronger incentive to produce works aimed at audiences on both sides of the Atlantic. This principle is obvious enough today in the adaptation of television offerings to a variety of markets. For example, the British TV serial *Upstairs, Downstairs* included an episode in which a German baker in London is persecuted during World War I. That episode had direct appeal to the German television market; but the entire series was made palatable to German views of the First World War, in a way that would not have been conceivable in the 1920s. "Transnational" television and movies today are the culmination of a process just beginning in the 1890s, when the two great national markets for literature in English began to merge.[69]

D.H. Lawrence is a well-documented case of conscious adaptation to the dual market. After the suppression of *The Rainbow* in 1915, and the rejection of *Women in Love* by many English publishers from 1916 on, Lawrence and Frieda could not survive on his English royalties. From late 1915 Lawrence had dreamed of moving to America: to escape the war, but also, he told Cynthia Asquith, because "I am pretty sure of selling my stuff if I am in America. . . . it is quite useless my trying to live and write here. I shall only starve." To Catherine Carswell he wrote "I believe America is my Virgin soil."[70] It took another four years for his confidence to bear fruit, but he was never again in want after the success of the privately printed U.S. edition of *Women in Love* in 1920 (followed by a trade edition). As Lawrence was finishing *Kangaroo* in Australia in 1922, he wrote to his American publisher "I must come to America and try to do a novel there."[71] He understood that he would have to turn away from the English social novel towards myth and romance, producing the kind of novel that required less knowledge of the English class system and therefore could appeal directly to American readers. Living as an expatriate from 1919 until his death in 1930 reduced Lawrence's commitment to English social issues; but the marketing of his work undoubtedly contributed to his leaving behind the intensely local concerns of his earlier novels.

Lawrence's trajectory could also be seen as a move from his working-class roots to the London intellectual upper-middle class, and then the class (if it can be called that) of expatriate bohemians and rentiers. An enclosed culture that offered a coherent object for fictional representation progressively dissolved into something with far more nebulous boundaries. Such a movement was consistent with the incentive, in the merged literary marketplace, to dilute local and national content in order to reach a mass transatlantic readership. For many intellectuals, this process would appear as a vulgarization of traditional British high culture. Concurrently, the journalistic practices of Harmsworth and Rothermere could be seen as a kind of Americanization from within, with radical populism washing away the authority of the traditional clerisy. Organicist intellectuals imagined American culture as invading England and driving native species to extinction, or dissolving the prestige culture of old-fashioned Englishness into a single Atlantic system that was driven solely by money.

Yet equally powerful counter-currents may flow within the Atlantic marketplace. An increase in the overall size of the market may not necessarily lead to a homogenization of the products being offered. Individual segments may become more promising for authors to exploit, leading to more variety rather than more uniformity. This could be true both horizontally, in terms of diversification of geographical or social settings, or vertically, in terms of stratification between high-, middle- and low-brow literatures. Michael Anesko has given a suggestive account of this kind of specialization:

> If the pressure to achieve bestseller status was made more acute by the evolution of a truly mass audience, the same conditions eventually fostered the recognition that smaller, more discriminating publics existed in tandem with it and might be capable of supporting writers of distinction.[72]

The emergence of such market segments was overdetermined – by the rise of the mass reading public, and by the merging of the Atlantic literary markets. Modernism, correspondingly, defined itself as both a literature that was hostile to the market, and one oriented to the European past rather than the Anglo-American commercial present. Pound and Eliot's American origins were effective in the way of negation: the last thing expatriates would desire would be for that which they had left behind to follow them to their new destination.

A final effect of the extension of copyright would be on canonicity in English literature. Before 1891 English writers looked to the domestic market for almost all their income and, generally, were still imbued with a conviction of their cultural superiority to the U.S. This superiority was threatened by the rise of America's population and economic power, which had so clearly surpassed Britain by 1900. But once English writing was routinely marketed in America, it was *offered up* to American readers, and proportionately reduced in authority. *Middlemarch* (1872) and *The Way We Live Now* (1874-5) were among the last novels of their kind, as complete and confident representations of a unitary culture. The establishment of the single Atlantic market made Englishness both relative, and a cultural commodity for a particular segment of the market. This may be most evident in generic fiction, rather than in more ambitious works. The detective stories of Arthur Conan Doyle, which began appearing in 1887, are fables of imperial rationality; their Englishness includes the hero's imperturbable self-possession when confronted with figures of the criminal or colonial margin. But by the 1930s, Englishness in the crime fiction of Agatha Christie and Dorothy L. Sayers had become a package of stereotypes for foreign consumption, quaint and unthreatening. Christie became the world's bestselling author of fiction on the strength of her idealized English village with its cast of stock characters.[73]

The Englishness of writers like Christie, and of the "Masterpiece Theatre" productions, makes no disturbing hegemonic claims on the rest of the world. Its market appeal rests on a representation of England as backward and mildly ineffectual: this is a version that "travels well" while others – Northern, industrial, lower-middle class, etc. – do not. This "Heritage style" extracts from the canonical tradition of English fiction a myth of an ordered social hierarchy, adds elements of kitsch and spectacle, and markets the result as essential Englishness. It might be argued that these images reflect Britain's relative decline in the twentieth century, with a national failure of nerve and obsession with past glories. But we are concerned here with the appeal of a Britain populated by the likes of Miss Marple, Lord Peter Wimsey, or Sebastian Flyte with his teddy bear at Oxford, to American readers or viewers. In Britain itself, such representations necessarily arouse conflicting responses, embedded as they are in contested class relations; most of these drop away on the Atlantic passage, and we are left with "truths" about Englishness that are a fulfillment of American desires, though satisfied by English cultural producers working to an external specification. This happens regardless of the hostility of writers like Evelyn Waugh to American culture: the American market took those elements of Englishness it wanted, whatever the intent of the original producers.[74] The same process, of course, was at work in the reverse direction, where the myths of the cowboy or the gangster were taken to represent American social reality in Europe.

Canonicity therefore tends to be put in question by the arrival of a single market for literature in English; and Britain, as it became a junior partner to the U.S., seems to have been the more vulnerable to such a loss of confidence. American literature had less to fear from an increased emphasis on market forces because it was already part of a more homogeneous money-culture and less influenced by prestige values. Yet literature in English as a whole has suffered a particular dispersal of authority – relative to other literatures such as French, German, Russian – as it first became bi-polar around the turn of the century, and then multi-polar with the rise of postcolonial literatures after World War II.[75] The kind of canonicity typical of nineteenth-century British works was necessarily implicated with British political and economic supremacy; and perhaps it can only be restored when the standards and types of an emergent postnational literature in English have become more settled.[76]

The Coming of Mass Journalism

The modern newspaper age began in 1896, when Alfred Harmsworth launched the *Daily Mail* with the slogan "a penny newspaper for a half-penny."[77] Newspapers and magazines, even more than books, benefited from mass literacy following the Education Act of 1870; and those periodicals that benefited the most were created specifically for the new market. Segmentation became the rule in journalism as much as in literature, and periodicals were even more clearly stamped with the signs of their intended audience (and therefore even more threatening to the guardians of high culture). The Harmsworth papers were aimed squarely at the growing lower-middle class of clerks and skilled workers, who wanted to be informed and entertained but who had not been able to afford the penny or more charged by previous daily papers.[78] A typical *Mail* reader lived in the South London suburbs and read the paper on the tram or train while going in to work. The recipe for the *Mail's* content included crime, the royal family, patriotism, and women's interests: so far as Harmsworth was concerned this was giving the punters what they wanted – and the proof was the size of the paper's circulation.[79]

The popular press affected the literary climate by showing that reading matter could be commodified through and through, and targeted precisely to the social position of its readers. Newspaper magnates became cultural bogeymen for critics to both left and right, whether socialists or upholders of the old prestige culture. The influence of the press seemed to be a horrid rebuff to Matthew Arnold's hopes for the civilizing mission of the clerisy. Mass-circulation newspapers did not civilize the newly-literate, but mobilized them into supporters of a vulgar, jingoistic consumer society. They confirmed the stratification of the populace by class, education and outlook, and made it clear that literacy was not an innocent extension of enlightenment. Once the readers of a particular paper had been targeted, surveyed, and enlisted, they could be kept loyal with the daily provision of a known recipe of content. This intimate and constantly reinforced relation with its readers made the popular newspaper into a much more effective cultural instrument than the vague and dispersed influence of books.

Within a decade or so of the founding of the *Daily Mail*, book culture had become literacy's junior partner, at least in terms of immediate influence on the mass of the population. Newspapers added greatly to the earning potential of those authors who could meet their needs, and a large new class of author-journalists emerged. Newspapers made successful writers into celebrities, and enabled pundits like Arnold Bennett or George Bernard Shaw to become intellectuals for the masses. Walter Besant praised newspapers for providing a "regular pyramid of easy incline" for writers to climb: they could start by freelancing for provincial newspapers and end as well-known authors with a column in a London daily.[80]

Arnold Bennett was both the most typical and most successful example of Besant's new model author. In *The Truth About an Author* – which was bitterly attacked for revealing an *economic* truth – Bennett called himself "an author of several sorts. I have various strings to my bow. And I know my business. I write half a million words a year." About 150,000 words of his annual output consisted of reviews: he boasted that he could look at a pile of new books and write a fifteen-hundred-word column about them inside sixty minutes, for a fee of three guineas. He admitted that he didn't read through the books: "the man in the street says, shocked: 'You are unjust.' And I reply: 'Not at all. I am merely an expert.'" Bennett expected to make at least ten shillings an hour for his journalism, but claimed that "when I am working on my own initiative, for the sole advancement of my artistic reputation, I ignore finance and think of glory alone."[81]

Earlier novelists, notably Dickens and Thackeray, had written great amounts of ephemera while also writing fiction to a canonical standard. But journalism, considered as an industry, had become far more powerful by the time Bennett came on the scene. Writers who lived in London were especially sensitive to journalism's influence and inducements. They became conditioned, for example, to a cycle of deadlines – short pieces of work produced in a short time. Such work necessarily reflected the stimulus of an immediate response from readers, topical content, and a quick pay-off. Journalism created a fashion cycle of ideas that was much shorter than previous swings of intellectual or literary opinion. And once accustomed to writing short pieces for ready money, novelists would find it hard to turn their backs on Fleet Street while slowly incubating a major work. Finally, the dominance of journalism worked against the principle of canonicity, as embodied in the authoritative, comprehensive and slowly matured text. When Pound defined literature as "news that stays news," he assumed that the two kinds of writing could, in the long run, be separated and opposed.[82] Yet journalistic culture was so powerful that it left no writer, and no kind of writing untouched.

What Money Can't Buy

As the fictional marketplace became more open and efficient by the beginning of the twentieth century, it should have carried the English novel to new heights. Yet most critics now would agree that the twentieth-century novel has regressed. Only one modern English novel, *Ulysses*, now stands as unquestionably great; and it was not elicited by the market but by modernist patronage, a regime to be discussed in the next chapter. The market now provides thousands of novels a year to suit every taste, but it has not delivered magisterial novels equivalent to those of Austen, Dickens, the Brontes, Trollope, Eliot or Hardy. Yet the financial rewards for novels are greater than ever before: £17 million for three novels by Barbara Taylor Bradford in 1992, for example, or a reputed £15 million for Jeffrey Archer's three-book contract in 1995.

Why is it that the market, such a complex, powerful and sensitive organization, cannot deliver certain goods at any price? The kinds of operas and symphonies produced before 1914 have no modern counterparts, though they are still "in demand." Many critics actively blame the market for a supposed decline in twentieth century culture, whether on the right (modernism, primitivism, medievalism, Leavisism) or on the left (everything from William Morris to the new-historicist demonizing of "commodification"). Such critiques assume some kind of idealized pre-market cultural economy (or post-market utopia, in the case of Marxism). Yet most art has been commodified from the beginning in the sense of not being a material necessity, and therefore something whose value is based on exchange rather than any objective estimate of the labor embodied in it. There is no connection between the amount of time spent writing a book and its perceived value. Further, the development of market society is only one of many seismic shifts since the Renaissance; one might just as plausibly argue that loss of religious belief, the spread of democracy, or technological progress are to blame for the decline of art.

The market is both a formal system of efficient exchange and, in any given society, an institution historicized by social interests external to it. This is why the market cannot elicit from a culture productions – romantic operas, religious paintings – that are not viable within a particular cultural situation, regardless of price. By the same token, institutions that seek to by-pass the market are not likely to be any more successful in producing high art on demand. The Soviet writers' unions, for example, specified a preferred literary form (socialist realism) and paid creators directly to make examples of the desired works. The effects of this command economy included a complete collapse of Russian fiction from its earlier achievements, much more dramatic than any decline of the novel in the West. In any case, the great Victorian novelists wrote for money too; though they produced within a literary marketplace that was less segmented, and less openly in conflict with prestige values. To speak of a general blight of commodification is too often to ignore the specificity of how markets can be embedded in all kinds of local situations.

This is not to say that the market always knows best, or to deny that markets affect the status of the goods they circulate. But cultural critics should admit their ignorance of precisely why "art happens," and should not assume that they can point the way to an alternative society whose art would be superior to that of the existing order. The new literary marketplace instituted its segmentation within a literary system that was more interconnected and extensive than ever before. In this system, the mode of production of popular culture became normative and tended to absorb the levels above it, reversing the old model of a Coleridgian clerisy regulating the baser elements below. The developments summarized in this chapter add up to a rationalization of capital employed in literary production, analogous to other sectors of the economy that were making the transition to twentieth-century consumer society.[83] But in the literary sphere, this process unfolded in a specially contested and contradictory fashion.

English literature has had a long affiliation with prestige culture values, and a correspondingly nostalgic orientation towards the past; within this tradition, many writers were bound to be affronted by the changes I have described.[84] But writing is also a tertiary economic activity, part of the service or knowledge sector that has become steadily more dominant over the past century in developed countries. The popular press of the 1890s was the first mode of mass entertainment, a uniform product reproduced and distributed by modern technology. Journalism thus inaugurated our modern "media society"; by the same token, it has become subordinated to the more powerful media that followed – radio, movies, television. In its affinity with journalism and the overall market for entertainment, literature belongs with the most dynamic sectors of post-industrial society, those that manipulate our strategic myths, symbols and financial instruments.

It is important, though, to see that the hostility of Victorian high culture to market forces initiated other projects than just the rejection or repression of popular writing. One group, led by people like Walter Besant and Arnold Bennett, adapted eagerly to the new constraints and opportunities. They may have lamented the rise of commercialism, but they followed Besant's rule that "There has never been any poet or any author who has in reality been unwilling to take all the money his works would bring in."[85] At the same time, they had to recognize that they had no power over the demand for their goods: they had to monitor the market on which they depended as carefully as a ship's captain observed the tides and the weather. Their subordination to the market defined their position as a literary class.

Meanwhile, to the extent that high culture was pushed away from the center of authority it sought to occupy new spaces that were defined by their distance from popular and commercially successful literary forms. These spaces included the *fin-de-siècle* movement of aestheticism and decadence; the rentier culture of those who did not need to be directly involved with market activities; and the modernism that developed after Ezra Pound's arrival in London in 1908. Rentier culture sought to distance itself from the market, but in a stance more of independence than of active opposition. Henry James's stories, according to Nigel Cross, assume that "art and profit are irreconcilable. This view leaves literature in the hands of a privileged, well-educated elite with private incomes – it leads, inevitably, to Bloomsbury."[86] The rentiers drew on inherited landed or financial wealth, either from the prestige classes or from commercial families who were moving away from active involvement in trade. Simultaneously dependent on the market and disconnected from it, the rentiers were numerous enough to evolve a distinctive way of life. Their distance from the market defined their creative sensibility, but their works were mainly distributed through the commercial publishing system.

Modernism, finally, proclaimed itself a root-and-branch enemy of the literary marketplace, and sought to establish a complete alternative system of evaluation and distribution. Modernist producers would be endowed (with resources largely derived from the rentier culture), and their work would appear in little magazines and private presses: organs uncontaminated by the menacing worlds of journalism and commercial literature. Rentiers and modernists both hoped to inhabit a separate sphere from the marketplace; the degree of their success will be taken up in the next two chapters.

Whatever their differences, all these formations separated literary values (and human values generally) from the daily imperatives of production and subsistence. Yet that which is not routinely traded in the marketplace acquires value from its rarity, making it more desirable as a badge of status. The separation of form from commodification opens up a wider range of literary possibilities; yet this freedom will in its turn be distilled into new genres that cannot escape the market's notice, once they have been validated by cultural leaders as exceptional and prestigious. In the long run, attempts to evade the vulgar commodity forms of the literary marketplace will be recuperated by that market's alertness to novelty and refinement – an alertness that leaves the literary producer with no innocent refuge.

8
English Literature and Rentier Culture

> *"For long past there had been in England an entirely*
> *functionless class, living on money that was invested they*
> *hardly knew where, the 'idle rich' . . . . They were simply*
> *parasites, less useful to society than his fleas are to a dog."*
> —George Orwell, "The Lion and the Unicorn"

The Fundholders

The emergence of a "Monied Interest" within the aristocracy went hand in glove with the rapid and exceptional development, in England, of a banking system. Walter Bagehot argued that it was the rise of banks that made England into "the greatest moneyed country in the world."[1] French landowners with extra funds would typically buy more land, or invest in mortgages, or simply keep their cash under lock and key at home. But their English counterparts had attractive opportunities for collective investment through banks, stock promoters, or purchase of government debt (the "funds"). This "concentration of money in banks" was the key to England's Victorian hegemony, creating a huge pool of capital for the expansion of trade and for new economic enterprises, whether domestic or foreign.[2]

The English rentier class can be defined as those who lived off financial wealth, which gave them a higher income than if they invested in land, and freed them from responsibility for an estate with its servants, laborers, and tenants. What might be called a rentier infrastructure was built up gradually from the late seventeenth century on. In *Moll Flanders* (1722) the heroine's capital is as unstable and promiscuous as she is herself. The secure and profitable placement of savings had to await the maturing of the banking system and of government borrowing. With no social security provided by the government (except for the Workhouse), and fewer people protected by the paternalism of landowners, the accumulation of private capital was the only remaining way to provide for old age; and it was quixotic to expect people merely to hoard their wealth when, in England at least, the financial system stood ready to give them a three to five per cent annual return. The need to finance the Napoleonic Wars first created a large and visible class of fundholders, and despite the complaints about the emergence of a parasitic class, the English economy rapidly outpaced those countries where wealth was kept under the bed.

Nonetheless, critics like Cobbett were right to note the formation of a new class, distinct both from the country gentry and from "trade." They could be seen in new London districts like Kensington, or in entire towns like Bournemouth or Cheltenham (which Edward Clodd called "the city of three per cents").[3] England had always had its idle rich, but by the later nineteenth century the scale of leisure had changed, as the country reaped the rewards of its global hegemony in trade and finance. Between 1855 and 1875, British overseas investments increased by five hundred per cent. In 1871, the census found 170,000 "persons of rank and property" without any stated occupation; most of these were women, so there must have been many more male rentiers who claimed a nominal profession but mainly lived off their capital.[4]

England had social values that drew people away from trade and towards the leisured lifestyle of the prestige classes, and a financial system that made it easy to draw an income on capital. Hirschman speaks of the tendency of newly enriched bourgeoisies to display "'spineless' subservience toward the well-entrenched aristocrats of the *ancien régime*"; and Max Weber emphasizes the barriers raised by "privileged status groups," who will never accept the *nouveau-riche* himself, but only "his descendants who have been educated in the conventions of their status group and who have never besmirched its honor by their own economic labor."[5] Such constraints may have motivated the French provincial merchants of the Renaissance whose typical ambition was to buy "noble land," and withdraw entirely from commerce.[6] But the English situation was less cut and dried. Many of the descendants of wealthy tradespeople and financiers did not assimilate into the landed gentry, but became a hybrid class: they mimicked gentry values in some degree, but did not shift their financial base from monetary assets to land. The defining quality of the rentier was detachment, whether from the responsibilities of land ownership, or from the heat and dust of the marketplace. George Eliot sends Daniel Deronda rowing dreamily down the river, "questioning whether it were worth while to take part in the battle of the world: I mean, of course, the young men in whom the unproductive labour of questioning is sustained by three or five per cent on capital which somebody else has battled for."[7]

It is crucial for Deronda's mentality that he has personal control over the management of his seven hundred a year. A collective rentier culture had long existed in England, and had sustained most of the nation's intellectual life: the Church of England (as well as its Catholic predecessor), the great public schools, and the universities of Oxford and Cambridge. These were institutions that measured their horizon in centuries and that traditionally lived off the modest but secure returns from land that had been bequeathed to them. Their cultural work was to reproduce and legitimate the established order, rather than to foster the creative freedom or self-cultivation of the individual.

The true rentiers had no institutional ties, and confirmed their dissociation by placing the bulk of their capital outside of England. The London Stock Exchange had its nucleus in the trading of East India Company stock, and continued to be oriented mainly towards foreign investments. Until the First World War, most domestic trade and industry was controlled by private companies in which no outsider could invest; so that in 1913 sixty per cent of the quoted value of the London Exchange was in foreign stocks.[8] The typical rentier had little financial interest in the success of British industry, which he was likely to disdain as a despoiler of the countryside and as the base for an uncouth class of nouveau-riche manufacturers. Many of the intellectuals who promoted the rural myth of organic Englishness had no actual ties to the land, but drew their family wealth from banking or finance: for example, William Morris, John Ruskin, Cardinal Newman, G.M. Hopkins, E.M. Forster.[9]

J.A. Hobson wondered if "Another century may see England the retreat for the old age of a small aristocracy of millionaires, who will have made their money where labour was cheapest, and return to spend it where life is pleasantest."[10] The rentier interest lay in cheap housing, an unspoiled countryside, low wages for service workers, and stable prices.[11] This would be specially true of those who wanted to enjoy independence and leisure on a modest income. In Gissing's *The Whirlpool* (1897), Harvey Rolfe can live comfortably in Wales on his private income of £900 a year; but his wife's ambition to be a concert violinist draws them into the financial and social whirlpool of London, where they must put their capital at risk in order to raise their income. The novel idealizes the way of life of the rural rentier, while lamenting that people are moving out of their three per cents into business ventures and financial speculation.

T.E. Lawrence feared another kind of whirlpool, as he prepared to retire from the army at the age of forty-six:

The assets are my cottage in Dorsetshire . . . 25/- a week, a bike. If to that I find myself in possession of a quiet mind, then I shall be fortunate. . . . I do not often confess it to people, but I am always aware that madness lies very near me, always. The R.A.F.'s solidity and routine have been anchors holding me to life and the world. I wish they had not to be cut.[12]

The 25/- (£1.25) was the interest on Lawrence's savings, on which he proposed to live for the remainder of his days. He believed that he was too mentally exhausted to write another book or undertake any responsible work; if required, he would do just enough to top up his capital to ensure his subsistence.[13] Whether it was someone like Lawrence with £65 a year, or George Orwell's father with his pension of £438 from the Opium Service, almost every village in England would have its quota of gentlefolk living on their "private means," and dabbling with hobbies or cultural pursuits.

But what value is there to such "unproductive" lives, dedicated only to the achievement of a quiet mind? Tony Tanner considers the question as it applies to many of the characters of Jane Austen:

> I just want to note the significance of the fact that Emma is rich – in money. It is not property, which for Jane Austen always carried distinct responsibilities and patterns of behaviour with it – or should do. Unlike money, property supplied a specific agenda of duties, actions and rewards. The danger of money, on the other hand, was that not only did it not provide any pedigree: it conferred no specific obligations.[14]

For those who believed, with Cobbett, that "all valuable things arise from labour," people like Emma Woodhouse and her father were the cause of "all our present misery."[15] To keep them in their idleness, others had to pay higher taxes to cover interest received by the holders of the national debt. In *The Idea of a Christian Society*, T.S. Eliot echoed Cobbett's concern about a national system that favored the trader or financier over the primary producer. "Money is always forthcoming," he complained, "for the purpose of making more money, whilst it is so difficult to obtain for purposes of exchange . . . [I am] by no means sure that it is right for me to improve my income by investing in the shares of a company."[16]

All such criticisms reflect the ideology that consumption is intrinsically suspect, unless justified by a balancing contribution on the side of production. Gissing's Everard Barfoot asks, rhetorically, "Why is the man who toils more meritorious than he who enjoys?"[17] But those who only consume, even on a modest scale, fall under Raymond Williams's censure of "those who wanted to live at a comfortable distance from all real work, in some fantasy of funded simplicity": fund-holders, simple-lifers, Bloomsburyites, and the like.[18] Bukharin's *Economic Theory of the Leisure Class* (written 1914) was a polemic against the "marginal utility" economics of von Bohm-Bawerk, which Bukharin called "a marginal theory of the marginal bourgeoisie."[19] The global shift in the West towards a consumer society was for Bukharin proof that an over-ripe capitalism was ready to fall from the tree:

> This stratum of the bourgeoisie is distinctly parasitical. . . . The 'sphere of activities' of these *rentiers* may perhaps be most generally termed the *sphere of consumption*. Consumption is the basis of the entire life of the *rentiers* and the 'psychology of pure consumption' imparts to this life its specific style. The consuming *rentier* is concerned only with riding mounts, with expensive rugs, fragrant cigars, the wine of Tokay. A *rentier*, if he speaks of work at all means the 'work' of picking flowers or calling for a ticket at the box office of the opera.[20]

The separation of rentier life from business and productivity often involved geographical withdrawal. In Gissing's *The Odd Women*, Everard Barfoot meets in Normandy a family called the Brissendens who represent the proper circle for a man whose private income has increased from £450 to £1500 a year: "He was making friends in the world with which he had a natural affinity; that of wealthy and cultured people who seek no prominence, who shrink from contact with the circles known as 'smart,' who possess their souls in quiet freedom. It is a small class, especially distinguished by the charm of its women."[21] *The Emancipated* presents a similar little group of rentiers in Naples, a mixture of the children of Yorkshire mill owners with would-be writers and artists, such as the painter Ross Mallard whose "patrimony was modest, but happily, if the capital remained intact, sufficient to save him from the cares that degrade and waste a life." The group is emancipated in several ways: from work, from England, from religion, and from Victorian gender roles (Cicely Doran is "a human being to be instructed and developed, not a pretty girl to be made ready for the market").[22]

The privileged consumption of such groups anticipates the development from leisure class to mass tourism. People like Gissing and E.M. Forster were able to spend long periods in Italy because travel and accommodation became relatively much cheaper for English visitors towards the end of the nineteenth century; in turn, their writings about Italy helped to make it an object of desire for the middle-class masses. Any new experience may fuel the modern consumption-driven economy, where, as Lawrence Birken observes, it is no longer the case that "useful things [are] desired, but that desired things [are] useful."[23] In this perspective, rentiers cease to be a marginal and stigmatized group; they too perform work of a sort, as pioneers of new kinds of consumption that will become normative when increased income and leisure permit.

Rentier Culture

Clive Bell's *Civilisation* seeks to justify the leisure class as a repository for "good states of mind":

> to live a highly civilized life a man must be free from material cares.... almost all kinds of money-making are detrimental to the subtler and more intense states of mind, because almost all tire the body and blunt the intellect.... those only who never had to earn money know how to spend it; they alone take it simply for what it is – a means to what they want.[24]

Bell is trailing his coat in such passages; it may not have been his fault that he could not produce original art or literature, but in *Civilisation* he writes as if the leisure class deserve to be kept like peacocks, for their ornamental qualities alone. His desire to "make it impossible for any one in the [endowed leisure] class by any means to increase his or her income" was a languid rejection of energy or ambition.[25] People like Bell made it easy for later critics to disparage rentier culture as inherently parasitic. Orwell, for example, blamed this class for the mediocrity of novelists like Galsworthy:

> When he sets out to depict what he conceives as the desirable type of human being, it turns out to be simply a cultivated, humanitarian version of the upper-middle-class *rentier*, the sort of person who in those days used to haunt picture galleries in Italy and subscribe heavily to the Society for the Prevention of Cruelty to Animals.[26]

D.S. Mirsky called the Bloomsbury Group "theoreticians of the passive, dividend-drawing . . . section of the bourgeoisie . . . extremely intrigued by their own minutest inner experiences."[27] Raymond Williams makes the Bloomsbury ideal of the "civilised individual" equivalent to the enjoyment of "privileged consumption," while Jennifer Wicke calls

Bloomsbury "an invented community, in intention almost a utopia of and for consumption."[28]

Yet Bell was surrounded by those who did produce as well as consume (and perhaps provoked Bell into writing *Civilisation* as a defensive manoeuvre). Vanessa Bell, Leonard and Virginia Woolf, Duncan Grant, J.M. Keynes, and E.M. Forster all worked obsessively (and used that work to supplement their income from investments). Bell ignored, also, the enabling role of ordinary rentiers as audiences or patrons for the creative members of their class. There is a distinction to be made between the passive enjoyment of leisure, and the active production of art that represents or expresses that way of life. Henry James understood his artistic production in the double sense of working his capital, and living off it. When invited to visit America, he responded: "My capital is *here*, and to let it all slide would be simply to become bankrupt."[29] Jean-Christophe Agnew observes that "The only thing Jamesian characters actually produce are effects"; but their effects are a return on their cultural capital, as well as on the economic capital that sustains their worldly position.[30] All of this requires active management of their heritage, though it was someone else who made the original accumulation; as James put it: "it takes an old civilisation to set a novelist in motion. . . . It is on manners, customs, usages, habits, forms, upon all these things matured and established, that a novelist lives."[31]

Bourdieu also elaborates the metaphor of artistic production as a return on capital:

> economic capital provides the conditions for freedom from economic necessity, a private income [*la rente*] being one of the best substitutes for sales [*la vente*], as Théophile Gautier said to Feydeau: 'Flaubert was smarter than us . . . He had the wit to come into the world with money, something that is indispensable for anyone who wants to get anywhere in art.' . . .
>
> It is also because economic capital provides the guarantees [*assurances*] which can be the basis of self-assurance, audacity and indifference to profit - dispositions which, together with the flair associated with possession of a large social capital and the corresponding familiarity with the field, i.e. the art of sensing the new hierarchies and the new structures of the chances of profit, point towards the outposts, the most exposed positions of the avant-garde, and towards the riskiest investments, which are also, however, very often the most profitable symbolically, and in the long run, at least for the earliest investors.[32]

Bourdieu privileges the dissociation of the avant-garde, paying little attention to the ways in which possession of economic capital may bind the writer to the established order. In his view, the avant-garde's formal innovation is sufficient to distinguish it from the "bread-and-butter" or "industrial" literature that is enslaved to the market. Orwell, conversely, takes Eliot's avant-garde early poems to be the opposite of revolutionary:

> Clearly these poems were an end-product, the last gasp of a cultural tradition, poems which spoke only for the cultivated third-generation *rentier*, for people able to feel and criticise but no longer able to act. . . . The qualities by which any society which is to last longer than a generation actually has to be sustained – industry, courage, patriotism, frugality, philoprogenitiveness – obviously could not find any place in Eliot's early poems. There was only room for rentier values, the values of people too civilised to work, fight or even reproduce themselves.[33]

Orwell's attack, philistine as it might be, does point to the unlikeliness of any substantial radicalism emerging from such a milieu. But the contradiction in his position was that he wanted the marketplace to be replaced by a kinder and gentler socialism, yet jeered at the rentiers for their lack of capitalist aggression. His criticism of them for being too civilized to fight or reproduce was a veiled sneer at Bloomsbury for its pacifism, homosexuality and childlessness. Nor did Orwell acknowledge the labor involved in rentier artistic production. Virginia Woolf could be said to have worked herself to death, the strain of composition finally overwhelming her sanity; Henry James was enormously productive in spite of the thousands of dinner invitations he accepted.

The rentier writer still had to enter the arena of the literary marketplace to reach any substantial audience. Earlier in the nineteenth century, writers with private means like Byron or Browning were eager to consolidate their early successes with the commercial exploitation of their reputations.[34] Possession of capital undoubtedly affected writers' sensibility and allowed them to work up their texts more carefully, or even to suspend production of their novels as Forster did. But only the marketplace could deliver a general readership, and the economic rewards that came with it.[35] Rentier writers might work in a different style from the commercial one; but work they did. Their double status as rentiers and producers appears in the examples of E.M. Forster, and of Leonard and Virginia Woolf.

Thinking About Money: *Howards End*

When he was eight years old E. M. Forster inherited eight thousand pounds from his great-aunt Marianne Thornton, who came from a well-to-do family of Victorian bankers. His father had died when Forster was a year old, leaving his mother completely detached from money-making and concerned only with the future of her infant son. She had about the same amount of capital as her son, ensuring him a comfortable home, and a Public School and Cambridge education. *The Longest Journey* deals with the emotional consequences of this secure and sheltered upbringing; *Howards End,* though not directly autobiographical, examines Forster's *economic* origins. The novel's motto, "Only connect . . ." is usually read as a plea for emotional openness; but Forster is equally concerned with the subtle connections between a class's mentality and how it gets its means of life.

Forster's paternal family was allied to the Clapham Sect, wealthy Evangelicals who campaigned against slavery abroad and vice at home.[36] Families like the Wilberforces, Thorntons, Stephens, Cadburys, Rowntrees, Frys, and Gurneys – some Evangelical and some Quaker – formed a party of conscience in nineteenth century society. Their comfortable way of life derived from old fortunes made in trade or banking; but they were sufficiently distant from the marketplace to evolve a morality separate from mere economic self-interest or unquestioned class code. It was precisely this kind of dissociation that irritated Orwell: "if you have embraced a creed which appears to be free from the ordinary dirtiness of politics – a creed from which you yourself cannot expect to draw any material advantage – surely that proves that you are in the right? And the more you are in the right, the more natural that everyone else should be bullied into thinking likewise."[37] In his awkward way, Orwell seemed to *want* behaviour to be determined by interest; whereas Forster's family tradition was that a large share of the wealth they had amassed should be directed to social activism and philanthropy.

The Bloomsbury Group came as a second generation of rentiers who justified their comfortable lives, not by charity, but by culture; this shift came partly by a drift from evangelical Christianity to agnosticism, partly by the replacement of direct concern for others with an emphasis on the refinement of personal life. In both respects, G.E. Moore provided the philosophical rationale for the change. Forster was an enthusiastic disciple of Moore, but he retained a much stronger social conscience than most others in Bloomsbury. *Howards End* is concerned with the inadequacy of living only by good states of mind, and the self-gratifying aestheticism preached by Clive Bell shows unattractively in the character of Tibby. What could be the worth or the use, Forster asked himself, of an entire class of people who lived on the labor of others? His part-time teaching at the Working Men's College, from 1902 onwards, helped sharpen his awareness of the gulf between his own comfortable existence and that of his hard-pressed students. In his darker moods he condemned himself as a milksop who lived with his mother, who was sexually backward, and who had been absolved by his inherited wealth from the need to seek a useful career.

Howards End starts from Margaret Schlegel's claim that: "independent thoughts are in nine cases out of ten the result of independent means."[38] But independent thoughts that are the result of economic privilege aren't really independent, or even virtuous; as Margaret puts it to her ladies' discussion group "the very soul of the world is economic":

> "That's more like socialism," said Mrs Munt suspiciously.
>
> "Call it what you like. I call it going through life with one's hand spread open on the table. I'm tired of these rich people who pretend to be poor, and think it shows a nice mind to ignore the piles of money that keep their feet above the waves. I stand each year upon six hundred pounds, and Helen upon the same, and Tibby will stand upon eight, and as fast as our pounds crumble away into the sea they are renewed – from the sea, yes, from the sea. And all our thoughts are the thoughts of six-hundred pounders, and all our speeches; and because we don't want to steal umbrellas ourselves we forget that below the sea people do want to steal them, and do steal them sometimes, and that what's a joke up here is down there reality – "[39]

This must be one of the first occasions in the English novel where a middle-class character announces his or her income (though the narrator often announces it to the reader). At a return of four percent, Margaret and Helen would have £15,000 in capital each, and Tibby £20,000.[40] Margaret's position is indeed "like socialism" in saying that consciousness is determined by its economic base, but neither she nor her creator are ready to jump from this premise to revolutionary conclusions. All they feel obliged to do is to make the connection between the Schlegels' class and those on each side of it: the Basts (with perhaps £150 a year), from the half-submerged yet aspiring lower middle class, and the Wilcoxes (with £30,000 or so), "whose hands are on all the ropes."[41]

The Uses of Capital

In *Howards End*, Forster was engaging two earlier works about connections across class lines: Gaskell's *North and South* (1855) and Shaw's *Widowers' Houses* (1892). Gaskell brings together the active and the contemplative lives, North and South, men and women. These oppositions are all finally reconciled in the union of Margaret Hale, daughter of a Southern vicar, with Mr Thornton, a rough-hewn Northern manufacturer. Forster may well have been influenced by Gaskell's novel in conceiving *Howards End* for he uses a similar dialectical structure, contrasting the morals and economics of the Wilcoxes and the Schlegels.[42] Spatially, he opposes town to country rather than North to South; but a more important difference between the two novels is that Forster's ends with the triumph of one side of his opposed forces, Gaskell's with a vision of complementarity. Margaret Hale and Mr Thornton have many disagreements, but at the end they arrive at a sentimental and economic union. Thornton has gone bankrupt in a trade recession, in spite of his competence and hard work, while Margaret has inherited money and real estate from a family friend who was a don at Oxford. She makes Thornton a formal proposal: "if you would take some money of mine, eighteen thousand and fifty-seven pounds, lying just at this moment unused in the bank, and bringing me in only two and a half percent. – you could pay me much better interest, and might go on working Marlborough Mills."[43] Thornton is so moved that he counters with his own proposal, that they should get married. Margaret's acceptance brings together the strong and the sweet, the entrepreneur and the rentier, North and South, industry and finance, in one of the most comprehensive of Victorian happy endings.

Margaret Hale, as a Victorian lady, need feel no qualms about becoming a passive investor in her husband's enterprise. But Forster could not rest easily with the idea of living on the fruits of his capital while others took on for him the struggle in the marketplace. "The education I received in those far-off and fantastic days made me soft," Forster wrote in 1946, "and I am very glad it did, for I have seen plenty of hardness since, and I know it does not even pay. . . . But though the education was humane it was imperfect, inasmuch as we none of us realized our economic position. In came the nice fat dividends, up rose the lofty thoughts, and we did not realize that all the time we were exploiting the poor of our own country and the backward races abroad, and getting bigger profits from our investments than we should. We refused to face this unpalatable truth." Forster himself did face it, however: "Ever since I have read

Widowers' Houses," he wrote in 1934, "I have felt hopeless about invest-ments."[44] He had read the play thirty-five years before as an undergradu-ate. Its hero is a genteel young man, Harry Trench, who has a private income but is also about to set up a medical practice. He has fallen in love with Blanche Sartorius, but is shocked when he discovers that his pro-spective father-in-law is a slum landlord. Trench is even more shocked to learn that his own capital is invested in a mortgage on one of Mr Sarto-rius's filthy hovels. Sartorius points out to him, however, that if he liqui-dates the mortgage and puts the money into government bonds, his income will fall from £700 to £250 a year. After consulting his con-science, Trench decides both to marry Blanche and join Sartorius in a speculation that promises to double his capital in two years. Since one cannot belong to the upper middle class without being an exploiter, he feels that he may as well be hung for a sheep as for a lamb.

Widowers' Houses demonstrates that social status is proportional to dis-tance from economic reality. At the bottom of the play's pecking order is the despised Mr Lickcheese, the man who actually squeezes the money out of the wretched slum-dwellers. Next comes Mr Sartorius, who owns the buildings but never sets foot in them. At the top are Dr Trench and his aunt Lady Roxdale, who have not even troubled to find out where their comfortable private incomes come from. Shaw's play suggests that the rich could "Only connect" with the sources of their income if they walked a few hundred yards to the nearest London slum. But the way of the world is that people who eat meat have no desire to live next to a slaughterhouse; and by the time of *Howards End,* the rentiers have re-moved themselves even further than in *Widowers' Houses* from the actual workings of their capital. The English investor now thinks in global, rather than just regional or national terms. So, on reaching their major-ity, the Schlegel sisters remove their inheritances from "the old safe in-vestments" and put them into what Forster archly calls "Foreign Things."[45] The safe investments would probably be Consols – British gov-ernment bonds – which for many decades had yielded a steady two and a half to three and a half percent. If we assume that Forster himself was in the same position as the Schlegels, his £8,000 would have yielded about £240 a year until he reached twenty-five, when he came into control of his money and was free to invest it more adventurously. We know that one of his new investments was in British American Great Southern Rail-way, an Argentinian railway which yielded about five percent.[46] The Schlegels' aunt, Mrs Munt, wants them to keep their money in Britain, if not in bonds. She persuades them to invest a few hundred pounds in her favorite "Home Rails"; unfortunately, "the Foreign Things did admirably and the Nottingham and Derby declined with the steady dignity of which only Home Rails are capable."[47]

The popularity of "Foreign Things" had a powerful influence on British economic development. From about 1855 to 1914, Britain exported capital on a huge scale. New portfolio foreign investment in this period amounted to well over four billion pounds. Two kinds of impulses promoted the shift of capital overseas. One was the straightforward economic motive that average returns were higher in foreign than in domestic investment. But there was also a cultural aversion to the root-and-branch transformation of society that would have been required to keep pace with Britain's technical and industrial rivals, especially in the United States and Germany. The possession of an Empire made it easier for Britain to avoid a head-on industrial competition with these countries, but did not fully determine that choice. In fact, sixty percent of her overseas investment in this period went to foreign countries, and only forty percent to the Empire.[48] The heart of the matter was that Britain's governing classes preferred a strategy of external development, whereby the City of London facilitated the transfer of massive capital resources overseas, at the expense of the traditional manufacturing industries of the North.

So far as Forster is concerned, however, industry has not been deprived enough. He does not question investment in Foreign Things because it is at the expense of Home Rails, but because immoral methods must be used to organize it. When Margaret Schlegel goes to visit Henry Wilcox at his office she sees on his wall a map of Africa, "looking like a whale marked out for blubber." The reader is surely meant to think of Gillray's famous cartoon of Napoleon and Pitt carving up the world like a Christmas pudding.[49] If in *Widowers' Houses* the issue is domestic exploitation, in *Howards End* it is Imperialism, and the application of the Imperial mentality to class rule in Britain.

Henry Wilcox is a self-deceiving Social Darwinist, who speaks complacently of "the battle of life" and cuts down the salaries of his clerks in the name of the "survival of the fittest."[50] Margaret becomes steadily disillusioned with him; she comes to believe that he does not stand for the control of savagery, but is himself an expression of it. Social Darwinism gives Henry an excuse to spurn Leonard Bast, the aspiring but unlucky working man. It encourages him to exploit the "subject races" for England's benefit, affronting Margaret's (and Forster's) anti-imperial or Little England sentiments. At home, the creed of the battle of life leads to the destruction of the cherished past, the pollution of the countryside by the noise and stink of the motor car, and the loss to the English people of what they most need: a sense of being securely rooted in their own particular corner of the earth. Margaret begins by contrasting the Wilcoxes' manly vigor with her own lack of worldly purpose; but she ends up repelled by the amoral use that the Wilcoxes make of their strength.

A Field of Hay

Howards End repudiates the Wilcox way of life as hopelessly philistine, materialist, and brutal. But Forster is left with the task of imagining a coherent alternative to the Wilcox culture of "red [i.e. red-brick] houses and the Stock Exchange," and of finding a way for the Schlegels to avoid complicity in any of the Wilcox undertakings – that is to say, with commerce, imperialism, modernity itself. The obvious candidate for an alternative British culture is pastoralism, such as Forster described in the conclusion of "The Abinger Pageant":

> Houses and bungalows, hotels, restaurants and flats, arterial roads, by-passes, petrol pumps and pylons – are these going to be England? Are these man's final triumph? Or is there another England, Green and eternal, which will outlast them? I cannot tell you, I am only the Woodman, but this land is yours, and you can make it what you will.[51]

But who exactly is the Woodman? C. K. Hobson's book *The Export of Capital,* published in 1914, is refreshingly explicit about the structural changes in the British economy that are the direct and intended results of capital export. He notes, for example, that "the decay of British agriculture [was] largely attributable to the development of railways in new countries."[52] These are the same railways that Forster personally invested in. Foreign investment may contribute to the decline of British manufacturing, Hobson notes; but when the profits are repatriated they are "likely to mean an increased demand for labour in certain kinds of industry – *e.g.* for artists, printers, dressmakers, domestic servants, gardeners, chauffeurs."[53] Finally, the depopulation of the British countryside after the Corn Laws was precisely what made it possible for the bohemian fringe of the middle class to move into their country cottages, play at being rustics, and imagine that a Woodman lived at the bottom of their garden.

Forster's pastoralism seeks to be a true alternative to modernity, rather than a fantasy of rentier detachment. His problem is how to uphold the civic and cultural virtues intrinsic to the rentiers' way of life, yet avoid complicity with the Industry and Empire that supply their dividends. He begins by sidestepping the charge that the rentier is a parasite who consumes, but does not produce. Helen Schlegel's belief that "personal relations are the important thing for ever and ever" assigns to work a purely instrumental value, to provide the comfort and leisure that are required for agreeable personal relations.[54] The Schlegels' younger brother Tibby is stigmatized, but for emotional rather than physical laziness. As his name suggests, he is an epicene young man who warms the teapot "almost too deftly." He is also a surrogate for Forster himself; Tibby's languid existence contrasts with the striving Wilcoxes, but morally he is no better than them:

> Unlike Charles [Wilcox], Tibby had money enough; his ancestors had earned it for him, and if he shocked the people in one set of lodgings he had only to move into another. His was the leisure without sympathy – an attitude as fatal as the strenuous: a little cold culture may be raised on it, but no art. His sisters had seen the family danger, and had never forgotten to discount the gold islets that raised them from the sea. Tibby gave all the praise to himself, and so despised the struggling and the submerged.[55]

Tibby is damned for his cold self-sufficiency, whereas his sisters are redeemed by their sympathy, their eagerness for connection with the world. These are specifically female traits, of course, and it is part of the female image that they are not expected to work. Middle-class women of this period can be thought of as rentiers by biological destiny; their vocation is to display their accomplishments, to be rather than to do. No one would expect them to be anything but passive investors.

Still, they have some work to do in the world – of an appropriate kind. One of their callings is to prevent change, which in Forster is almost always for the worse. In 1907, the year before he began *Howards End,* the Georgian mansion of the Thornton family, "Battersea Rise," had been torn down and its site "completely covered with very small two-story houses."[56] Forster had given money to a campaign to save the house and garden, but nothing could be done. *Howards End* is named after a house which is saved – even if the red tide of semi-detached houses is lapping at its fringes – and which ends up in the hands of the preservationist Schlegels. When property is rightly transmitted and cherished from one generation to another it acquires a kind of spiritual patination; it contrasts, in the novel, with dwellings that are merely passed around by the marketplace and torn down when they cease to be profitable, like the London house where the Schlegels are living at the beginning of the book. The rentier is a preserver of the aura, the precious "spirit of place"

that is threatened by the onrushing chaos of modernity. A society dominated by "new men" would have no traditions, no landmarks to guide
the succession of generations; the rentier does not build but she guards
the ancestral rites, like the pigs' teeth embedded in the elm at Howards
End.[57]

The Schlegel sisters end the novel with a more substantial vocation
than their earlier life of concert-going and tea-drinking in London. They
have become traditional female providers of nurture: Helen cares for her
infant son by Leonard Bast, Margaret cares for her husband who breaks
down after his son's conviction for Bast's manslaughter. They are farmers, raising hay on the meadows around the house. And Margaret will be
a philanthropist, giving away half her capital over the next ten years.
When she dies the house will pass to her nephew, the living symbol of
union between the bourgeois Schlegels and the proletarian Basts.

Forster's own life imitated his art. His inherited capital was greatly increased by his earnings as a writer after the success of *Howards End* in
1910 but he gave away much of what he had, either to charities or to his
friends. In 1931, after some ups and downs in his financial affairs, he
joked that "I am not again making the mistake of investing, or even of
letting it lie in the Bank. I shall bury it to be disinterred as wanted."[58] In
1934 he started a lively controversy on the issue of ethical investment in
Time and Tide. He described how he went to South Africa in 1929 and was
appalled by the treatment of black workers in the mines at Kimberley; on
his return, he sold his shares in a Belgian mining company. Now, he
wanted to encourage the readers of *Time and Tide* to get rid of investments in arms companies. Several readers wrote in to point out flaws in
this advice, but Forster stuck to his point. "You can bowl anyone out on
his investment list," he responded, "but I deny that all lists are equally
harmful or harmless and that one need not bother, and I think it would
be healthier if people talked openly about the contents of their lists and
did not conceal them like illegitimate children."[59]

Still, a code of personal conduct does not necessarily provide the basis
for a credible vision of society as a whole. The Schlegels take their sensitivity *to* the countryside, rather than imbibing it *from* the flowers, trees,
and farm laborers. Rentier culture is a sheltered offshoot of finance capital with irredeemably urban roots, no matter how many individual
rentiers enjoy their mobile consumption in the shires or Tuscany. Nor
could such a pastoral retreat provide any general solution to the "Condi-
tion-of-England" issues that are presented in the body of the novel.[60]
Margaret's strategy for dealing with the modern world is simply to wait
until it renounces its own vital principle:

Because a thing is going strong now, it need not go strong for ever,"
[Margaret] said. "This craze for motion has only set in during the last
hundred years. It may be followed by a civilization that won't be a
movement, because it will rest on the earth. All the signs are against it
now, but I can't help hoping, and very early in the morning in the garden I feel that our house is the future as well as the past."[61]

Again, there is a contrast with the more positive outlook of the other
Margaret in *North and South*. When she revisits her old village in the
South, Margaret Hale is at first dismayed not to find the rural Eden she
had remembered in her Northern exile:

A sense of change, of individual nothingness, of perplexity and disappointment, overpowered Margaret. Nothing had been the same; and
this slight, allpervading instability, had given her greater pain than if
all had been too entirely changed for her to recognise it. . . .

Wearily she went to bed, warily she arose in four or five hours' time.
But with the morning came hope, and a brighter view of things.

"After all it is right," said she, hearing the voices of children at play
while she was dressing. "If the world stood still, it would retrograde
and become corrupt. . . . Looking out of myself, and my own painful
sense of change, the progress of all around me is right and necessary. I
must not think so much of how circumstances affect me myself, but
how they affect others, if I wish to have a right judgment, or a hopeful
trustful heart."[62]

Margaret Hale is in fact connecting with the body of society in and beyond her village, while Margaret Schlegel has chosen to sever herself
from it. Throughout the novel, most of the significant actions have been
initiated by more vital characters: the Wilcoxes, Leonard Bast, her sister
Helen. At the end, Henry Wilcox is reduced to a cipher in order to remove an inconvenient force from the plot, much like the sudden deaths
of unwanted characters in other Forster novels. And Henry's personal defeat is made into a facile allegory of the withering away of the class he belongs to. "I'm broken – I'm ended" he whimpers to Margaret; but what he
represents surely is not.[63]

Good liberal that he was, Forster was well aware of the case that could be
made against his pet causes. He feared that those on the frontier of scientific thought would "abandon literature, which has committed itself too
deeply to the worship of vegetation."[64] We can see another danger too:
that English literature would waste away on its vegetarian diet – clinging

to archaism and nostalgia while failing to engage the contemporary passions of the ordinary citizen. In his creative career, Forster remained a perpetual Edwardian, even though he lived until 1970. That period was the golden age of rentier culture in England, which is why it figures so prominently in England's nostalgia industry today. Everyone wants "a room with a view," but England is peculiar in its insistence that the view should be of the eternally sunlit meadows of the past.

Leonard and Virginia Woolf: "A Little Capital"

"The private finances of people seem to me always interesting; indeed they have so great an effect upon people's lives that, if one is writing a truthful autobiography, it is essential to reveal them." This is Leonard Woolf's rationale for giving, in his autobiography, a detailed account of his and Virginia's income and expenses from 1924 to 1939.[65] Still, he was often candid without being altogether complete. Leonard was much more devoted to left-wing politics than Forster was, but his use of the term "private finances" suggests that he expected to keep them separate from his activities in public life for the Labour Party. Where Forster – and even T.S. Eliot – worried about profiting from the labor of others, Leonard blithely acknowledged that "It is extremely pleasant to have plenty of money."[66]

When she decided to marry Leonard, Virginia described him as a "penniless Jew"; he actually had about £600 in cash and investments, mostly derived from winning £690 on the Melbourne Cup sweepstake in 1908.[67] George Duckworth, acting as Virginia's guardian, wrote to Leonard two days before the wedding, asking him to settle some money on Virginia, or else assign ten percent of his income to a life insurance policy.[68] Having given up his job with the Colonial Service, Leonard was not well placed to comply with either request. The economic base for the marriage was Virginia's capital: £9,000 that she had inherited from her father in 1904, her brother Thoby in 1906, and her aunt Caroline in 1909.

Invested conservatively, the joint capital of the Woolfs would yield about £400 a year. They needed at least twice that amount to live comfortably and pay Virginia's medical expenses, which in some years were as much as £500. For the first thirteen years of their marriage they made up the balance mainly by journalism and Leonard's work as an editor. After *Mrs Dalloway* and *The Common Reader* were published in 1925, Virginia had a large and steady income from her books: royalties averaged more than £1,500 a year until her death and the Hogarth Press gave her about £750 a year more, largely derived from the success of her books. But as their income had risen dramatically, from 1925 to 1935, Leonard and Virginia "fundamentally . . . had not altered their way of life."[69] The fixed cost of running the Woolf household held steady at about £1,200 a year from 1927 to 1939. Careful management thus left them in the thirties a discretionary income that averaged about £1,500 a year. Some of this went on personal indulgences, but they steadily increased their wealth in property, in the Hogarth Press, and in financial investments.

In 1915 the Woolfs leased a Georgian house in Richmond, Hogarth House. Five years later they bought the house and its twin, Suffield House, for £2,000. After they moved to a leased house in Tavistock Square in 1924 they sold both Richmond houses, apparently at a profit.[70] Monk's House, Rodmell, was bought as a country home in 1919 for £700. In 1928 Leonard bought an adjoining six-acre field for £450; he added an acre to his garden and leased the rest to a local farmer. In 1932 he bought two cottages in Rodmell, later occupied by the Woolfs' housekeeper, Louie Everest, and by their gardener.[71]

Leonard liked to boast that the capital invested in the Hogarth Press was only £136, to buy the original presses and type; all expansion after that was paid for out of profits.[72] When John Lehmann bought a half share from Virginia, in 1938, the business was valued at £6,000.[73] It would hardly be fair to call the Hogarth Press a profitable investment, because its increased value derived from years of shrewd judgment and grinding effort by its owners. They took relatively little income out of the business, and the money they got from John Lehmann was really deferred compensation rather than profit.

Walking round Tavistock Square, Leonard told his office-boy that "a little capital was one of the most important things in life."[74] The Woolfs' capital was kept as a strategic reserve, not to be drawn on for ordinary living expenses. The return on this capital amounted to £310 in 1924 and rose gradually to £802 in 1939.[75] Statements of the Woolfs' investments for 1930 and 1935 appear in Figure 1 below.

What kind of investor was Leonard (for there is no evidence that Virginia was actively involved)? In the twenties and thirties he held mainly common stocks, with a few bonds. At the end of 1930 they were worth 64% of what he had paid for them, and by July 1932 only half as much, at £5038. They then rose steadily, and from 1933 onwards Leonard made substantial further investments; dividend yields also improved. Leonard rarely sold stocks once he had bought them, and then only ones that showed a profit; perhaps he disliked selling a loser because he would then be admitting that he had made a mistake in buying it.

In 1920, Leonard had written that the real motive for European expansion in the nineteenth century was "markets, raw materials, and profits."[76]

```
10 Nov  1930          Value of Investments
                      Purchase price    10/11/30
300 French 4½     69¾  203 .19  6  20A  61   0  0
2 Royal Dutch     57¾  116  1I  0  28   56
35 Shell          6    223   2 11   4½ 148  15  0
18   do           5 7/16 99  18  6   4½  76  10
£175 G " R       112⅞  199  16  8  72  126
185 United Dair  21/1½ 199  17 11 21/3 201   1
70 Dormanr Long  14/3   51   o  6  4/9  16  12
200 Fed Seleng   30/-  304   8  6 10/) 101   9  6  ?
£200 Ind Invest        200        15/- 150         ?
85 Bajoe Kid    327/16 298   0  5   1   85
80   do           3    243   3  6   1   80
630 Toyo Tin     15/6  501   6  0  2/-  63
220 Ceylon Para  9/9   110   1  0  3/9  41   5  0
4715 B.A. Gt S  108⅞  788  12  8  76  543   8
200 Coats        75/9  769  19  6 59/3 592  10  0
20 Am Col      17 15/16 359  16     3½  65
113 Ceb P Mang    6    678        2½ 279  10
10 Shell          1     10        4½  42  10
126 Met El S     46/3  295   7  3 41/3 257  16
41   do          30/-   61  10  0 41/3  92   5  0
75 Imp Tob     133/7½ 510  11  5 95/9 358  11  5
44   do         125/-  279      6 95/9 126  10  0
29   do         bonus             95/9 158  16  9
220 Imp Chem    25/9½ 289  17  3 20/7½ 226   8  0
32   do          23/-   36  19  0 20/7½  32  16  0
82 Courtaulds  4x5/32 367  11  3  2½ 205
72 Cables B      81     58   6  4  15   10  16  0
60 Napier        51/9  159  11  0 10/6  31  10  0
53 Agr Bank       8    424   0  0   8  424   0  0
70 Gramoph       4½   292   7  3  2½ 175       0
£360 Cables 5½  96½  351  18  0  72  259   4  0
£535 do A        64½  350   9  6  25  133  15  0
120 Napier bonus                  10/6  63   0  0
95 Col Gram      3½   351       5  2½ 250
£2113 i o Oas    348  399   7  9 355  401   3  0
395 Shell 7½   24/9½ 500   3  /. 25/- 494

                     10088  13  6      6410  0  6
```

```
                       Value of Investments 8/8/35
  Royal Dutch          26    52
  Shell Ord            3½  192
  175 G & R            50    86
  185 Un. Dairies      30/- 280
  7 Dorman Long        19/9
  1800 Fed Selangor    2/4½  137
  200 Ind Inv          ?    100
? 165 Maj. Kid.        28/9  237
? 630 Toyo             2/3   70
  220 Cayl Para        ½/9  41
  £715 S A G, S.       20   142
  200 Coats            65/- 650
  20 Am Col    5 13/16  116
  113 Cent Prev        4    452
  172 Metesco          53/9 461
  146 Imp Tob          7½  1073
  72 Cables B          7½    5
  160 Napier           13/9 123
  165 E & Was          26/6 219
  4535 Cables A        26/4 138
  2226 Imp C Oas       216½ 485
  395 Shell 7%         33/3 637
  270 Swed Mat M       19/6 263
  2477 Con £1 B.       120½ 570
  2385 Port Com        107½ 403
  100 Tate & Lyle      85/7½ 427
  210 Am Metal         12/10½ 240
  20 Am Col     5 13/16 116
  65 Enf Cable         104/9 327
  11 Metesco           53/9  29
  150 Ass Cement       51/9 433
  190 Ford             35/6 337½
  220 Austin 5/-       55/- 605
  308 Am Mat           22/10½ 350
  65 Austin 10½/-
  Bank Balance              1794/140
  Total                     10516
```

Figure 1:   Leonard Woolf's investments for 1930 and 1935. *Manuscript Section, University of Sussex Library.*

He proposed that imperialism should be replaced by a system of mandates, in which Europeans would serve the economic and cultural interests of the local inhabitants. The "railways and economic concessions extorted" from countries like China should simply be given back.[77] It is intriguing, therefore, to find that Leonard invested more than forty percent of his and Virginia's capital in imperial ventures like Shell Oil, Federated Selangor, Ceylon Para, or Bajoe Kidoel.[78] E.M. Forster's portfolio was not unlike Leonard's in size and kind; but he was full of qualms of conscience about his private income, and tried to practise what we would call today ethical investing. There is no evidence that Leonard bothered about such concerns.[79] One might call his investment decisions hypocritical; but perhaps it was more a lack in him of any impulse to question or regret his own acts. Virginia was painfully aware of such traits in Leonard:

> L. is very hard on people; especially on the servant class. No sympathy with them; exacting; despotic. . . . His extreme rigidity of mind surprises me; . . . What does it come from? Not being a gentleman partly:

uneasiness in the presence of the lower classes: . . . His desire, I suppose, to dominate. Love of power. And then he writes against it.[80]

The Woolfs' housekeeper, Louie Everest, was paid 12/- (60p) a week from 1934 to 1940; this bordered on stinginess, even though she worked part-time and had a cottage provided. Sometimes she would return to Monk's House in the evening for a meeting of the Rodmell Labour Party.[81] Leonard doesn't seem to have found such occasions embarrassing, or even to have seen the joke.

The enemies of Bloomsbury saw it as the aesthetic fringe of Orwell's class of parasites. But the Woolfs, rich as they may have become, were the opposite of idle. Leonard has described the intense concentration that Virginia devoted to her writing; for himself, he noted simply that "I have always felt the urge, the necessity, to work and work hard every day of my life."[82] The first effect on the Woolfs and their friends of having a private income was to foster an ease of outlook and freedom to set their own intellectual standards. This is how Virginia distinguished herself from the members of the Working Women's Guild:

> When people get together communally they always talk about baths and money: they always show the least desirable of their characteristics – their lust for conquest and their desire for possessions. To expect us, whose minds, such as they are, fly free at the end of a short length of capital, to tie ourselves down again upon that narrow plot of acquisitiveness and desire is impossible.[83]

When Virginia speaks of the artist's need for £500 a year (in *A Room of One's Own*), she assumes that the marketplace by itself will not provide adequately for the artist. The market may have supported English literature from Walter Scott to Arnold Bennett, but Woolf expects the serious modern novel to be in some degree unpopular and unprofitable; so private wealth must give the contemporary artist what the market will not. In her own writing, Woolf drew a line between journalism, which she wrote to pay current expenses, and her creative work, which for the first fifteen years of her career yielded only some £20 a year (how the classics of modernism later became immensely profitable is another subject).

We need also to distinguish between Leonard's attitude to money and Virginia's. Even when very comfortably off, Virginia would suffer "panics in the middle of the night about money." "Like my father," she observed, "I can always conjure up bankruptcy. But unlike my father Leonard has no money complex. So we can rub along cutting a servant, cutting clothes; but otherwise not encroaching on capital yet."[84] Virginia was quite unworldly about money, and did not have her own cheque book until 1927 (though she then found it "a great advance in dignity"). Still, her New Year's resolution for 1931 was "To care nothing for making money."[85] Money came in, all the same, for the rest of her life.

Leonard had a firmer grip on the money question. When he was eleven his father died and left the family "extremely poor"; but further ups and downs convinced Leonard that "money is not nearly as important as we are inclined to believe."[86] Important or not, Leonard was good at making it. There was a strict, almost puritanical quality to his money management: work hard; keep your expenses under control; don't speculate; never borrow; pay your workers the going rate or less; buy property and blue chips and hold on to them. In his political writings, Leonard argued that economic motives were the true determinants of policy; and he gave detailed financial information in his autobiography in the belief that it was both interesting and important. At the same time, the Bloomsbury ethic recognized money as no more than a means to such higher ends as cultural appreciation or friendship. For Virginia, one feels that money was indeed no more than that; but with Leonard, his behavior suggests that money satisfied deep desires – for power, security, control over his everyday life – that he was little inclined to acknowledge. But, as I have argued throughout this chapter, rentier culture was about the art of detachment.

9
Paying for Modernism

"Why in Chrisst's name we arent all millionaires I dont know."
—Ezra Pound to James Joyce, 22 November 1918

Modernists and Rentiers

If we want to know who paid for Victorian fiction, the answer is simple: its readers. Victorian novels were produced almost entirely under direct signals from the market. Publishers paid for a novel in one lump on acceptance of the manuscript, according to their judgement of its success: for example, £3,000 for Trollope's *The Way We Live Now* (1873) or £10,000 for Disraeli's *Endymion* (1880).[1] The novelist provided the middle class reading public with an agreeable work, which until the death of the three-decker in 1895 was close to being a standard commodity; and the price was a measure of how well the task of literary production had been achieved.

It was Ezra Pound's aim to establish a modernist literary economy in isolation from the literary marketplace. But someone still had to pay for modernism; this chapter will examine where the money came from, what modernism's supporters expected for their money, and how the practice of modernist writers in England was shaped by the sources of their support.[2] The direct source of money for much of early modernism was a regime of patronage; but I will be arguing that the market was not easily or permanently shunned, even if modernism's relation to it was one of complex intermediacy.

In the last two decades of the nineteenth century, two developments prepared the way for the modernist mode of literary production: the re-structuring of the literary marketplace, and the establishment of an alternative to market forces in what I have called the rentier culture. The market was changed by a general increase in prosperity, and by the near-universal literacy achieved in Britain by 1900. Mass literacy did not produce sweetness and light, but rather literary production for mass taste. Journalism became the dominant form; even "serious" writers came to depend on it for a substantial part of their income, and all writers had to recognize that they were now more a class defined by its relation to the market than a profession defined by its place in a prestige order.[3] It is against the background of this new system that we can best understand Pound's project: not just to "make it new" at the level of the individual work, but also to construct a fully articulated counter-system for modernist literary production.

Rentier culture had already distinguished itself from market-sensitive art by elaborating an ethic of refinement. It is no coincidence that Henry James wrote his classic defense of the art novel, "The Art of Fiction," in response to Walter Besant, who, as a "good steady man of letters," argued that "he who works for pay must respect the prejudices of his customers."[4] The art novel assumed a certain leisured sensitivity both in its readers, and in the characters it represented. The modernists were even more hostile than James to such marketable talents as Besant or Arnold Bennett, and based their aesthetic on resistance to literary commodification. Yet support for this resistance was largely derived – through the mediation of patronage – from the rentier culture; so that the modernists were dependent on the independence of those with greater means than themselves. They were both subordinate to rentier culture, and concerned to distinguish themselves from it.

If rentier culture offered an escape from the vulgarities of the literary marketplace (including the vulgarity of popular success), and an affinity with the oppositional stance of late Victorian aesthetes and decadents, why did it not satisfy the literary aspirations of figures like Yeats, Joyce, Eliot and, above all, Pound? In part, certainly, because they were all outsiders by nationality. They mistrusted the embeddedness of rentier culture in the most privileged stratum of English society, with all the exclusiveness and complacency that were by-products of this status. A culture so intimately linked to the established order could scarcely function as a true avant-garde of the Continental type. Further, for an artist to have a private income was largely a question of luck, so it would be difficult to base an ideologically coherent movement on such a randomly distributed resource. Some people who had private incomes would not be modernists, and some people who were modernists would not have private incomes. Early modernism, in defining itself as a movement of cultural insurgency, felt the need to sharpen its differences with the rentiers on one side and commercial writers on the other. Yet this oppositional stance often co-existed with a craving, often only thinly disguised, for absorption and acceptance. Culturally, Pound and Eliot both envisioned the re-establishment of a conservative order; Eliot had a private income from his father's estate, and Yeats, Eliot and Pound all married into the British rentier class with an eye to social and material enrichment.

Where rentier writing shows a tropism towards refinement, sensitivity and exclusiveness, modernists show a more aggressive and deliberate attempt to make their works "unmarketable." "Modernism," Terry Eagleton argues, "is among other things a strategy whereby the work of art resists commodification, holds out by the skin of its teeth against those social forces which would degrade it to an exchangeable object."[5] The road away from the market could lead only to some form of patronage – whether self-patronage, in the writer's private income of rentier culture, or patronage from outside supporters of the modernist agenda. Modernism was indeed a patronage culture, yet this status entailed two nagging difficulties. One was that literature – unlike the plastic arts – still faced the imperatives of reproduction and circulation, even if this was done outside of mass-market channels. Literary works whose production was supported by patronage were offered for general sale once they were complete, and patrons supported not only individual writers but their distinctive means of distribution: the little magazine and the avant-garde press. It would prove hard to maintain the distinction between a modernist prestige culture whose sole currency was the critical approval of mandarins like Pound or Eliot, and a market mechanism that translated approval into cash sales (and, eventually, sales that were very large).[6] Exclusiveness does not conflict with commodification; it may even be the highest form of it. Patronage allowed the young modernist writers to survive while they labored at forms too esoteric for the commercial literary culture. Yet the projects they undertook, in subsidized obscurity, were grandiose in scale and in breadth of cultural reference; their implicit aim was to progress from their avant-garde coteries into the public sphere of the great capitals.

The other problem with modernist patronage was its gender. Those who were active in the Social Darwinist milieu of pre-1914 capitalism – virtually all male – found their primary satisfaction in the struggle itself, rather than in any of the leisure arts. Like Forster's Wilcoxes, they were likely to look down on the cultural sphere as effete and feminized – at best, a place where their wives or artistic children might blamelessly pass their time.[7] John Quinn was probably the only one of the main patrons of modernism who contributed money that he had made himself. The others either inherited their money or, like Lady Rothermere, spent on culture part of their husband's profits from business. It is not surprising that most of modernism's patrons were women, though this did not inhibit male modernists from biting the hand of the gender that fed them. Andreas Huyssen has attributed the suspicion towards women of modernist male writers to "the increasingly marginal position of literature and the arts in a society in which masculinity is identified with action, enterprise and progress – with the realms of business, industry, science, and law."[8] The male writer may embrace this marginality, cultivating his "imaginary femininity" through identification with aestheticism, homosexuality, or female eroticism and hysteria. From Flaubert to Eliot, Joyce, and D.H. Lawrence, male authors responded to the popularity of "women's" literature by re-colonizing its emotional territory for the profit of masculine high art.[9] Yet at the same time, they resisted feminine cultural hegemony, or even women's desire to speak for themselves: the author of Molly Bloom's soliloquy preferred the actual women in his life to wear long dresses and be silent. When Eliot warned against "the Feminine in literature" he meant women writers and their demands, but also the feminine in American culture that stood for the refinement or repression of male energies.[10] Pound explicitly voiced his desire to exclude women from the modernist movement: seeking John Quinn's support for a proposed new review in 1915, he wrote: "You will see that I have included hardly any feminine names. I think active America is getting fed up on gynocracy and that it's time for a male review."[11]

Leslie Fiedler has spoken of a nineteenth century American literary culture that was "simultaneously commercialized and feminized" – to the consternation of "serious" male authors. The purchasing power of the female reader generated the successful female popular author, a constant target for modernist misogyny.[12] Women's power as consumers and sponsors of art made them, for Pound and Eliot, threats to the artist's phallic autonomy. The modernists routinely produced work of *ressentiment* against the milieu that sustained them: generic satires like Eliot's "Portrait of a Lady" or Pound's "Portrait d'une Femme," or personal ones like the treatment of Ottoline Morrell in *Women in Love* and in Huxley's *Point Counter Point*. Another characteristic response was for the male modernist to divide his female loyalties between a sexual muse and a chaste patron; he thus evaded the danger to his masculine image if he should both sleep with a woman and take money from her. Yeats's concurrent dealings with Olivia Shakespear and Lady Gregory, or Joyce's with Nora and Harriet Shaw Weaver, followed this pattern. When the two categories were confused, trouble was sure to follow, as in D.H. Lawrence's triangles with Frieda and Lady Ottoline Morrell, or Mabel Dodge Luhan. Lawrence was unusual in accepting patronage only if he was desperate, and paying it back as soon as he could; but accepting it from a woman was specially repugnant to him.

Female patronage allowed Yeats, Pound, Hemingway and Joyce to wait out the market's early rejection of experimentalism, and to do so in a milieu much more agreeable than the stereotypical garret of the avant-garde artist. Olivia Shakespear, for example, was at the center of a nexus of social support for modernism.[13] With her husband's £1,000 a year and some money of her own, she gave sexual and social comfort to Yeats. Lady Gregory, his platonic patron, lent him money as needed and lodged him for summers at Coole. Thanks to her, Yeats recorded, he was enabled "through the greater part of my working life to write without thought of anything but the beauty or the utility of what I wrote. Until I was nearly fifty, my writing never brought me more than two hundred a year, and most often less, and I am not by nature economical."[14] Pound's writing brought much less than £200 a year, and he steadfastly refused to take regular employment. Margaret Cravens apparently gave him £200 a year until her suicide in 1912; two years later, Olivia Shakespear finally agreed that Pound should marry her daughter Dorothy, whose income was also about £200.[15] Humphrey Carpenter observes that Pound's "access to Dorothy's income inevitably affected the nature of his literary work in the years following the marriage. It freed him not only from the necessity of earning his living but even of considering his audience."[16] This was a freedom that Pound enjoyed for all his subsequent career, as Dorothy, through successive gifts and inheritances, became steadily richer.[17] The long roll-call of women who supported modernism financially or morally makes it evident that, even as male modernists decried the influence of female culture, they were profoundly indebted to it, sometimes even for their very survival as artists.[18]

Patronage and Form

Orientation to the market assumes acceptance of an already existing commodity form; patronage enables the writer to produce something relatively unconstrained either formally or temporally. The ideal-typical example is the composition of *Ulysses* and *Finnegans Wake* by a method of gradual accretion, whereby each successive draft of an episode is longer and more complex, and the *Wake* as a whole is an accretion on its predecessor. A similar aesthetic appears in the composition of Pound's *Cantos*. Joyce's project of relentless densification of an original narrative core could not have been carried through without Harriet Weaver's support. To use up seven years for *Ulysses* and sixteen for *Finnegans Wake* was not a commercial rate of literary production; repeatedly Joyce told his patron that he needed more time, and wanted her to send more money. With-

out his subsidy Joyce would have had to write more numerous but sim-
pler books, as commercial novelists have always had to do.

Joyce's decisions about form were, of course, over-determined; and financial circumstances can scarcely explain every local particularity of his
works. But Harriet Weaver's decision to endow Joyce with a substantial
block of capital – effectively without conditions – gave him the security
to push his fictional method to its full extension.[19] In both Joyce and
Pound, we observe an imaginative ambition to pile up riches; to combine
comprehensiveness and fineness of detail to achieve works that aggre-
gate in themselves every formal and thematic resource of their literary
era. Distinguishing his aims from those of the Balzac – Zola – Arnold
Bennett line of realism, Pound observed that "Not everything is interesting or rather not everything is interesting enough to be written into novels, which are at all but the best a dilution of life."[20] Such novels, written
for the market, were unproblematic representations of everyday life that
were immediately re-circulated as literary commodities. Modernist masterworks, in contrast, issued from a tertiary mode of production in which
pre-existing representations were accumulated and re-combined in order
to create new values – a process that, both in the financial and literary
systems, took place at a remove from the markets that provide for primary needs of consumers.

Modernist production is no longer the representation of a coherent social reality, but a piecing of shards into a structure whose value depends
on the labor of reconstruction devoted to it by its author. The ineluctable
secondariness of this imaginative work leaves the author with the task of
restoring a shattered inheritance, to make it yield something on which to
live. The shattering itself is blamed on the disruptive industrial and commercial power of the nineteenth century, when "all that is solid melts
into air," and European organic society is deprived of its integrity. The
modernists, coming at the end of the nineteenth century regime of capitalist accumulation – and benefiting from it, of course – feared that their
time might be one of cultural exhaustion. This sense of dissolution was
made literal in Eliot's selling off, after his father's death in 1919, his
shares in the Hydraulic Press-Brick Company, which his family controlled. The power and glory of his inheritance meant nothing to Eliot,
since he wished only to diversify his holdings and have a reliable supple-
mentary income. Just as the rentier withdraws from direct participation
in business to cultivate a more refined style of life, so does the modernist
take up a secondary or indirect relation to literary production. Yet both
rentier and modernist author (and all the more one who combines both
positions) are haunted by their loss of primary productivity or usefulness

– something that could have been achieved by actual participation in business in the one case, or by success in an unproblematized literary genre in the other.

Modernism and the Market

Modern literary theory has proposed the subordination of the writer's subjectivity to impersonal authorship systems of genres, ideologies, or discourse-formations. Yet these structuralist models have taken little note of the literary marketplace, which also reduces authors to "price takers" faced with an established mass taste that they cannot easily influence. One of the most imposing manifestations of the market is that it has its own preferences in subjectivity, so that any pristine authorial sense of self must be alienated – in both a psychic and an economic sense – in order to be "realized." The only escape from those market preferences, for the modernist author, seems to be through irony, fragmentation and pastiche. Jameson suggests that traditional generic writing can only persist in popular rather than high culture:

> the generic contract and institution itself . . . falls casualty to the gradual penetration of a market system and a money economy. With the elimination of an institutionalized social status for the cultural producer and the opening of the work of art itself to commodification, the older generic specifications are transformed into a brand-new system against which any authentic artistic expression must necessarily struggle. The older generic categories do not, for all that, die out, but persist in the half-life of the subliterary genres of mass culture, transformed into the drugstore and airport paperback lines of gothics, mysteries, romances, bestsellers, and popular biographies.[21]

Jameson's argument has been widely influential; but it goes too far in reducing modernist literary practice to a simple reaction against the alienation of subjectivity into commodity. There is an evident difference in the writing practice of a Trollope who writes two thousand words every day before breakfast, and a Joyce who takes a whole day to decide on the order of words in one sentence. Patronage did insulate the modernist writer from the immediate demands of a market that wanted a steady stream of predictable works. Yet modernist works, even if they arrived at the market more intermittently and by a more circuitous route, ended up as commodities too. Just as being a rentier can be said to mystify the relation between an income and its origin, so does literary patronage mystify the relation between the production of a work and its ultimate destination.

In trumpeting that "Nothing written for pay is worth printing. ONLY what has been written AGAINST the market," Pound sought to establish a modernist myth of economic innocence.[22] The myth has flourished since, in such instances as Van Gogh's inability to sell his paintings, Joyce's difficulty in getting his early works published, or Malcolm Lowry's *Under the Volcano* selling three copies in North America in the year of its publication. It proposes an irreducible hostility between the vision of modernist art and the philistine world of popular taste. The paranoid and hermetic features of modernism can then be justified by Nietzsche's maxim that "The strong always have to be defended against the weak." Yet a salient feature of literary modernism is the speed with which it established itself in the literary marketplace that it professed to despise, and the hegemony that it achieved after World War II – and, in spite of the canon wars, still enjoys.[23]

Lawrence Rainey has examined the scaling-up of modernist distribution from avant-garde journals of tiny circulation like *The Egoist* or *The Little Review*, to *The Dial*, and finally to the mass-market *Vanity Fair*. Scofield Thayer and James Sibley Watson Jr. contributed $220,000 between 1920 and 1922 to support *The Dial* – money that bought them a key role in the popularizing of modernism in North America:

> When Pound suggested in May and August [1922] that [*The Waste Land*] be published by *Vanity Fair*, his proposal looked forward to modernism's future, to the ease and speed with which a market economy could purchase, assimilate, commodify, and reclaim as its own the works of a literature whose ideological premises were bitterly inimical toward its ethos and cultural operations. These distinct moments were mediated by what, in the early 1920s, was modernism's present: the sensibility epitomized by the *Dial*, a form of production supported by massive and unprecedented patronage that facilitated modernism's transition from a literature of an exiguous elite to a position of prestigious dominance.[24]

Rainey goes on to argue that these three American journals – *The Little Review*, *The Dial*, *Vanity Fair* – "are best viewed not as antagonists who represented alien or incompatible ideologies, but as protagonists who shared a common terrain, whose fields of activity overlapped and converged at crucial points within a shared spectrum of marketing and consumption." The twentieth-century avant-garde is no longer an enclave of artistic integrity, holding itself aloof from the swamp of commercial-ism; rather, Rainey argues, it "played no special role, possessed no ideo-logical privilege; instead it was constituted by a specific array of marketing and publicity structures that were integrated in varying de-grees with the larger economic apparatus of its time. Its typical endeavour was to develop an idiom, a shareable language that could be marketed and yet allow a certain space for individuation."[25]

Rainey's essay is a cogent riposte to the modernist myth of *l'art pour l'art*; but his revisionism – like much new historicist writing on com-modification – is too monolithic. That *The Waste Land* and Pears Soap both benefited from marketing campaigns tells us something about modern culture, but not everything; and the distinctions need to be ob-served as well as the convergences. Soap or cars are uniform goods that can be sold only in a single transaction. A modernist literary text could be sold repeatedly in different segments of the market; that is why *The Waste Land* or *Ulysses* had such complex publishing histories. Their mar-ket could be segmented both through outlet (the little magazine, the bound volume) and through time: early sales to buyers attracted by a rhetoric of scarcity, later the unlimited edition for the mass market. The same principle still prevails comprehensively for books in English, with a hardbound first edition being followed by a cheaper paperback.

Exclusivity was the very soul of the rentier culture out of which mod-ernism emerged. As a class formation, it was hostile to "trade," marketing and mass consumption; it mimicked aristocratic values, and followed Eu-ropean (as opposed to American) conventions of old money behaviour. To assert its separateness and superiority, this class favored modes of con-sumption that were intangible (in the sense of refinement of manners) or that highlighted exclusive, artisanal or patinated goods.[26] Much of the rentier style can, of course, be de-mystified. Commodification affects all classes in the early twentieth century, and a rentier way of life is often underwritten by such occluded articles of manufacture as Tarrant's Black Lead (in Gissing's *In the Year of Jubilee*), the Eliot family's bricks, or the unmentionable object produced by Merton Densher's New England fac-tory in *The Ambassadors*. Nonetheless, the economic milieu that incu-bated modernism did manage to distance itself from the brute material realities of the literary marketplace where writers like Gissing, Wells or Arnold Bennett had to make their way.

Pound insistently attacked Bennett because he believed himself to be a fundamentally different kind of writer; and with reason. The complexity and allusiveness of Pound's and Eliot's poetry, their condescension to-wards everyday life and everyday people – let alone their decision to write poetry rather than fiction – *did* exclude them from the Bennett market. The commercial success of some modernist works in the 1920s and after could scarcely have been predicted, nor does it make sense to view this success as the pay-off for a deliberate campaign by modernist writers to commodify their productions. The "integration" (Rainey's term) of modernism into contemporary market capitalism occurred in various ways, and as the result of various forces. The market became interested in modernism rather than the other way round: *Women in Love, Under the Volcano,* and even *Ulysses* ended up as movies after their authors' deaths because they were famous enough to become "properties," regardless of their authors' original artistic intentions. Other modernists saw that they could dilute their style into commercial viability, as in Hemingway's classic trajectory of experimentalism, commercial success, and artistic decline. Rather than expose the marketing of *The Waste Land* as mere commodification, we need to explore in detail the segmentation of the literary marketplace, the nature of the product cycle for literary works, and the interaction within the market site of formally differentiated monetary and prestige systems.

Circulation, Refinement, Patronage

An *objet d'art* does not move through the same channels as a mass consumer product; but this differentiation only confirms the market's capacity to value and circulate everything, from a bar of soap to a reputation. The market has always been a sensitive register of the refinement and scarcity of a good; in transgressing the normal expectations of genre, modernist works achieve a particularity – a kind of ontological scarcity – that is a crucial element in their value. In their material embodiment, too, modernist first editions typically sell for at least a hundred times more than the price at which they were first offered. When the work is unique, such as a sculpture or painting, increases in market value have often taken on a legendary quality of excess. In consequence, those searching for good "investments" try to buy earlier and earlier in an artist's career. The market history of recent decades has conclusively refuted the modernist work's original claim to be an anti-commodity. It is rather a super-commodity: something whose canonical status rests on a collective evaluation, and whose worth is almost completely dissociated from the original investment in its production.

Rainey, again, has shown in fascinating detail how the first edition of *Ulysses* was "crafted" as a specially desirable and exclusive object of purchase; a kind of instant antique. He finds this marketing campaign

appallingly misguided; in effect, the great betrayal of the modernist movement at the very moment of its triumph in the *annus mirabilis* of 1922:

> [the modernists] were eager to demonstrate that their work could be
> successful now and to construe market success as a justification for
> their aesthetic and cultural claims, certain that no grounds existed
> for legitimate dialogue with either critical discourse or mass opinion.
> Yet in forfeiting demands for public sanction to the operations of the
> marketplace, the participants in the first edition of *Ulysses* commit-
> ted a grave mistake from which the history of the avant-garde has
> never recovered – and never will. . . . The "success" of *Ulysses* was an
> illusion that concealed a cultural and philosophical disaster of im-
> mense consequence, one that reverberates in every debate about cul-
> ture and patronage, art and the market, now taking place. . . . The
> invisible hand of the market is not a moral or rational agent, and it
> can never be a substitute for processes of mutual intelligibility and
> critical justification.[27]

I find it difficult to share Rainey's indignation over the enterprise at
Shakespeare and Co. First, the entire antiquarian book trade in the 1920s
was caught up in a bubble where "scarce" editions were fabricated right
and left, and rare volumes by authors like Kipling and Galsworthy
fetched ludicrous prices. The market dealt with that as it deals with all
bubbles, and in the context of the time the price asked for *Ulysses* was fair
dealing. Second, the villain of Rainey's scenario can only be Joyce himself. Was he "guilty" of driving one of the hardest bargains ever made
with a publisher by claiming 66% of the net profits (he had already sold
the manuscript to John Quinn before publication)?[28] But *Ulysses* was a
hard book to write; and it is no coincidence that it is perhaps the only canonical work of English literature whose hero is a lower-middle class
businessman. Finally, to lament the imbrication of modernism with
market capitalism can only be fruitful if things can be imagined otherwise: that modernism could have preserved its literary qualities while
basing itself on some other economy. Rainey himself has shown how
Pound tried to do just that by approaching Mussolini as a state patron in
1923-24; comment on the outcome of that initiative is superfluous.[29]

Modernism's early status in the market was achieved as an appreciation of refinement. Whether published or offered for sale as an object,
the exchange value of the avant-garde work of art is measured by its distance from the crude utility of staple and tangible goods; yet the highest
values in the market have always accrued to things furthest removed

from practical use. When we consider the employment of capital, similarly, we observe the gradient from the extraction of raw materials at the periphery, to their working-up in manufacturing centers, and on to tertiary functions of finance and distribution in the metropolis. The task of the economic critic is to try all the links of the chain: to note, for example, how in the thirties the composition of both *Finnegans Wake* and *The Cantos* was being supported by investments in the Canadian Northern Ontario Railway, a part of the colonial extractive infrastructure traditionally popular with metropolitan rentiers. Canadian Northern 4% bonds figured prominently in the investment portfolios of both James Joyce and Dorothy Pound. Neither Joyce nor Ezra Pound would have had the slightest interest in the culture of Northern Ontario, of course; but to reap a yield from a position of detachment and disinterest was precisely the point of the London capital market. Frank Lentricchia, expressing a typical kind of new historicist antipathy to capitalism, has argued that the modern economic order works "to so establish and saturate the conditions of creativity as to eliminate all social spaces that might be hospitable to the personality of idiosyncratic imagination."[30] But – and here I agree with Rainey – the social space of modernism is closer to a final stage of capitalism than a genuine site of opposition to it.

Although modernist writing could not exist outside of capitalism, it would be crude to assume that all capitalist commodities comprise a passive, undifferentiated mass. The modern literary marketplace – like market society as a whole – includes many active sub-cultures of readers and producers. There are markets for detective stories, for pornography, for self-help books, for screenplays, for avant-garde poetry, and so on down the list. All respond in particular ways to market forces, though some works break out of their categories and "cross over" into a wider and more lucrative market segment (as most modernist masterworks eventually succeeded in doing). But just as literary value can be defined as everything in a work that exceeds the formal requirements of its genre, so does "high" literature exceed the market conditions under which it is produced. It is not merely that these conditions fail to explain all the specificities of literary works, and the formal differences between them; it is also that, *pace* the new historicism, the status of these works as tradeable goods does not render trivial the ability of many of them – *The Way We Live Now*, say, or *The Wings of the Dove*, or *The Waste Land* – to articulate the most searching critiques of market society.

Where modernism should be situated, therefore, is in certain enclaves comprehended by market society, yet with a relative autonomy within it.

In these enclaves works were "traded" by critics and other cultural brokers who determined distribution and reception. Audiences could "invest" in authors according to how their works were priced in the stock exchange of modernist reputations. Bourdieu has spoken of cultural capital as a realm opposed in principle to economism: "There is an economy of cultural goods, but it has a specific logic."[31] Yet relative autonomy, in my terms, means that the specificity of the cultural sphere is bounded by its economic constraints. The avant-garde resembles other prestige system proto-markets (marriage, sports, literary criticism) that look implicitly to a settlement day when status tokens from the one market are cashed out for banknotes from the other. At the level of material subsistence, the modernist cultural enterprise was supported by real money that necessarily came from the market economy, whether directly or indirectly: from inheritances, patronage, allowances from parents, jobs in Lloyds Bank or the Trieste Berlitz School, and so on.

Modernist patrons and clients alike understood the linkages between the modernist and the commercial literary systems. Scofield Thayer and James Watson, like Lady Rothermere, Lady Ottoline Morrell, Harold Loeb, Nathalie Barney, and many others, used their money – not all of them had a great deal of it – to gain entry into literary circles and bask in the reflected glory of the writers they assisted. But they used their money because they could not have gained entry on their talent, and everyone understood the difference between what patronage could and could not buy. Because the people involved in these transactions – writers and patrons – each had something the other lacked, and because the transactions involved money (though more than just money changed hands), does not mean that modernist production was determined through and through by the marketplace in the sense that, say, the novels of Gene Stratton Porter were.[32] A patroness provided venture capital for the development of works that were not yet viable in the commercial market; she did not give a reward (as she would have during the renaissance), but made an investment, both in the artist's future development and in the transformation of public taste. Her own profit, if it accrued, would be in literary prestige rather than money, as she gained a position of honor in the living pantheon of modernism.

Pound's relations with John Quinn help to correlate cultural practice with a patron's status within capitalism. Among the major patrons of modernism, Quinn was perhaps the only active man of affairs, a corporate lawyer in New York. His patronage was more opportunistic, more directive, and closer to the market than that of women like Harriet Weaver; but it is ironic that his "masculine" shrewdness produced only modest and cautious support for Pound's editorial schemes. Quinn reserved his serious money for tangible objects: works of art by such artists as Matisse, Brancusi, Picasso, Rousseau.[33] His literary interests found a focus in actual books and manuscripts: he sold his manuscript of *Ulysses* to the Rosenbach Foundation, paid $10,000 for Conrad manuscripts between 1911 and 1919, and accepted as a gift from Eliot the manuscript of *The Waste Land*.[34]

Quinn took for granted the implicitly commercial relation between patron and producer in the visual arts. However much the patron might consider himself a friend and benefactor to the artist, at the end of the day a material object changed hands at a price set by negotiation, and the price arrived at was an index of the balance of interest in the relationship. Pound's solution to this awkwardness was that Quinn should only buy from artists whose work was still cheap:

> My whole drive is that if a patron buys from an artist who needs money (needs money to buy tools, time and food) the patron then makes himself equal to the artist, he is building art into the world. He creates.
>
> If he buys even of living artists who are already famous or already making £12,000 per year, he ceases to create. He sinks back to the rank of a consumer.[35]

The trouble with this advice was that the patron expected the artist to *become* famous before long. If he did not, it was a mistake to buy his work; if he did, the patron was simply a shrewd investor who bought in advance of a rise. Pound himself played the same card in urging Quinn to buy drawings by Wyndham Lewis: "As to Lewis, I think his prices will soar like Matisse's when once they start."[36] No line that Pound might draw between poor and rich artists could obscure the desire of any artist to sell high, and of any patron to buy low, as Carter Ratcliff has argued:

> Western art gains its entrepreneurial flavor from the Western self. We define ourselves in competition for economic profits that, thoroughly examined, reveal other aspects – social, cultural, esthetic. Likewise, the most transcendentally esthetic behavior or image reveals motives in some sense economic. The esthetic is an aspect of the economic, as the economic is an aspect of the esthetic.[37]

No one knew this better than Quinn; and Pound knew it too in his own way, hard as he fought to change the actual workings of the economic/ esthetic system that he encountered when he moved to London in 1908.

The development of the modernist market segment under the regime of patronage was a relatively brief episode in literary history, enabled by conditions that could never again be reproduced. By 1933, Pound himself was already casting a backward eye at the moment of modernism; though he was not inclined to give any credit to Western capitalism for what had been achieved:

> It is no answer to say that 'my' programme in art and letters has gradually been forced through, has, to some extent, grabbed its place in the sun. For one thing, I don't care about 'minority culture'. I have never cared a damn about snobbisms of writing *ultimately* for the few. Perhaps that is an exaggeration. Perhaps I was a worse young man than I think I was.
>
> Serious art is unpopular at its birth. But it ultimately forms the mass culture.[38]

"Ultimately" is an important term here. New historicist arguments tend to assume that because the destination of modernism is commodification – in the form, say, of a modernist classic that sells half a million copies a year, or Van Gogh's "Irises" selling for $59 million at Sotheby's – the commodification was implicit in the very moment of conception. But modernist patronage was not just a screen, behind which commercialism pulled all the strings of reputation and financial reward; rather, it was a specific regime that deserves to be examined, in all its complexity and contradiction, within the historical conjuncture that made it possible.

10
T.S. Eliot's Personal Finances, 1915-1929

All men are ready to invest their money
But most expect dividends.
                    —T.S. Eliot, Choruses from 'The Rock'

Literary Life

One of Ezra Pound's most successful creations is the myth of the economic martyrdom of modernist writers; as Hugh Kenner puts it, "there was no mechanism to translate into food and lodging what these men gave to the life of the mind."[1] Pound was generously concerned for the well-being of the writers he sponsored, but also he relentlessly ground the axe of his dislike for the literary marketplace, for journalism, and for the financial system as a whole. T.S. Eliot became "Exhibit A" in Pound's indictment of the English literary world, and many others were drawn into the cause of providing Eliot with the proper conditions for writing poetry. Eliot himself responded to Pound's campaign with a mixture of embarrassment and collusion. This chapter gives an accounting of Eliot's actual financial position in his first fourteen years in London, by way of comparing myth and reality.

Until 1915 (when he was twenty-seven) Eliot had been a student, almost entirely supported by his father. He met Ezra Pound in London in September 1914, who encouraged him to think of himself as the most important poet of the younger generation. In the following June Eliot made the two most important decisions of his life: he married Vivien Haigh-Wood, and he decided to become a writer in London rather than a professor in the United States.[2] Two days after the wedding, he induced Pound to write a long letter to his father Henry Ware Eliot, presenting "some sort of apologia for the literary life in general, and for London literary life in particular." Pound ended with Henry Ware Eliot's expected contribution to establishing his son in his chosen career:

As to exact sums, or the amount a man actually needs to begin on, I should think that if a fellow had five hundred dollars for the first year and two hundred and fifty for the second he ought to be able to make the rest of his keep and get decently started.[3]

Pound was proposing that a writer could live in London on a thousand dollars a year (£200), of which Eliot's father was being asked to provide half.[4] This was modest enough, given that Mr Eliot owned a great deal of St Louis real estate and the biggest single block of shares in the Hydraulic Press-Brick Company of St Louis, whose stationery was headed "Largest Manufacturers of Face Brick in the World."[5]

So far, the affair was an utterly Jamesian one. Henry Ware Eliot was rich—a multi-millionaire by today's values—but he had a wife and five other children, and the Press-Brick company had not paid a dividend since 1913.[6] Although Tom was not expected to be a brick-maker, his parents did want him to be a Harvard professor of philosophy, and they knew nothing of the young woman whom their son had suddenly married. Vivien's father, Charles Haigh-Wood, was also a millionaire in modern terms; he was a landscape artist who lived off his investments and the rents from a great deal of property, including fourteen semi-detached houses he owned in Kingstown, Dublin.[7] He gave Vivien £1,000, yielding a private income for her of £50 a year. Eliot went to the U.S. alone to see his family a month after he married, and his father agreed to continue providing a moderate amount of financial support.

The first year of the Eliots' marriage was economically painful for both of them. Both had enjoyed leisure and comfort all their lives; now Tom had to take his first job, as a schoolteacher at High Wycombe for less than £3 a week.[8] He and Vivien had no regular home; they lived either with Vivien's parents in South Hampstead or, for some months in 1915, sharing Bertrand Russell's London flat. Russell had taken pity on his former Harvard pupil for being "desperately poor." Eliot was not truly poor, but he certainly exuded an air of desperation. Russell told Eliot's Harvard supervisor, J.H. Woods, that "It has driven me almost to despair to see his fine talents wasting."[9] Russell's remedy was to give Eliot £3,000 worth of "engineering debentures."[10] As an opponent of the war, Russell thought it wrong to draw income from an arms merchant; Eliot was a neutral and also needed the money, which would have amounted to £180 a year at six percent. It seems that the Eliots continued to draw this income for nearly twelve years.

Not content with the return from the debentures, Eliot drifted into a continuing financial dependence on Russell. He accepted regular contributions to his living expenses and the shared use of a country cottage, and tolerated Russell's expensive presents to Vivien of dancing lessons, silk underwear, and the like. In August 1916 Russell wrote to Ottoline Morrell: "one thing that attracted me to [Vivien] was that it seemed clear one could make her happy by the very simple method of spending a certain amount of money."[11] Given Russell's evident sexual interest in Vivien, the situation came close to Eliot being paid for being a complaisant husband. This is not the place to speculate about the emotional dynamics of the *ménage-à-trois*; but Eliot seemed to tolerate a painful relationship in part because of the money involved, while at the same time feeling trapped by it.

In March 1916 the Eliots finally set up house on their own, in a flat at 18 Crawford Mansions; Tom's father paid the rent of £65 a year, and his mother and older brother Henry sent him regular gifts that made the total family support somewhat more than £100 a year.[12] It is likely that Vivien's family also helped out with cash and supplies; they were certainly well able to afford it. Tom and Vivien engaged a servant who, he later told his mother, "does all sorts of things that no one else would do, and is almost like a trained nurse when either of us is ill." If she left, he continued ingenuously, "we should never get another at anywhere like such low wages."[13] Eliot was already starting to earn some money from his writings, and had the potential to establish himself, as Pound had wished, as an independent man of letters.[14]

The great impediment to Eliot's following such a career was Vivien's health: she suffered from nervous prostration, gynecological problems, and colitis. She had worked briefly as a governess before their marriage, but could not undertake paid work after it, and needed frequent rest cures in the country. Eliot does not specify her medical expenses, but they must have run into well over a hundred pounds in most years.[15] His own health also became uncertain, from a combination of overwork and worry about the state of his marriage; this required consultations with specialists and periodic rest cures for him too. Trying to write poetry and literary journalism, while also teaching school (a profession for which he was unsuited by temperament), was more than he could cope with; at the end of 1916 he resigned from Highgate School. The first two years of the Eliots' marriage had been financially precarious, but they had received at least twice the amount of Tom's earnings as gifts from his parents, Vivien's parents, and Russell. This pattern of combining work and dependency would continue.

Eliot the Banker

In the first months of 1917 Eliot tried to support himself solely by lecturing and writing, but soon realized that he could not do so. He went to Charles Haigh-Wood for help, who in turn asked his friend L.E. Thomas, chief general manager of the National Provincial Bank, to provide a letter of recommendation.[16] On the strength of this, Eliot was given a menial and temporary job in the Colonial and Foreign department of Lloyds Bank in March 1917, at £130 a year. The General Manager of Lloyds, E.J. Harrison, recalled later that Eliot "was then in a rather desperate condition."[17] Eliot's critics have routinely described him as "a bank clerk," conjuring up a picture of him dealing out shillings and pence across the counter, as James Joyce actually did in Rome for eight months in 1906-7. Joyce complained that work in the bank was leading to his "mental extinction" and quit; on his last payday he got drunk, was robbed of his money, and fled Rome with the few crowns left at home with Nora.[18] Eliot, by contrast, liked the bank; and the bank liked him. He was given routine work at first, but he never waited on customers and his qualities as a man of business were quickly recognized. His salary doubled in just over a year, and by November 1923 he was earning £605 a year, more than four times what he had started at.[19]

Six weeks after he had started work Eliot, by Vivien's account, was full of satisfaction:

> Now that Tom has taken so extraordinarily to the City . . . he is considering, to my *great* astonishment, taking up Banking as his *money-making* career! We are all very much surprised at this development, but not one of his friends has failed to see, and to remark upon, the great change in Tom's health, appearance, spirits, and literary productiveness since he went in for Banking. . . . He is *extremely* interested in finance, and I believe has a good deal of hitherto unsuspected ability in that direction. If he can push on in Banking, and in the course of a year or two secure a sufficient income from it, there is no reason why he should not obtain through it his greatest ambition: viz: a congenial and *separate* money-making occupation - *of a sort* that will leave his mind and brain fresh enough to produce good literature, and *not to have to depend on writing for money at all*. This is what he has *always* been hoping for - he has never altered.[20]

Eliot's own report, equally positive, was: "I am getting on nicely in my work at the bank, and like it. . . . It is not nearly so fatiguing as schoolteaching, and is more interesting. . . . I want to find out something about the science of money while I am at it: it is an extremely interesting subject."[21]

Eliot remained under a great nervous strain during his years at Lloyds, but this derived from difficulties with Vivien and his compulsion to take on more literary work than he could comfortably handle. His hours at the bank must often have been a respite from the tensions that awaited him at Crawford Mansions. When he broke down in 1921 the bank gave him three months' leave with pay. E.J. Harrison, his boss, dealt with such matters in a bluff but kindly way. When an employee asked to extend his sick leave after a diagnosis of "neurasthenia," Harrison granted the request, adding: "I know from bitter experience that neurasthenia is 'the very dickens.'"[22] The bank stood by Eliot during his breakdown, and he in turn felt gratitude for the security afforded him by his employment at Lloyds.

In March 1919 Eliot was offered the position of assistant editor at *The Athenaeum*, which he turned down in favor of staying at Lloyds. Apart from his reservations about becoming a full-time journalist, he had just been transferred into more interesting work in a new "Information Department," analyzing international economic and political developments. His salary was still less than the £500 offered by *The Athenaeum*, but it was secure, and he (rightly) expected it to exceed £500 before too long.[23] By March 1923, when he refused the offer of Literary Editor of *The Nation* at £400 a year, he would have lost £200 a year by leaving Lloyds.[24]

In September 1923 Eliot began to contribute regularly to the *Lloyds Bank Monthly*.[25] His creative and intellectual writings professed a distaste for the world of commerce typical of the Coleridgean "clerisy"; but his sensibility was sufficiently dissociated for him to have a successful eight-year career in the bank, and to enjoy many of the rituals of life in the City. His father, after all, was an intellectual who chose to go into business and did very well at it; and included in Eliot's character was the determination also to become a man of substance and prove himself a worthy son.

Family Business

In assessing Eliot's literary exile, we should not underestimate the simple need—whether or not he could articulate it—to put an ocean between himself and his parents' expectations of him. At the same time, his worries over Vivien's health (and his own ability to support her) made it impossible for him to do without the actual and potential financial aid that his parents could provide. Despite their misgivings about Vivien, Eliot's family continued to provide the young couple with a steady flow of financial assistance. Apart from Henry Ware Eliot's payment of the rent on

Tom and Vivien's London flat, Charlotte Eliot sent regular checks for clothing, while his brother Henry provided cash for incidentals. In October 1916 Vivien thanked Henry for "these constant five poundses"; in 1917 five became ten, and in 1918 Henry seems to have sent a regular fifty dollars a month. In July 1919 Vivien told Mary Hutchinson "The money trouble is always cropping up," and Henry helped out with substantial gifts through 1921.[26] Henry's support in this period would have averaged about £100 a year. Since Tom's salary at the bank was rapidly increasing, the main cause of the "money trouble" must have been medical attention for Vivien, plus her extended stays in country cottages and seaside hotels. But they still managed to visit Paris regularly (in part, perhaps, to shop for Vivien's always-fashionable clothes); while Tom went for tours of rural France in 1919 and 1920, treatment by Dr Vittoz in Lausanne in 1921, and a rest cure in Lugano in 1922.

Central to Eliot's monetary outlook was his status as the cherished younger son of a wealthy Midwestern family. On 3 January 1919 his father reported "Tom is now independent," presumably on the evidence of his letter to his mother saying: "the salaries of the whole bank staff are going to be very largely increased all round, and I may get another rise of my own at Christmas, besides."[27] Four days later, Henry Ware Eliot died at the age of seventy-five, leaving his manuscripts to his son Henry, a gold cane to Tom, about $3,000 worth of shares in the Hydraulic Press-Brick company to each of three daughters, and the residue to his widow.[28] The estate was probated at $258,159 net, divided between $117,807 in shares (mostly in Hydraulic Press-Brick preferred) and $128,000 in real estate.[29] As befitted a brick-maker, Henry Ware Eliot had been an inveterate buyer of building-lots in St. Louis.

The vacant lot, that great symbol of American hopefulness, figures prominently (though not hopefully) in Eliot's early poems.[30] Once Henry Ware was dead, his family quickly renounced their industrial heritage. The two sons remained in Chicago and London, and Charlotte moved to Cambridge, Massachusetts in September 1920. Henry did not have confidence in the long-term future of the Hydraulic Press-Brick Company; in the 1920s he systematically sold off the family's shares, moving the proceeds into a diversified portfolio of stocks and tax-exempt bonds. The potential for controlling and developing the company meant nothing to Henry or Tom, since they were only interested in having a reliable income from the family fortune. Henry also moved to liquidate—with some difficulty—the family's lots in St. Louis.

Early in 1920, Charlotte Eliot gave each of her six children 225 preferred shares of Hydraulic Press-Brick. Valued at $30 for probate, they had risen to $55 as the company benefited from the postwar building boom. Tom sold his in November at that price, and turned over $12,000 to Henry to invest for him. Henry invested Tom's money conservatively at seven percent. In the summer of 1923 Charlotte gave Tom another 120 shares, which he sold at $64. He now had an inherited capital of about $19,000, on which he earned $1,400 a year.[31] When his mother died (she was eighty in 1923) he could expect to get about another $35,000, depending on Henry's success in selling off the family inventory of lots.

The only blemish on Tom's rosy prospects was Charlotte's disapproval of Vivien. When the estate was settled, Charlotte wanted to give Tom his shares in trust rather than outright. Perhaps getting wind of this, Tom wrote to her in October 1920, telling her that if he died, he wanted Vivien to receive his inheritance; Henry seems to have convinced his mother to give Tom the shares without conditions.[32] Charlotte finally met Vivien in the summer of 1921, and was confirmed in her mistrust; the following year she told Henry she was worried that Maurice Haigh-Wood, now a young man about London, would sponge off his sister and brother-in-law.[33] When she made her will in 1923 Charlotte left Tom and Margaret's shares of her estate in trust, while the other children's shares were given without restriction. Tom would receive the income on his share quarterly; if he pre-deceased Vivien, she would receive the income as his widow, but would be cut off from Eliot family money if she re-married.

Bel Esprit

The origin of "Bel Esprit" was John Quinn's proposal for a collective organization to support writers, with Pound himself to be the first beneficiary.[34] Able to live well enough on Dorothy's income and his own modest earnings, Pound suggested supporting Eliot instead. In March 1922 he launched his campaign "that T.S. Eliot be endowed for life, at such rate per year as will enable him to leave his job in Lloyd's bank, and give his entire time to literature."[35] Pound's crusade was set off by the completion of *The Waste Land*, and the positive impetus behind his efforts was the hope that Eliot would write more poetry of similarly high quality if he were freed from daily cares. Negatively, he wanted to rescue Eliot from the twin evils of journalism and business. Pound did not make it explicit, but much of the urgency of his campaign must have derived from his belief in Major Douglas's scheme of "Social Credit": it was not just that Eliot worked in business, but that he worked in a *bank*, the Vatican of the great economic swindle.[36]

Pound probably did not know that Eliot was already endowed, with a private income larger than his own; but the scion of the Hydraulic Press-Brick Company was certainly more exigent than Pound about his standard of living: "I Don't think 300 a year however [from Bel Esprit] is a living income for me, especially with vagueish guarantees. . . . I shall not stand in the way of your finding out just how much money can be got and how many people will give it for the arts in any form, *only* I do not at present find 600 a penny too much and cannot accept one bed room as being liberty in comparison with my present life."[37] Eliot enjoyed both his work at Lloyds and the income it brought, and he was deeply worried about Vivien's medical costs and future prospects. Nonetheless, he could not bring himself to simply tell Pound to stop canvassing on his behalf.

Ottoline Morrell's "Eliot Fellowship fund" became the English off-shoot of Bel Esprit in July 1922. Virginia Woolf was the most active fund-raiser for the scheme, but Eliot probably did not receive more than a hundred pounds from all this Anglo-French concern, and he paid a much higher price in embarrassment and ridicule. Too many people recognized that Eliot was comfortably off from his job at Lloyds alone, apart from the private resources they knew nothing about. Bel Esprit came back to haunt Eliot in 1931, when his former friend Richard Aldington satirized him as Jeremy Cibber, a poet who supports himself by working in a department store:

Yet with all this fame he refused to leave the haberdashery, . . . Was this inability to make up that mighty mind, or was it a supreme touch of chic? In either case it turned mere publicity into fame. A great genius in a haberdashery department! How too remarkable! What a disgrace! Why doesn't somebody do something? People became most agitated:
   'Do you know Cibber's *still* in the haberdashery?'
   '*No!* You *don't* mean it?'
   'My *dear*, I thought he was *scraping* it in by thousands!'
   'Oh, it's that awful wife of his.'
   'How I loathe that woman!'
And so on.[38]

Where Pound could succeed in boosting Eliot financially was in arrangements for the U.S. publication of *The Waste Land*, with the help of John Quinn in New York. Lawrence Rainey has examined the protracted negotiations that led to the poem's publication in *The Dial* and in book form by Boni and Liveright, and to Eliot's receipt of the *Dial* award of $2,000 for 1922. His total receipts for the poem amounted to about $2,800, plus

Quinn's purchase of the manuscript of Prufrock for $140.[39] All of this seems to have been added to Eliot's capital, as were the incidental sums he received from Bel Esprit.[40] Indeed, by the summer of 1923 Eliot's private income (including the Russell debentures) must have been substantially more than the £300 that Pound sought to provide for him through his embarrassing and ineffectual publicity campaign. It is all the more surprising, then, that in June 1923 Eliot was still permitting Virginia Woolf to solicit contributions for him. Only in November 1924 did he make it unequivocally clear that he did not need the money (he refused a residual sum of £50) and the fund was wound up by returning its funds to the original donors.[41]

Comfortably Off

On 16 March 1924, Henry Eliot reported to his mother that Tom's total income was about $5,000 a year; this would include $1,400 on his capital, $3,000 from the bank, and $600 in literary earnings. In addition, there would be about £50 from Vivien's capital (and perhaps other aid from her family), perhaps £30 from investing the *Dial* prize and other donations, and £180 from Bertrand Russell's debentures, for a grand total of £1,265 a year or $6,300. In the same year, the Woolfs had an income of £1,047; so that they had been raising money for a couple who were at least twenty percent better off than they were themselves (and who, unlike the Woolfs, could expect major inheritances within five years).[42]

Eliot resigned from Lloyds Bank in the spring of 1925 and joined Faber and Gwyer a few months later, accepting a salary that was twenty percent less than he had received at the bank.[43] He was not yet able to live on his literary earnings, but work at a publisher would be more congenial than at Lloyds, and he could now exert an even stronger influence on the London literary world. Scarcely seated in his editor's chair, he arranged for Faber to issue his collected poems—including *The Waste Land*, to which the Hogarth Press had reprint rights. Eliot ignored this obligation, and also brought Herbert Read over to Faber from Hogarth; the Woolfs were not happy with the business practices of someone they had devoted so much effort to helping.[44]

Going to Faber did not substantially change Eliot's financial situation; such change would come from two deaths. Charles Haigh-Wood died of lung cancer on 25 March 1927, after years of ill health. He left his estate in a family trust, with equal shares in the income for Vivien, her brother Maurice, and her mother Rose. Eliot and Maurice controlled the trust. Apart from an unknown amount in securities, the Haigh-Wood estate included the fourteen small Dublin houses (rented at £60 a year each), a family mansion in Ireland, a large house in Anglesey and another in London for his own use, a house for his sister-in-law in London, and houses rented out in Surrey and in Bury. Maurice estimated that the annual income of the trust was over £4,000 a year, so Vivien's share would have approximately doubled her and Eliot's income.[45]

In 1925 Eliot had been writing Bertrand Russell plaintive letters, appealing for help in dealing with Vivien.[46] Three months after his father-in-law's death he returned Russell's debentures, accompanying them with a scathing attack on Russell's lecture "Why I am Not a Christian."[47] A week after sending the letter, Eliot was baptized and received into the Anglican church.

Charlotte Eliot died on 10 September 1929, leaving Tom the income on his share of the estate. Henry estimated this at $2,000 a year in 1923, but he was a shrewd investor and Tom's sister Charlotte had pre-deceased her mother; the income may have been as much as $3,000.[48] Money would never again be a problem for Eliot, though after his separation from Vivien in 1933 he lived very frugally. When *The Cocktail Party* opened in New York in 1950 his royalties were for a while £570 a week; his estate when he died in 1965 was only £105,272, but for years he had been giving money away.[49] Some of the recipients—Wyndham Lewis, Dylan Thomas, Roy Campbell—were writers, as "desperately poor" as Eliot had been, by repute at least, at the start of his career.

11
The Way We Write Now

> *The idea that money, patronage and trade automatically*
> *corrupt the wells of imagination is a pious fiction, believed by*
> *some utopian lefties and a few people of genius such as Blake*
> *but flatly contradicted by history itself. . . . On the whole,*
> *money does artists much more good than harm. The idea that*
> *one benefits from cold water, crusts and debt collectors is now*
> *almost extinct, like belief in the reformatory power of flogging.*
> —Robert Hughes, "Art and Money"

Plain Living and High Thinking

English fiction of the nineteen-thirties did not have much concern with money, except as an instrument of injustice. After the war, the Labour regime undertook to set money straight, with the slogan "Fair Shares for All" and income tax peaking at ninety-seven and a half percent. The loss of overseas investments, the dissolution of the Empire, the erosion of private capital by taxes and inflation, and relative industrial decline all contributed to a lowering of monetary expectations. At the end of Kingsley Amis's *Lucky Jim*, a decent job and a flat in London provide Jim Dixon with a rosy outlook; and however far they moved to the right, writers like Amis and Philip Larkin never set their economic sights much higher than that. Money could never disappear from literature altogether, but for several decades it seemed to offer little food for the imagination.

In the thirties and after, many English writers and intellectuals hoped to see fulfilled their long dream of a virtuous culture divorced from commerce and the market. Whether this culture was to be communal (on the left) or heroic (on the right), it would at least put in their place the lower-middle classes who "fumble in the greasy till." Given the premise that "trade" was ignoble, either collectivism or reaction could offer the prospect of anti-economic alternative societies. Left or right, anti-clerical or clerical, the English mandarins agreed that the market was baneful to culture: it was vulgar, frivolous, and had no principles beyond those of philistines doing as they liked. It claimed to be a self-regulating system, which for many intellectuals raised the spectre of people going about their business without any care for order or justice. Both right and left were suspicious of the amorality of the market (though it could be argued, of course, that the market was more demo-cratic than the various kinds of godly rule that intellectuals and politi-cians wanted to set over it). This amorality seemed especially threatening in the production and distribution of cultural goods, which the market degraded to mere commodities. The market threatened national iden-tity, and was a Trojan horse for the Americanization of England.

The governance of schools, universities, the British Broadcasting Corpo-ration, the British Council all reflected the establishment's fear of a mar-ket-determined national culture. Radicals like Raymond Williams and Richard Hoggart, in the fifties and sixties, went so far as to propose that *all* culture should be understood "as the antithesis of and the antidote to the self-interested world of the capitalist market."[1] In this "left-culturist" anal-ysis, according to Alan Sinfield, "commerce was the problem and state funding the answer."[2] Left-culturalists found (and still find) their natural home in state-funded sectors and institutions, where cultural activities can be situated apart from the market and, in principle, above it. This is also the base for most literary study and research. Yet literary production in the West remains stubbornly attached to the literary marketplace and to commercial publishing. Even where creative writing has been institu-tionalized in universities, those who teach it are credentialled by their suc-cess in the market, and the measure of success for their students is that they should become professional writers in their turn (ideally, so success-ful that they need never teach creative writing!).[3] The socialization of liter-ary production – in the Writers' Unions of the U.S.S.R. and other Eastern Bloc countries – proved an almost complete failure, due to the stultifying effects of central ideological control and the inability of a command econ-omy to respond to the tastes of individual readers. The Russian writer Olga Nadimova has explained how the old system worked:

> It is the same both with the committees of the publishing houses and with the Union of Writers. Some of them, they themselves they write a book; and it is worthless. But because of their position they can approve that it can be printed, in an edition of several million copies. We do not have the royalty system that you have in the West, that you earn royal-ties on how many copies of your book are sold. Here you are paid for how many are printed. So you see if you are in a position of power, you can order yourself a fortune and one for your friend. Then you will see the situation that the book appears in large numbers of copies in the bookshops, and it sits and sits on the shelves because no one wishes to buy it. So finally it is recalled, and it is pulped. Then what can happen is hard to believe: but it is true, a new edition of the book

appears, reprinted on its own recycled paper. This is a good system yes? I think you would call it in your country 'Alice in Wonderland'.[4]

Alan Sinfield points to two weaknesses of the left-cultural agenda: it places the responsibility for good culture in the hands of an elite of meritocratic functionaries, and it naively assumes that the capitalist state will be happy to support an effective cultural opposition.[5] Yet subsidized culture in Britain can support admirable work in museums, universities, theater companies, and the like; the point, surely, is that this is achieved in a cultural sphere of *reproduction*, whereas the market remains dominant for cultural *production*. The reproductive sector has long enjoyed a combination of state support and private endowment, and massive new funds are now being provided by the National Lottery; reproductive culture is safe and respectable, in England, in a way that productive culture seemingly cannot be. There is even a strong "right-culturalist" movement that wants the state to support traditional high culture (seen as a repository of national and conservative values) or, alternatively, emphasizes the economic potential of the arts for stimulating tourism and urban renewal.[6]

For productive culture, though, the market devil continues to have the best tunes, even when they are the protest songs of a Caryl Churchill, Dennis Potter or David Hare. Writers on the left have to live, and reliance on the market is inescapable if they are to work at their craft full-time. That some, incidentally, become wealthy may create a moral dilemma for the individual, but is not in itself an invalidation of leftist convictions.[7] The deeper question is how the literary marketplace confers vitality even on works that are, in their formal content, opposed to it.

Making a Come-back:
Drabble, Amis and Churchill on Money

John Vernon speaks of how money in the nineteenth century novel "flares up as a force in itself," only to die down in the twentieth century. "In our age," he suggests, "money as a representation tends to disappear into what it represents: forms of power on the one hand and the accumulation of commodities on the other."[8] But the election of Mrs Thatcher in 1979 put money back at the center of concern. Under the flag of monetarism, the imperatives of the financial system took priority over both traditional Labour issues of equity, and the consumerism of Macmillan's "You never had it so good" in the 1950s. If you got money right, Thatcher claimed, everything else would follow, as individual energies were unleashed in pursuit of

wealth. Traditional English barriers to money-making needed to be demol-
ished, whether they had been erected by the snobbery of the prestige
classes, or the concern of the Left for Fair Shares.

It goes without saying that the English clerisy were not happy with the
cultural implications of monetarism. Nonetheless, money did make a
comeback in literature, if only as an object of repugnance and denuncia-
tion. Yet this repugnance could not be altogether credible: even among
writers on the Left, money was shown bringing new warmth to the
half-frozen limbs of Britannia. Money, they concede, is life; and even the
wrong sort of life must be welcome after the paralysis afflicting the country in the 1970s under Heath, Wilson and Callaghan. It is money that stiff-
ens the sinews, summons up the blood, and cures the English disease of
not wanting; and especially on the Left, it carries the thrill of the forbidden.

Margaret Drabble's three novels of the nineteen-seventies, and especially the last of them – *The Ice Age* – are pioneers of the revival of money
in English fiction. As a self-conscious "condition of England" novel, *The
Ice Age* registers the dissolution of the postwar Fair Shares consensus, and
its replacement by a society of consumerism and speculation. The
novel's historical moment is the recession of the early 1970s that puts
into question the confident expansion of the fifties and sixties. Its hero,
Anthony Keating, is at the end left stranded in a communist prison; this
allows Drabble to evade the vision of personal and national resolution
that typically concludes condition of England novels such as *North and
South* or *Howards End*. Drabble does recognize that some great change is
in the air, though she is uncertain of its nature. This social agnosticism
reflects her self-division, between recognizing the cracks in the postwar
social contract, and holding on to the fundamental beliefs of Labourite
welfarism. In retrospect, we see that the novel foretells the end of compromise and consensus: Margaret Thatcher became Prime Minister in
1979, two years after *The Ice Age* was published.[9]

Anthony Keating is the son of a Church of England clergyman who
epitomizes the social disposition of the Coleridgean clerisy:

> throughout his childhood, Anthony had listened to his father and
> mother speaking slightingly of the lack of culture of business men, of the
> philistinism and ignorance of their sons, of commercial greed, expense
> accounts, business lunches. Under the massive yellow sandy shadow of
> the cathedral wall, the Keatings sat safely in their extremely attractive,
> well-maintained eighteenth-century house (it went with the job) and lis-
> tened to good music, and laughed over funny mistakes in Latin proses,
> and bitched about the Canon's wife who had a pronounced Lancashire

accent, and they economized in small ways, for they were not well off, and had to appear better off than they were.[10]

Keating follows the beaten track for his class to Oxford and the BBC; he has conventional left-wing views (though both his parents voted Tory) and feels "that there was something not very nice about money." He takes one step down the primrose path by moving from the BBC to commercial television, but his real conversion strikes in 1968 when he is editing a television interview with the property developer Len Wincobank:

> it struck him, suddenly, with a dazzling flash: how could he not have noticed it before? The truth was that Len Wincobank was a genius, about ten times as intelligent, ten times as perceptive, ten times as alive as Austin Jones [the interviewer]. Austin Jones, in comparison, was a boring somnambulist, a ventriloquist's dummy, mouthing without conviction or information or even any intelligence the obligatory provocative questions: questions which were based on an utterly false premise, the premise that he and the viewers lived in a society which disapproved of the profit motive and which condemned private enterprise. No wonder, thought Anthony, no wonder I have been so bored and so half-hearted, for so long.[11]

Keating decides that he wants "to stop being a gentleman and become a business man"; he goes into property development and is buffeted by the cross-currents of the early 1970s. He is an economic innocent, set between Len Wincobank on one side and, on the other, an Oxford friend who has become a classics don, Linton Hancox. Wincobank is a working-class boy turned successful speculator, while Hancox is an impoverished cultural reactionary, embittered by the decline of classical studies: "A pond, out of which the water had slowly drained, leaving Linton stranded, beached, useless. Unable to adapt, unable to learn new skills, obstinately committed to justifying the old ones – and alas, as so often happens, ruining quite unnecessary and disconnected parts of himself in his willed, forced, unnatural, retrogressive justification."[12] Keating won't become much of a business man, but at least he bestirs himself and avoids the fate of Hancox – who stands for the whole class of traditional British intellectuals, freezing and slowly running out of money in their country cottages.

In *The Ice Age* and its two predecessors (*The Needle's Eye* and *The Realms of Gold*), material questions are again placed at the center of fictional concern. Perhaps Drabble was influenced in doing this by writing her biography of Arnold Bennett (1974), that supremely money-minded English novelist. Certainly, she attempts in *The Ice Age* to enter into the preoccupations of a wide spectrum of English types, instead of staying within the conditioned reflexes of those Oxbridge arts graduates who – in Anthony Keating's view, at least – "had killed the country, sapped initiative, destroyed the economy."

Early in the novel, Drabble surveys "the state of the nation" in the recession of the winter of 1973-74.[13] Unlike similar visions of the whole in, say, *To the Lighthouse* or *Howards End*, Drabble avoids conclusions and registers the diversity of individual fates. The earlier novels relied on the narrative authority of a liberal humanism secure in its own virtue, and dissociated from the mundane concerns of the lower-middle or working classes. In *The Ice Age*, the normative Englishman and woman are now the classless "new businessman of the sixties," Len Wincobank, and his secretary/lover Maureen Kirby. Anthony Keating's heart attack stands for the collapse of the old humanism of "Oxbridge arts graduate values," whose irrelevance is supposed to be the novel's point. But characters like Keating will not really be marginalized until the arrival of Thatcher, Britain's first lower-middle class Prime Minister.[14] Drabble herself tried to rally intellectual opposition to Thatcher in the late 1980s, but her novels since 1979 have shown a good deal of uncertainty about where in society a base for that opposition might be found.

Martin Amis's *Money* (1984) is also a kind of satire on Thatcherism; yet there is in it remarkably little sign that the author remains, in real life, a Labour voter.[15] He has said, apropos of *Money*, that "The society one is writing about is to do with decline rather than decadence. . . . I would say I am not terribly interested in disapproval."[16] It is a society where "money went wrong ten years ago" – in 1973, that is, the year of the Arab oil crisis. The hero of *Money* is an Englishman in New York, John Self, who has gone from a culture with some residual gentility to one where money is "the only gauge of anything, the only measure."[17] In theory, this should be a great simplification of the problem of living – except that money itself has gone mad, and Self with it, hearing voices in his hotel room: "First, of course, is the jabber of money, which might be represented as the blur on the top rung of a typewriter . . . compound terrors and greeds."[18]

Self gets his sex from prostitutes, excited by the way cash can call forth desire; with his girlfriend Martina, who is upper class and "old money," he is impotent. Amis's point seems to be that prestige goods, "the things money can't buy," have gone out of circulation in America, and will soon be gone in England too. For Evelyn Waugh this would have been a decline and fall, but with Amis it seems closer to the necessary re-vitalization of an old country by the injection of a new, amoral energy (this is, after all, what Anthony Keating thought he was doing in becoming a property developer). But when everything is reduced to the money-motive, as it is in Self's world, the novel is enfeebled by the disappearance of any rival moral system.

As money becomes the all-in-all during the nineteen-eighties, an author like Amis finds it hard to generate a significant moral conflict, or to have any plot beyond characters having either more money, or less. One recourse, for Amis, is to a verbal inflation corresponding to the monetary one in the world of the novel: a crackling, demotic language itself becomes a form of action. Another is to focus on acts of consumption that can make inroads on the stock of money: the mindless use of liquor, cigarettes, prostitutes, junk food. The "moronic inferno" that Amis called America is the condition of any society driven entirely by money.[19]

Caryl Churchill's play *Serious Money* (1987) shows the difficulty, in the 1980s, of carrying on the critique of Cobbett and Ruskin. The play begins with a scene from Thomas Shadwell's *The Volunteers*, a satire on the new Stock Exchange written in 1692; someone is explaining that "it's no matter whether it turns to use or not; the main end verily is to turn the penny in the way of stock jobbing, that's all."[20] If the argument between the financial economy and the "real" economy of use-value has been going on for three hundred years, can it really be the best stick to beat Thatcher with? To set up as a modern Cobbett, Churchill would have to invoke a virtuous organic society that is being corrupted by traders and speculators. In *Serious Money*, though, all the dramatic conflicts are internal to the ruling class: they are between public schoolboys and barrow-boys; between land and money; and between England and America. The money market is where they confront each other, because no other social contradictions remain visible after the defeat of the miners' strike in 1984, and because in the world of the play the most important aspects of Thatcher's rule are her abolition of restrictions on international capital movements (1979) and the "Big Bang" deregulation of financial markets (1986).

Serious Money assumes that in the new City of London, the old privileges of class and gender are being dissolved. As Scilla, an upper-class stockbroker, puts it:

> I found O levels weren't much use, the best qualified people are street traders.
> But I love it because it's like playing a cross between roulette and space invaders.[21]

When "Jake" is praised as "the only public schoolboy what can really deal," he retorts "That's because I didn't go to university and learn to think twice." So far so good; but the market is both "fair" (to those hitherto excluded) and a place where, to succeed, you have to be "greedy and completely amoral."[22] In *The Way We Live Now*, the traditional code of the landowning classes was a restraint, in principle at least, on speculative greed; in *Serious Money* there is no longer any code, just a life-style. The American dealer "Zac" asks:

Why do the British always want land?
(In Paris or New York you live in an apartment, why do the English need gardens?)

Jake.
You're not upper class without it, you're too American to understand.

Zac.
You don't make money out of land, you make money out of money.[23]

Land in England has traditionally been a positional good that aligns its owner with the old prestige classes. Zac is right that money turns over faster in the financial markets; but land has been the place in England to salt those profits away and turn oneself into a country gentleman. In *Serious Money* land may still be desired, but it has nothing to do with legitimation, trusteeship or public service. As one character observes, "sexy greedy *is* the late eighties," and there is no moral authority to regulate the great roulette wheel of the City.

Serious Money is not, however, a deadly blow to Thatcherism. Representation always contains an element of recommendation: showing the market from inside, Churchill also conveys its quality as a spectacle. Then, there is the ambiguity in Churchill's presentation of the "barrow-boys" and the female traders: if it's good that they are outwitting the old upper classes, why condemn the "amorality" of the market that was happy to give them their chance?[24] The prejudice against barrow-boys in the 1980s echoes Cobbett's complaints about Jews and Quakers in the 1820s: that the market rewards people who lack self-restraint, and who don't have a stake in the community.

Finally, the play makes no attempt to present a moral alternative to the traders. No *deus ex machina* comes at the end to close down the casino and restore order to society; nor is there any mention of the Labour Party as a potential savior.[25] The West End run of *Serious Money* began a month after Thatcher was elected to her third term, and the play closes with the cast singing an anthem to the Tories, "Five More Glorious Years."[26] The audience for *Serious Money*, like that for *Private Eye,* enjoyed laughing at its own vices; but it is unlikely that anyone was moved by the play to renounce them. The real joke was that their friends were back in power, they were getting serious money in real life, and no leftist play could spoil their fun.

Serious Money appeared at a time when market values had triumphed in England over both the collectivist ideals of the left, and the paternalism of the old Tory "wets." The triumph became global in 1989 when the Berlin Wall came down and Leninism with it. Since then, the major rivalries have been between different economic strategies and national interests within capitalism, rather than between capital and Labour at home, or between West and East abroad. Even Labour's landslide victory in 1997 depended on their acceptance of Thatcherite economic principles and the curbing of union power within the party.[27] In such an era, the condition of England question can no longer be resolved by the ideals of liberal humanism – we are all Wilcoxes now – but rather by a sober assessment of the niche that English society may find for itself within the new global system. The future of literature then becomes inseparable from the structures peculiar to the London publishing industry, and their relations with the complementary center of New York.

Publishing Today

Chapter Seven described the revolution in the literary marketplace of the 1880s and 1890s, which determined the economics of English literature for most of the twentieth century. In the 1980s and 1990s there has been another seismic shift, to what may be called a postmodern literary system. The perfect representative of that system is Martin Amis's *The Information*: a novel that both satirizes the new realities of the market for fiction, and is itself the "guilty thing surprised" of which it speaks.

Here is Amis on the subject of his reputed £500,000 advance from HarperCollins for *The Information*:

> There's also this idea, perhaps, that writers should be underpaid. I mean, if you're interested in rich people you'd do better to go and visit a few publishers. They're the ones with the big houses, but no one seems to get that. There's a continuing myth that they are wonderful

people, like wine merchants or antique dealers – all they want is their five-per-cent profit. People don't understand that that's all gone. . . . We're talking about conglomerates now.[28]

Publishing used to occupy a liminal position in the English class system: it was a trade, certainly, but publishers were also gentlemen, typically with Oxbridge educations and private means. Now, almost all the old gentlemanly publishing houses have been absorbed into corporate conglomerates where they survive only virtually, as imprints – one brand name in a portfolio, each required to be a "profit center." [29] Any loyalty that an author might have to a particular publishing house would be delusional when it is News Corporation, Bertelsmann, or Time Warner that sits at the top of the organizational pyramid. Such conglomerates are transnational; their holdings in British publishing are provinces that are largely self-governing, so long as they meet their quota of tribute to "Rome" (corporate headquarters, which need not be in New York or London).[30]

Contemporary publishing is shaped by the fading of personal loyalties between author and publisher, the shortening of perspectives, and a movement back towards the Victorian practice of investing a large capital sum to purchase a book. This is not to argue that commerce has driven out morality and creativity: publishing was always a business, and it is now conducted not in a worse way, but in a different way. "Loyalty" may have meant that publishers gave authors more time in which to prove themselves, but also that authors were expected to stick with publishers who gave them less than their books were worth. In the old days, loyalty often meant a personal relationship with the firm's founder or proprietor, like William Heinemann or Alfred Knopf; now editors typically stay with a firm for only three or four years, so that a "loyal" author would still have to follow his or her editor from one firm to another.

Stable relationships are now more likely to be between authors and their agents, than between authors and publishers.[31] The gatekeepers of the literary marketplace are now young agents, trying to establish themselves by building a "stable" of new writers; agent and writer each have a long-term stake in the other's success. Authors and agents are on the same side in terms of their direct economic interest; whereas for a publisher, payments to authors are a cost of production and thus a charge against profit. A leading New York publisher liked to say that "the agent is to the publisher as the knife is to the throat." If agents and authors have been allied against publishers for a century now, it may be a sign of the times that in two recently notorious book deals this loyalty broke down. Martin Amis was criticized for switching from Pat Kavanaugh to Gillon Aitken when selling rights to *The Information*. One accusation against Aitken was that he approached authors to drop their existing agents, promising them bigger advances; this is precisely the criticism leveled against aggressive publishers in the 1890s, that they wooed authors away from rival houses. More radical yet was Jeffrey Archer's decision to represent himself in a reputed £15 million deal for three books, on the ground that it was cheaper to pay a fee for professional services as needed than to pay a standard agent's commission (normally ten to fifteen percent).[32]

The shortening of perspectives means that an author's career now tends to break down into a series of auctions for individual works, or for a bundle of future books. A publisher, similarly, thinks in terms of buying a literary property rather than taking on an author. To the extent that the single-book deal predominates, modern publishing is moving away from the logic of the royalty system, which was to build up a body of work that would eventually yield a steady income. Stability now tends to be found only at the very top, with the twenty or thirty "brand name" authors that every publisher wants. Joseph Epstein reports that of the hundred best-selling books in the U.S. from 1986 to 1996, sixty-three were written by six authors.[33] In 2000, J.K. Rowling sold four times as many books as the runner-up bestselling author.[34] Such authors have so much bargaining power that they can effectively turn their publishers into distributors, and take most of the profits for themselves.

The conglomerates have taken over British publishing in the past twenty years because it has traditionally been an under-capitalized business: private resources could not fully underwrite the rapid expansion after World War II, and by the 1970s most publishers were in debt to the banks and vulnerable to cyclical downturns. The wave of takeovers introduced new equity capital and a bias towards further expansion. Publishers are now likely to acquire a promising new book by offering an advance equal to the total expected royalties – in effect, this is a return to the Victorian system of outright purchase. By paying the estimated royalties up front, a well-capitalized publisher is only sacrificing three or four years' interest on the money. Shrewd authors realize that it is better to get the biggest possible advance, because then the publisher will have a strong incentive to promote the book, having put a substantial sum at risk.

The squabble over *The Information* was partly over the meaning of an advance: is it a speculative investment by the publisher, or a loan against the author's future earnings? A.S. Byatt argued "that you should be paid what you earn": i.e. take a moderate advance, followed by whatever comes in from the book's actual sales.[35] Against this is the argument that any price paid by a knowledgeable buyer – in this case the high bidder, HarperCollins – is legitimate. As Richard Curtis observes, "Sometimes publishers deliberately overpay to acquire a coveted author. That author's books may become a loss leader to make some kind of statement to the publishing industry, to authors and agents, and to the press."[36] That *The Information* failed to earn its advance is no more significant than that most movies lose money: big media companies need blockbusters, and know that they must eat losses to get them.[37] Winslow Farrell argues in *How Hits Happen* that cultural markets are becoming more unequal and disorderly, which implies that there may be no such thing as a "rational" advance.[38] Publishers may feel that paying too much to literary novelists like Martin Amis or Salman Rushdie is a relatively small risk compared to the multi-million pound cost of acquiring top-selling commercial authors.[39]

The literary agent Carole Blake has observed that "publishing has become almost synonymous with marketing."[40] This cannot be true for most of the 90,000 plus titles published annually in Britain, and 140,000 in the U.S.[41] The few hundred top books, however, are now distributed in a much more targeted way. Traditionally, power and status within publishing lay with acquisitions editors; the marketing department took care of the nuts and bolts of distribution, sending out ill-paid salespeople to make the rounds of provincial bookstores. Now, the marketers have power from the beginning in deciding what books should be acquired and how they should be sold. Under the old regime, publishers would acquire a certain number of books for their lists, in the expectation that some would sell well and make enough profit to keep the house going. Under the new one, marketers look much more carefully at a book's chances of profit, before it is acquired; when it is published, they intervene much more actively in the market to guarantee its success. With the end of the Net Book Agreement, top books can be sold in supermarkets or "big box" retailers, literally on the principle of "Pile High, Sell Cheap."

When a book itself becomes news, a promotional loop is set up whereby, for example, people may buy *The Information* out of simple curiosity about a book for which such a large advance was given. The marketing campaign for the paperback edition was actually based on this theme, encouraging people to buy the book to decide for themselves whether it was worth what was paid for it! The curiosity necessarily extends to the author of the book as a newsworthy personality; perhaps it is *only* the author that they are curious about, as Richard Nann's agent explains in *The Information*:

'Writers need definition. The public can only keep in mind one thing per writer. Like a signature. Drunk, young, mad, fat, sick: you know. It's better if you pick it rather than letting them pick it. . . .

People are very interested in writers. Successful ones. More interested in the writers than the writing. In the writers' lives. For some reason. You and I both know they mainly sit at home all day.'[42]

Sales of bestselling books are now driven by their authors' appearances on television and radio, and effective self-presentation is at least as important as the book itself.[43] Inevitably, publishers have moved towards marketing the author and making the book an afterthought:

The conglomerates that dominate publishing are still greedy for big names. Unfortunately, there are not enough authors with the required cachet; new stars have to be found. Hence the signing up of actors, models and comedians.[44]

Century publishers paid £700,000 in 1987 for the first novel of actor Joan Collins, star of *Dynasty*. In 1996 she was sued by Random House of New York to return an advance of $1.2 million paid her as part of a two-book contract, on the grounds that the manuscript she delivered was unpublishable (the suit failed).

The phenomenon of the celebrity novel necessarily draws "serious" writers into the same media culture. All movies now require their stars to do publicity and promotion around the time of release; publishers, similarly, require their leading authors to undertake publicity tours, as insurance that their books will earn their advance. *The Information* provides no place to stand outside this system: Richard Nann is tormented by having to tag along with his rival Gwyn Barry's American publicity tour, but the worst of Richard's torment is that his own novel is too obscure to justify a tour for him. Without the external machinery of a successful author's life, Amis would have no such novel to write; so how could anything in the novel wish itself out of existence? Amis's satire cannot escape complicity with its supposed target.

If the ideal of intrinsic literary merit is to survive at all, it may be within the contradiction between the publisher's "front-list" and "back-list." The front-list – consisting roughly of books published in the current year – is entirely subject to the fashion-cycle, to publicity, and to a new title's struggle to earn its advance. The back-list – books that remain in print for more than a year and continue to sell – typically provides forty to sixty percent of a publisher's revenues, and a higher percentage of profits (since back-list titles have already covered their editorial and publicity costs). A solid back-list provides the foundation for a more speculative front-list; though in a time of retrenchment – as in British publishing after the end of the Net Book Agreement in 1995 – publishers will tend to prefer front-list books that have potential to move to the back-list, rather than having a merely topical appeal. Yet it is now more difficult for publishers to promote their back-lists, because so much retail space is occupied by current offerings, which themselves have only a few weeks to find an audience. As the saying goes in the pop music business: "here today, gone today."

A successful back-list can build a bridge from the current bestseller to the segment of the book market supported by schools and mass higher education. With the extension in 1995 of copyright in the U.K. from fifty to seventy years after the author's death, the achievement of canonicity – through the collective judgment of those who teach literature – becomes even more valuable.[45] Both authors and publishers who have an eye to the long run must look primarily to the educational market, satisfying an academic rather than a popular taste. As with the lending libraries in the nineteenth century, the relatively small group of teachers of English literature can determine very large sales. The stacks of hundreds of copies of a literary novel to be found in a university bookstore at the beginning of term may not be so different, as a marketing phenomenon, from similar stacks of a current bestseller in an airport or shopping center.

Gatwick and Heathrow are now the two leading centers for sales of trade books in England; along with the universities, they seem to be places where reading is holding its own. Whatever the differences between airports and universities as sites of literary circulation, both show the workings of what Frank and Cook have called the "winner take all society."[46] Penguin Classics sell over 25 million copies a year, mainly to the educational market: an average of 17,000 copies for 1400 titles. Despite ideological attacks on the Canon, a small number of titles will continue to be the focus of literary studies, even if individual books come into or fall out of favor. On the high street, more and more display space in bookstores is now taken up with multiple copies of bestsellers – a trend that is being accentuated by the end of the Net Book Agreement.[47] Greater emphasis on marketing and publicity, along with more general economic tendencies towards inequality, focuses the demand for books on a small group of well-known authors, whose status now resembles that of bankable movie stars. There is a widening gap between them and the "mid-list" authors who find it more difficult to make even a moderate income as full-time writers.

Since about 1980, the distribution of income has become substantially more unequal in both Britain and the U.S., and everything indicates that changes in the literary marketplace over the same period have worked to give a larger share of total rewards to bestselling authors.[48] In theory, the existence of the "great rewards" that Walter Besant called for a century ago should entice a larger number of talented people to become writers. But the really large rewards go to commercial rather than literary writers, which suggests that these talents will be directed towards producing bestsellers, not masterpieces.[49] Almost all people who try to become movie stars or professional athletes simply fail; in writing, tens of thousands will succeed in getting something published. The steady increase in the number of titles suggests that more people are achieving a minimum standard of competence; whether sheer quantity will lead to more masterpieces in the long run remains an open question. Jason Epstein has predicted that distribution of books over the internet will bring about a new golden age for publishing by keeping every title "in print." There is certainly a potential for change, given that writers, like farmers, capture only a very small percentage (surely less than ten percent for writers) of the final price at which their product is sold.[50]

In Chapter Seven I discussed the paradox that markets are the most efficient way of meeting demands, yet are often incapable of supplying cultural goods at any price. No matter how great the rewards we offer, we cannot produce another Rembrandt or Mozart or Kafka; nor can we specify a social context that will ensure the appearance of genius. Some might predict a decline for British high culture as the country becomes more Americanized and more integrated into the homogenized forms of global entertainment industries. This fits the Marxist scenario of the degradation of Western culture, over the past century or more, by the shift to a near-universal commodification. Fredric Jameson proposes, as a corollary, that only art that is *not* commodified can be good:

> The only authentic cultural production today has seemed to be that which can draw on the collective experience of marginal pockets of the social life of the world system: black literature and blues, British working-class rock, women's literature, gay literature, the *roman québecois*, the literature of the Third World; and this production is possible only to the degree to which these forms of collective life or collective solidarity have not yet been fully penetrated by the market and by the commodity system.[51]

One could make debating points by asking Jameson for the exact date when culture was vitiated by the market (what was Shakespeare writing for?), or by pointing out that his "authentic cultural products" all come to our attention through the marketing channels of global media. No doubt Jameson would view such success (of reggae, post-colonial fiction, etc.) as the corruption of an originary authenticity; but markets have always drawn in new resources from the periphery to the center, and in the process have hybridized what they bring into circulation.

This drawing-in is a specific function of London and New York. Cities like Calcutta and Shanghai may be flourishing centers of the third-world literature mentioned by Jameson; but it is literature in the vernacular for a local audience. For this literature to be globalized, it must pass through the capitals, as Aijaz Ahmad observes:

> countries of the Third World have little direct access to each other's cultural productions. Indians, for example, don't import novels from Latin America. We read only those Latin American novels which get translated and published in English, in places like London and New York. In order to read such novels critically, an Indian would typically read the scholarship about Latin America that is produced in the same Atlantic zones. . . . my knowledge of such novels is highly mediated, virtually determined by the complexes of knowledge assembled in Anglo-American universities and publishing houses.[52]

The international literature that emerged in the 1980s under the banner of "post-colonialism" added a further level of globalization. It was predominantly written in English, by authors based in the West, and working within Western fictional traditions. To call this literature post-colonial was ambiguous: it proclaimed a break with previous eras of Western dominance, but it also assumed that the identity of non-Western countries and peoples was entirely determined by the impact on them of Western colonial incursions, or of their status as immigrants to the West.[53] The boom in post-colonial literature was mainly created in London and was deeply implicated in the workings of a globalized literary marketplace. London publishers saw the possibilities of a new and profitable line of merchandise, as they had earlier profited from the feminist boom and the literary theory boom. This is not to denigrate post-colonial writing itself, or to jeer at the ways in which leftist intellectuals may be rewarded by Western publishers or universities. Rather, my point is that non-market cultural practices are deeply vulnerable, once the market moves to absorb them. Their only remaining habitat would be in the few enclaves "red-lined" by global capitalism: areas of civil strife, much of Africa, closed-door regimes like North Korea, Afghanistan or Myanmar. Whatever their future, these regions are improbable launching-pads for the kind of cultural redemption that Jameson hopes for.

There is a kind of convergence, then, between Jameson's hopes for a margin on the left opposed to commercial society, and Ezra Pound's for a traditionalist culture of the right. Both visions see commodification as the enemy, and both seem too exiguous to sustain a counter-culture outside the market. In Britain, such a counter-culture would find a firmer base in the remaining strongholds of prestige values, where hostility to the market is backed up by high status and by public and private endowments. This sector overlaps with a rentier culture that may be larger than ever, even if it is no longer so clearly visible as in the milieus of Forster, Galsworthy or Henry James. Old money still accumulates in Britain, and new wealth enters the country from the international wealthy who admire the British way of life. The impact of this money is clear in such endowed cultural institutions as the ancient universities, the Royal Literary Fund, the older art galleries and museums and the Anglican Church (insofar as the church still counts as a patron of culture). We can add those institutions, such as the British Council, the BBC or the National Theatre, whose operating budgets are supported by the state but which are influenced by "old money" values and distance themselves from pure market forces. Massive new support for this sector is now being provided from the National Lottery, which in Britain is effectively a tax on the working class to support high culture.

It is hard to define the precise effect on English literature of endowed cultural institutions. Many writers are partly supported by this sector, or make it the setting for their fiction; it is one of the crucial peculiarities of the English, and its influence might be assessed through a comparison with cultures of common heritage – such as Canada or Australia – where it is less developed.[54] But that writers find subsistence outside the market gives no guarantee about the quality or type of work they may produce. Money can ensure results in the reproductive sector, when it is a matter of hiring singers for Covent Garden or filling the Getty Museum with art; but much of the recent vitality in the novel has come from regions – Africa, India, Latin America – insulated from the direct influence of metropolitan literary marketplaces.

Old money in English culture also operates at the individual level, where inherited wealth may buy leisure for literary pursuits. This kind of rentier existence is less visible than earlier in the century, when Orwell would sneer obsessively about young men with private incomes. Writers with money of their own no longer stand out as a distinct social type, perhaps because they blend into a common upper-class consumer culture. Nor is there a credible equivalent to the modernist bohemia, where young people went to live modestly and produce masterpieces. The rentier lifestyle visible in places like Santa Fe, Tuscany or Monaco, if involved with culture at all, is now oriented towards consumption rather than production. Most important, the end of modernism means that there is no longer a cultural space that validates the anti-commercial and esoteric literary work. Whatever the writer's source of income in the phase of production, the completed work will be directed towards material success and renown in the marketplace; and if someone were to write a new *Ulysses*, the market niche labeled "cult novel" would be there waiting for it.

The grand theory of the death of literature by commodification is inconsistent with another leftist claim, that English culture has declined because of the relative failure of the English economy. England's loss of pre-eminence in the twentieth century was inevitable, given its population and resources, though anti-industrial tendencies in English culture may have speeded the decline. But it would be hard to prove that the industrial superiority of Germany, the United States and Japan was a direct cause of success in the art of fiction (and still harder for the socialist realism that celebrated the Soviet Union's five-year plans). Industrialism has, in general, been a barren subject for fiction, except when it has played the role of cultural villain.

If English literature has declined in this century, it has not been because of any single, dominant cause such as industrial backwardness or the commodification of writing. The literary history of the United States, Canada and Australia suggests that good literature will not appear until its host society has achieved a certain degree of complexity, and has accumulated a past sufficient to feed the imagination – a cultural capital requiring a hundred and fifty years or more to achieve. Beyond this, great literature cannot be produced on demand, whether from market forces, desire for prestige, or the cultural decrees of Stalin or Mao. In considering the economics of English literature today, we can say something about works that are typical, but probably very little about the occasional, unpredictable masterpiece.

At the everyday level, English writing is in a healthy state, and will surely continue so. The location of economic activity tends to be remarkably stable, and probably more so for tertiary activities than for manufacturing. London has remained the global leader in specialized financial services for three hundred years. English-language publishing may be a larger industry in New York now than in London, but London retains its lead internationally: about thirty percent of British book production is exported, whereas U.S. publishers sell few books abroad. Britain's relatively weak performance in manufacturing in this century may not reflect weakness in national character or institutions, but rather a historical bias of the British economy towards finance and other tertiary activities. As this sector of the economy steadily increases, worldwide, Britain may regain an economic and cultural advantage over the "metal-bashers."

Another asset for British writing and publishing in the future is the rise of English as the first truly global language. Frank and Cook argue that competition between languages is winner-take-all: once a critical point has been passed, the leader will steadily move ahead of its rivals. English first established itself as a world standard for technical communication and is now an all-purpose *lingua franca*; about 1,200 - 1,500 million people have some knowledge of it.[55] Literary writers in many countries now compose and publish in English rather than their local vernacular.[56] A century after the merging of the American and British literary marketplaces, the rest of the world is now beginning to be absorbed into the English-language literary system. This starts with the global dissemination of English bestsellers in translation, and of subtitled movies and television programs, and will probably result in English becoming the first choice for global literary production, as it has already become for scientific communication.

It might be argued that globalization threatens established hierarchies, dispersing cultural activities more widely and diluting the power of capitals like London and New York. English writers have lived in the countryside for two centuries or more; American writers are even more widely dispersed and are often identified more with their regions than with a metropolitan literary scene. The consumption of writing is certainly more widespread, at least for those books taken up by the global mass media:

> The same kinds of trade agreements that have brought workers in Toronto into direct competition with workers in Chicago have also brought workers in Kyoto into direct competition with workers in Munich and Johannesburg. And each year a growing share of people in all these places will read books by the same authors, see films by the same directors, and buy clothing by the same designers.[57]

However, this widening of the market calls for ever-increasing sophistication in the design and marketing of goods. For books, this means that, regardless of where they are written or read, bestsellers are made in London and New York, as surely as film stars are now made in Hollywood and *only* there. Geoff Mulgan has argued that "the core areas of key value added still depend on geographical proximity" – that is, on strategic centers where there is a concentration of talent and where there can be fruitful unplanned meetings between top performers.[58] These centers support interlocking relations between clusters of skills: not just book editors, but also artists, reviewers, newspaper reporters, television presenters, agents, accountants.

It may seem a depressing prospect that the future of English literature should be so controlled by these market institutions, however finely attuned their workings may be. But if any margin of innocent cultural production remains, sheltered from global market forces, it is surely a shrinking one – just as global tourism renders elusive the mythical "unspoiled" destination. Literary diversity may be restricted to what is adaptable to the market, yet diversity may increase in absolute terms. And diversity may be the reliable quality that future readers can expect: no longer the *Bleak House* or *Middlemarch* that sums up a culture, but books that express one of many contending perspectives, as the only adequate representations of the society of difference-in-proximity that we now inhabit.

Notes

Chapter 1   Introduction: The Peculiarities of the English

1 Hirschman, *The Passions and the Interests. Political Arguments for Capitalism Before its Triumph* (Princeton: Princeton University Press 1997), p. 69.
2 Quoted in Hirschman, pp. 39-40.
3 Bourdieu, "A Reasoned Utopia and Economic Fatalism," *New Left Review* 227 (Jan/Feb 1998), 127.
4 Trollope, *Dr Thorne* (London: J.M. Dent, 1908), p. 10.
5 On this strain in the *Manifesto* see, for example, Marshall Berman's *All That is Solid Melts into Air: The Experience of Modernity* (New York: Simon & Schuster, 1982).
6 On an aspect of Marx that still resonates in current opposition to globalization see Stanley Moore, *Marx Versus Markets* (University Park: Pennsylvania State University Press, 1993).
7 Jonathan Dewald, "The Ruling Class in the Marketplace: Nobles and Money in Early Modern France," in Thomas Haskell and Richard Teichgraeber, eds. *The Culture of the Market: Historical Essays* (Cambridge: Cambridge University Press, 1993), p. 45.
8 Smith, *Lectures on Jurisprudence*, ed. R.L. Meek, D.D. Raphael and P.G. Stein (Oxford: Oxford University Press, 1978), p. 352. The quotation is from lectures given in 1762-63.
9 *An Inquiry into the Nature and Causes of the Wealth of Nations*. Ed. Edwin Cannan. 2 vols. (Chicago: University of Chicago Press, 1976), I, p. 18.
10 *Lectures*, p. 192.
11 Thomas J. Lewis, "Persuasion, Domination and Exchange: Adam Smith on the Political Consequences of Markets," *Canadian Journal of Political Science* XXXIII: 2 (June 2000), 283.
12 Smith, *Lectures*, p. 452.
13 Representative works are Marc Shell, *Money, Language, and Thought: Literary and Philosophical Economies from the Medieval to the Modern Era* (Berkeley: University of California Press, 1982); Jean-Joseph Goux, *The Coiners of Language* (Norman: University of Oklahoma Press, 1994). It is dangerous to equate theories of language (which shift from a substantive to a Saussurean perspective) with the actuality of the evolution of money, over time, towards "de-materialization." Language was de-materialized from the beginning, whereas money progressed from precious metal, to paper, to the intangible electronic media of the present. For an excellent cultural history of money, see James Buchan, *Frozen Desire: An Inquiry Into the Meaning of Money* (London: Picador, 1997).
14 In what follows, I subsume these two movements under the "new historicist" banner; for distinctions between them see, for example, the collection edited by Kiernan Ryan, *New Historicism and Cultural Materialism: A Reader* (London: Arnold, 1996).

15 *The Economics of the Imagination* (Amherst: University of Masachusetts Press, 1980).

16 Quoted in Aram Veeser, ed., *The New Historicism* (New York: Routledge, 1989), p. xiv.

17 Veeser, p. xiv. In Britain, following the lead of Raymond Williams, cultural materialists were more inclined to attempt a revision of the base/superstructure model, rather than simply considering it obsolete. See Williams, *Marxism and Literature* (Oxford: Oxford University Press, 1977).

18 Kevin Dettmar and Stephen Watt, eds., *Marketing Modernisms: Self-Promotion, Canonization, Rereading* (Ann Arbor: University of Michigan Press, 1996), p. 6.

19 Veeser, xi. In general, I prefer in this book to speak of the market system rather than of capitalism because writers and other cultural producers are, typically, neither capitalists nor employees.

20 See David Shumway, "The Star System in Literary Studies," *PMLA* vol. 112, no. 1 (January 1997): 85-100. I address some related issues in "The University in Pieces: Bill Readings and the Fate of the Humanities," *Profession 2000*, 89-96.

21 Gallagher, "Marxism and the New Historicism," in Veeser, p. 45.

22 "Is there Class in this Class," in Veeser, p. 226.

23 I argue this view in "'A Sort of Notch in the Donwell Estate': Intersections of Status and Class in Austen's *Emma*," *Eighteenth-Century Fiction*, vol. 12, no. 4 (July 2000): 533-548.

24 Sean Burke, *The Death and Return of the Author: Criticism and Subjectivity in Barthes, Foucault and Derrida.* 2nd ed. (Edinburgh: Edinburgh University Press, 1999). The emergent field of "print culture studies" tends to finesse the issue by concentrating on genres and discourses, thereby passing over in silence questions of individual authorial strategies.

25 Apart from the *Journal of Cultural Economics* itself, representative works include Dick Netzer, *The Subsidized Muse: Public Support for the Arts in the United States* (Cambridge: Cambridge University Press, 1978); Bruno Frey and Walter Pommerehne, *Muses and Markets: Explorations in the Economics of the Arts* (Oxford: Basil Blackwell, 1989); and Tyler Cowen, *In Praise of Commercial Culture* (Cambridge: Harvard University Press, 1998). In none of these books does Foucault's name occur in the index; conversely, books of this school are rarely cited by literary critics. However, the 1998 Exeter conference on economic criticism opened up some discussions between cultural economists and new historicists.

26 For a more cautious view than Cowen's see Russell Keat, *Cultural Goods and the Limits of the Market* (Houndmills: Macmillan Press, 2000).

27 Furet, *The Passing of an Illusion: The Idea of Communism in the Twentieth Century* (Chicago: University of Chicago Press, 1999), pp. 4-6. The most comprehensive recent refutation of the idea that communism was in principle superior to capitalism because "its intentions were good," is Stephane Courtois et al., *The Black Book of Communism: Crimes, Terror, Repression* (Cambridge: Harvard University Press, 1999).

28 Furet, p. 502.

29 *The General Theory of Employment,, Interest and Money* (London: Macmillan, 1973), p. 380. Hayek goes further in claiming an intrinsic radicalism for the liberal ideal: "true liberalism is still distinct from conservatism, and there is danger in the two being confused. Conservatism, though a necessary element in

any stable society, is not a social program; in its paternalistic, nationalistic, and power-adoring tendencies it is often closer to socialism than true liberalism . . . . A conservative movement, by its very nature, is bound to be a defender of established privilege and to lean on the power of government for the protection of privilege. The essence of the liberal position, however, is the denial of all privilege, if by privilege is understood in its proper and original meaning of the state granting and protecting rights to some which are not available, on equal terms to others." Friedrich Hayek, *The Road to Serfdom* (Chicago: University of Chicago Press, [1954]), pp. ix-x.

30 "The Peculiarities of the English," in *The Poverty of Theory and Other Essays* (London: Merlin Press, 1978). Here and throughout, I use "English" consciously to indicate that I am not attempting to deal with the specific economics of the "Celtic fringe," and its associated literatures.

31 Quoted in David Cannadine, *Class in Britain* (New Haven: Yale University Press, 1998), p. 186.

32 Walter Michaels, *The Gold Standard and the Logic of Naturalism* (Berkeley: University of California Press, 1987), p. 93.

33 In 1900, well over half of all wealth was held by one percent of the population: W.D. Rubinstein, *Wealth and Inequality in Britain* (London: Faber & Faber, 1986), pp. 89-91.

34 Dickens, *Great Expectations* (Harmondsworth: Penguin, 1965), p. 229.

35 *Wealth of Nations*, II, p. 439.

36 See, for example, Bruce Collins and Keith Robbins, eds. *British Culture and Economic Decline* (London: Weidenfeld & Nicolson, 1990); Corelli Barnett, *The Audit of War: The Illusion and Reality of Britain as a Great Nation* (London: Macmillan, 1986).

37 Ingham, *Capitalism Divided? The City and Industry in British Social Development* (London: Macmillan, 1984).

38 Martin Wiener, *English Culture and the Decline of the Industrial Spirit 1850-1980* (Cambridge: Cambridge University Press, 1981).

39 Vernon, *Money and Fiction* (Ithaca: Cornell University Press, 1984).

40 Brinley Thomas, "The Historical Record of International Capital Movements to 1913," in John H. Dunning, ed., *International Investment: Selected Readings* (Harmondsworth: Penguin, 1972), pp. 39, 34.

41 The shift from the productivism of Adam Smith and the political economists to modern consumerism is of great interest, but beyond the scope of this book. See Neil McKendrick, John Brewer and J.H. Plumb, *The Birth of a Consumer Society: The Commercialization of Eighteenth-Century England* (London: Europa, 1982); Colin Campbell, *The Romantic Ethic and the Spirit of Modern Consumerism* (Oxford: Basil Blackwell, 1987); John Brewer and Roy Porter, eds. *Consumption and the World of Goods* (London & New York: Routledge, 1993).

42 Authors may evade market imperatives by having private means, but it is significant that there have been so few successful efforts at direct resistance by controlling demand or supply. The Soviet writers' union ensured privileges for its members, but produced little worthwhile literature. In Germany, a cartel of poets from 1902 to 1933 enforced a minimum fee of 50 pfennigs per line for reprinting in anthologies, but failed when too many poets were willing to accept less (see Frey & Pommerehne, *Muses and Markets*, p. 181). Perhaps the most successful writers' collective existed at the *New Yorker*, where writers

were given an office and a regular income as an advance against future contributions; see Ved Mehta, *Remembering Mr Shawn's* New Yorker (Woodstock, NY: Overlook Press, 1998).

43 Jameson, "Reification and Utopia in Mass Culture," *Social Text* 1 (1979), 140.

44 Quoted in N.C. Edsall, *Richard Cobden: Independent Radical* (Cambridge: Harvard University Press, 1987), p. 11.

45 For an example of productivist literary theory, see Pierre Macherey, *A Theory of Literary Production* (London: Routledge & Kegan Paul, 1978).

Chapter 2   Who's Who: Land, Money and Identity in Trollope

1 Trollope, *An Autobiography* (Berkeley: University of California Press, 1947), p. 90.

2 Ibid., p. 91.

3 Jonathan Swift, *The Correspondence of Jonathan Swift*, Volume II, ed. Harold Williams (Oxford: Clarendon Press, 1963), p. 373.

4 See Juliet McMaster, "Trollope's Country Estates," in John Halperin, ed., *Trollope Centenary Essays* (London and Basingstoke: The Macmillan Press, 1982), pp. 70-85.

5 *The Way We Live Now* (Oxford: Oxford University Press, 1982), I, p. 132.

6 *Phineas Finn* (London: Oxford University Press, 1937), I, p. 207.

7 *Mr Scarborough's Family* (Oxford: Oxford University Press, 1989), p. 389.

8 *Phineas Redux* (London: Oxford University Press, 1937), I, p. 146.

9 G.E. Mingay, *Land and Society in England 1750-1980* (London: Longman, 1994), p. 65.

10 Lawrence Stone in *The New York Review of Books*, 2 March 1989, 12. See also Lawrence Stone and Jeanne C. Fawtier Stone, *An Open Elite: England, 1540-1880* (Oxford: Clarendon Press, 1984).

11 For aristocratic involvement in property development see David Cannadine, *Lords and Landlords: The Aristocracy and the Towns, 1774-1967* (Leicester: Leicester University Press, 1980).

12 See Walter L. Arnstein, "The Survival of the Victorian Aristocracy," in Frederic Cople Jaher, ed., *The Rich, the Well Born, and the Powerful* (Urbana: University of Illinois Press, 1973), pp. 203-57.

13 Open ballots were also an incentive for landlords to grant only short leases to their tenants, so that they could be denied renewal if they opposed their landlord's election candidates; this applied to many urban tenants as well as tenant farmers and others dependent on the goodwill of their local aristocrat.

14 *The Prime Minister* (London: Oxford University Press, 1938), I, p. 146.

15 For example, when Sir Francis Baring died in 1810, two-thirds of his estate of £625,000 was in land and only £68,500 remained as capital in the family merchant bank. By the 1880s the Baring family held two peerages and had accumulated 89,000 acres in Hampshire. Philip Ziegler, *The Sixth Great Power: Barings, 1762-1929* (London: Collins, 1988), pp. 51, 188.

16 Vernon, *Money and Fiction: Literary Realism in the Nineteenth and Early Twentieth Centuries* (Ithaca: Cornell University Press, 1984), pp. 7, 17, 33-34. The "paper money men" constituted the so-called "Banking School," who welcomed the ability of the banks to create money by issuing notes as required

by the growth of commerce. They were opposed by the "Currency School," who wanted banknotes to be tied directly to gold reserves and whose views prevailed in Peel's Charter Act of 1844.

17 See Walter Benn Michaels, *The Gold Standard and the Logic of Naturalism* (Berkeley and Los Angeles: University of California Press, 1987).

18 *The Prime Minister*, I, p. 374. Land sold in the nineteenth century for about thirty-five times its annual rentals, equivalent to the steady three percent paid on government bonds. This was considered the "natural" and reliable return on capital, appropriate to a stable ruling class whose unearned income freed them for the task of governing England. Cf. Archdeacon Grantly's reasons for buying land, even when it yields only two and a half percent: "Land is about the only thing that can't fly away. And then, you see, land gives so much more than the rent. It gives position and influence and political power, to say nothing about the game." *The Last Chronicle of Barset* (London: Penguin, 1986), p. 612.

19 *The Prime Minister*, II, p. 37.

20 Ibid., I, p. 274. The doctrine is now standard practice in U.S. commodity markets, where less than one percent of futures contracts traded are actually settled by delivery of the goods.

21 *The Prime Minister*, II, p. 70.

22 *The Way We Live Now*, I, pp. 279, 277.

23 See Tony Tanner, "Trollope's *The Way We Live Now*: Its Modern Significance," *Critical Quarterly* 9, 3 (Autumn 1967), 264-65.

24 Georg Simmel, *The Philosophy of Money*, trans. Tom Bottomore and David Frisby (London: Routledge and Kegan Paul, 1978), pp. 221, 223, 225.

25 Ibid., p. 221.

26 William Cobbett, *Rural Rides* (London: Dent, 1957), I, pp. 163-164.

27 Ibid., I, p. 97.

28 Cf. Adam Smith, "The capital, however, that is acquired to any country by commerce and manufactures, is all a very precarious and uncertain possession, till some part of it has been secured and realised in the cultivation and improvement of its lands. A merchant, it has been said very properly, is not necessarily the citizen of any particular country. It is in a great measure indifferent to him from what place he carries on his trade; and a very trifling disgust will make him remove his capital, and together with it all the industry which it supports, from one country to another." *Wealth of Nations*, I, pp. 444-45.

29 For Trollope's attitudes to Judaism see R.H. Super, *The Chronicler of Barsetshire: A Life of Anthony Trollope* (Ann Arbor: University of Michigan Press, 1988), index under "Jews, Jewish."

30 Edgar Rosenberg has analyzed Augustus Melmotte as an anti-semitic stereotype of the dishonest financier: *From Shylock to Svengali: Jewish Stereotypes in English Fiction* (Stanford: Stanford University Press, 1960), pp. 140-50.

31 *The Letters of Anthony Trollope, Volume II, 1871-1882*, ed. N. John Hall (Stanford: Stanford University Press, 1983), p. 585.

32 Melmotte may also be linked with Claude Melnotte, a gardener's son who impersonates the Prince of Como in Bulwer-Lytton's drama *The Lady of Lyons* (1838). See J. Joyce, *A Portrait of the Artist as a Young Man* (New York: Viking, 1964), pp. 97, 99.

33 The notes are transcribed as "The Dramatis Personae Plan" in John A. Sutherland, "Trollope at Work on The Way We Live Now," *NCF* 37, 3 (December
1982): 472-93. It reinforces my point that Trollope first called the Melmotte
character "Samuel" or "Emanuel Treegrene" (an anglicization of
"Grunebaum"?), then erased and wrote "Augustus Melmotte." Nonetheless,
critics persist in simply taking it for granted that Melmotte is of Jewish origin.
Apart from Rosenberg, see Bertha Keveson Hertz, "Trollope's Racial Bias
Against Disraeli," *Midwest Q* 22, 4 (Summer 1981), 372-91; and Derek Cohen,
"Constructing the Contradiction: Anthony Trollope's *The Way We Live
Now*," in Derek Cohen and Deborah Heller, eds., *Jewish Presences in English Literature* (Montreal: McGill-Queen's University Press, 1990), pp. 61-75.
34 *The Way We Live Now*, I, p. 32.
35 Ibid., I, pp. 106-107. There are indications that Melmotte got his first substantial capital by marrying Madame Melmotte (I, p. 33); if so, he launched his career as a swindler not as a Jew, but by imposing on the Jews.
36 Annie's parents eventually accepted her marriage, partly because it was
agreed that bride and groom would each retain their religion. Compare, in
The Way We Live Now, the proposal made by the Jewish banker Brehgert to
Georgiana Longestaffe that their sons should be brought up as Jews, their
daughters as Christians. After Meyer Rothschild's death his only child
Hannah made a similar marriage, to the Earl of Rosebery (to whom she
brought a fortune of some two million pounds). Derek Wilson, *Rothschild: A
Story of Wealth and Power* (London: André Deutsch, 1988), pp. 217-25, 263-64.
37 *The Prime Minister*, I, p. 275. Later, when hard pressed, Lopez does forge a
name (like Melmotte), posthumously ruining Sexty Parker and his deserving
family (II, p. 328).
38 Ibid., I, pp. 3-4.
39 Cf. *The Prime Minister*: "We all know the man, – a little man generally who
moves seldom and softly, – who looks always as though he had just been sent
home in a bandbox. Ferdinand Lopez was not a little man, and moved freely
enough; but never, at any moment . . . was he dressed otherwise than with
perfect care. Money and time did it, but folk thought that it grew with him, as
did his hair and his nails." (I, p. 6).
40 Ibid., I, p. 35.
41 Ibid., II, p. 209.
42 Trollope's most sustained and explicit anti-semitism is directed against a Jew,
Mr Emilius, who has gone to the theoretical extreme of assimilation by becoming a Church of England clergyman:
43 *The Prime Minister*, I, pp. 92-93.
44 Trollope, *Autobiography*, pp. 10, 14.
45 Ibid., p. 301.

Chapter 3   The Market for Women

1 Land was the central good for feudalism, but other appurtenances of the aristocratic lifestyle also were excluded from the market. In his discussion of medieval forests, Oliver Rackham notes: "Venison was no ordinary meat: it was a
special dish for feasts and the honouring of guests. It was beyond price – I

have not a single record of a sale or valuation – and a haunch was a gift that money could not buy. . . . The king bestowed deer on favoured subjects, often in honour of their weddings, graduations, consecrations, pregnancies, and other festive occasions." *The History of the Countryside* (London: Weidenfeld and Nicolson, 1995), pp. 125, 135.

2 For the influence of money on the French aristocracy in the sixteenth and seventeenth centuries, see Jonathan Dewald, "The Ruling Class in the Market-place: Nobles and Money in Early Modern France," in Thomas Haskell and Richard Teichgraeber, eds., *The Culture of the Market: Historical Essays* (Cambridge: Cambridge University Press, 1993), pp. 43-65.

3 See Gayle Rubin, "The Traffic of Women: Notes on the Political Economy of Sex," in Rayna R. Reiter, ed., *Toward an Anthropology of Women* (New York: Monthly Review Press, 1975).

4 Henry James, *The Wings of the Dove* (Harmondsworth: Penguin, 1965), p. 7.

5 John Habakkuk, *Marriage, Debt, and the Estates System: English Landownership 1650-1950* (Oxford: Clarendon Press, 1994), pp. 1-2. A life tenant could not sell, lease, or will his land, or mortgage it for a term beyond his own life. Settlements were typically renewed in each generation: for example, when he married the heir-apparent would settle the family estate on his first son.

6 Mary Lyndon Shanley, *Feminism, Marriage and the Law in Victorian England, 1850 - 1895* (Princeton: Princeton University Press, 1989), p. 8.

7 Quoted in Adeline Hartcup, *Love and Marriage in the Great Country Houses* (London: Sidgwick & Jackson, 1984), p. 16.

8 Trollope, *Framley Parsonage* (Oxford: Oxford University Press, 1980), pp. 457, 452.

9 Habakkuk, pp. 5, 172.

10 Madame Goesler, the widow of a banker (who may have been Jewish) appears in Trollope's *Phineas Finn* and *Phineas Redux*; Miss Dunstable, whose father invented a successful patent medicine, is in *Framley Parsonage* and *Doctor Thorne*. Habakkuk notes that an aristocrat would expect a larger dowry when marrying the daughter of a merchant than a woman from his own caste; beauty could also be part of the equation (p. 151).

11 Trollope, *The Claverings* (Oxford: Oxford University Press, 1986), pp. 3-4.

12 Hartcup, p. 91.

13 *The Claverings*, p. 42.

14 Ibid., p. 331.

15 Ibid., p. 32.

16 Georg Simmel, *The Philosophy of Money* (London: Routledge & Kegan Paul, 1978), p. 383.

17 *The Claverings*, pp. 481, 480.

18 From the sixteenth century, equity was the province of the Court of Chancery, which was absorbed into the High Court in 1873.

19 Lee Holcombe, *Wives and Property: Reform of the Married Women's Property Law in Nineteenth-century England* (Toronto: University of Toronto Press, 1983), p. 38.

20 Widows would also be expected to move out of the family home when their sons married, into a dower house.

21 Ralph Thicknesse, "The New Legal Position of Married Women," *Blackwood's Edinburgh Magazine* 133 (1883): 207-220. Quoted in Holcombe, p. 218.

22 Simmel, pp. 378, 376.
23 Walter Benn Michaels, *The Gold Standard and the Logic of Naturalism: American Literature at the Turn of the Century* (Berkeley: University of California Press, 1987), pp. 20-21, 28.
24 Karl Marx, *Early Writings* (Harmondsworth: Penguin, 1975), pp. 193, 182.
25 *The Claverings*, pp. 120-27.
26 *Framley Parsonage*, p. 574. This is Trollope's description of Griselda Grantly after she becomes the wife of Lord Dumbello; the tone is in fact ironic, but it conveys the conventional wisdom about aristocratic marriage.
27 In *The Way We Live Now*, Georgiana Longestaffe bargains for a house in town as well as the one her fiancé already has at Fulham; she is rightly punished when he prefers to break the engagement (II, pp. 276-278). The same scenario is repeated in a comic mode when Miss Thoroughbung, the brewer's daughter, demands of Mr Prosper that she should have a pony-carriage with two ponies after their marriage. *Mr Scarborough's Family* (Oxford: Oxford University Press, 1989), pp. 408-414.
28 Trollope, *Phineas Finn* (London: Oxford University Press, 1937), chapters 40, 72.
29 *Phineas Redux* (St Albans: Panther Books, 1973), p. 634.
30 James, *The House of Fiction: Essays on the Novel by Henry James*. Ed. Leon Edel (London: Mercury Books, 1962), p. 105. Trollope's typical "American girl" is Winifred Hurtle in *The Way We Live Now*.
31 James, *The Wings of the Dove* (Harmondsworth: Penguin, 1965), p. 22.
32 Ibid., p. 55.
33 Ibid., p. 35.
34 Ibid., pp. 129, 82.
35 Ibid., pp. 85, 118, 106.
36 Ibid., pp. 57, 181.
37 Ibid., p. 348.
38 Jean-Christophe Agnew, "The Consuming Vision of Henry James," in Richard W. Fox and T.J. Jackson Lears, eds., *The Culture of Consumption: Critical Essays in American History, 1880-1980* (New York: Pantheon, 1983), p. 79.
39 Agnew, p. 94.
40 *Wings of the Dove*, p. 231.
41 Agnew, p. 84.
42 James, *House of Fiction*, p. 244.
43 *House of Fiction*, pp. 227, 75.
44 Though James, like Trollope, lived predominantly on his literary earnings; see Chapter 8 below.
45 Agnew, p. 100.

Chapter 4   Money, Marriage, and the Writer's Life: Gissing and Woolf

1 Allowing for inflation, Gissing's dream of £300 a year in the 1890s roughly corresponds to Woolf's £500 in 1929.
2 *The Collected Essays, Journalism and Letters. Volume IV: In Front of Your Nose*

1945-1950 (Harmondsworth: Penguin, 1970), p. 487. For Orwell's early interest in Gissing, which probably included taking Gissing's first name for his pseudonym, see Bernard Crick, *George Orwell: A Life* (Harmondsworth: Penguin, 1982), p. 213.

3 Lionel Tarrant in *In the Year of Jubilee* (London: J.M. Dent, 1994), p. 342.

4 *Collected Essays IV*, p. 488.

5 *Down and Out in Paris and London* (London: Secker & Warburg, 1986), p. 207.

6 Gissing, *New Grub Street* (Harmondsworth: Penguin, 1985), p. 37.

7 *New Grub Street*, p. 256.

8 Gissing himself produced fifteen novels in twelve years (1885-1897), and felt that he was killing himself with work.

9 Duncan Porter and Peter Graham, eds., *The Portable Darwin* (London: Penguin, 1993), pp. 356-57. The quotation is from *The Descent of Man, and Selection in Relation to Sex* (1871).

10 *New Grub Street*, p. 523.

11 Ibid., p. 526.

12 *The Odd Women* (New York: New American Library, 1983), p. 334.

13 In fact, Barfoot's offer was made as a test of Rhoda's love, and he is willing to marry her legally, though Rhoda's objections to marriage would still remain (p. 299).

14 *In the Year of Jubilee*, pp. 354-55.

15 Ibid., p. 356

16 Ibid., p. 21.

17 Gilman, *Women and Economics: A Study of the Economic Relation Between Men and Women as a Factor in Social Evolution*. Ed. Carl N. Degler. (New York: Harper & Row, 1966), pp. 118-19.

18 *New Grub Street*, p. 394.

19 Ibid., p. 550.

20 Ibid., p. 397.

21 Ibid., pp. 397-98.

22 See the savage portrait of the Peachey sisters in the opening chapter of *In the Year of Jubilee*.

23 *The Essays of Virginia Woolf. Volume I: 1904-1912.* Ed. Andrew McNeillie (London: Hogarth Press, 1986), p. 357.

24 Zwerdling, *Virginia Woolf and the Real World* (Berkeley: University of California Press, 1986), p. 105.

25 Woolf, *A Room of One's Own* (New York: Harcourt, Brace, 1929), pp. 12-13.

26 Ibid., pp. 15, 39.

27 "It is only for the last forty-eight years that Mrs Seton has had a penny of her own" (p. 38). Writing in 1928, Woolf mis-dates the Married Women's Property Act as 1880 instead of 1882.

28 *Room*, pp. 63-64.

29 *The Flight of the Mind: The Letters of Virginia Woolf. Volume I: 1888 - 1912* (London: Hogarth Press, 1975), p. 155.

30 *Room of One's Own*, p. 64.

31 *The Diary of Virginia Woolf. Volume I: 1915-1919.* Ed. Anne Olivier Bell (London: Hogarth Press, 1977), pp. 253-54.

32 *Diary II*, p. 155 (3 Jan. 1922). Woolf did return to reviewing, though mainly in *The Nation*, of which Leonard became literary editor in 1923.

33 Quoted in Hugh Kenner, *A Sinking Island: The Modern English Writers* (London: Barrie & Jenkins, 1988), p. 160.
34 *Room of One's Own*, pp. 120-21.
35 Woolf, *Three Guineas* (London: Hogarth Press, 1938), p. 162.
36 Ibid., pp. 166, 168.
37 Ibid., p. 169.
38 *Letters* I, p. 214.
39 *Room of One's Own*, p. 67.
40 Woolf, *The Captain's Death Bed and Other Essays* (London: Hogarth Press, 1950), p. 101.
41 Ibid., pp. 92-93.
42 Forster, *Howards End* (Harmondsworth: Penguin, 1975), p. 72.

Chapter 5   Conrad and the Economics of Imperialism: *Heart of Darkness*

1 For Said's wary view of post-colonialism see his Afterword to the 1994 edition of *Orientalism* (New York: Vintage). Post-colonialism is usually dated from Bill Ashcroft, Gareth Griffiths, and Helen Tiffin, *The Empire Writes Back: Theory and Practice in Post-colonial Literatures* (London: Routledge, 1989).
2 *Wealth of Nations*, II, pp. 131-132.
3 Jean Darcy, *Cent Années de Rivalité Coloniale* (1904); quoted in Leonard Woolf, *Empire and Commerce in Africa: A Study in Economic Imperialism* (New York: Howard Fertig, 1968. 1st. ed. 1920), p. 27. "Nowadays, the expansion of a race beyond its frontiers is the condition of its survival, the modern form of the struggle for existence . . . in these times of universal competition, whoever fails to advance falls behind, and who falls behind is drowned by the tide."
4 *The Times*, 5 May. Salisbury was then Prime Minister. Conrad referred to Salisbury's comments in a letter to Cunninghame Graham, *The Collected Letters of Joseph Conrad*, Ed. Frederick Karl and Laurence Davies (Cambridge: Cambridge University Press, 1983 –), II, p. 228.
5 For internal differences within Marxist theories of imperialism, see Anthony Brewer, *Marxist Theories of Imperialism: A Critical Survey* (Second edition, London: Routledge, 1990).
6 Patrick K. O'Brien, "The Costs and Benefits of British Imperialism 1846-1914" *Past and Present* 120 (August 1988), 173-174. The total overseas investment in this period was £3163 million, more than twice as much as was invested in the British domestic economy. Sixty-one percent of overseas money went to foreign countries (mainly the U.S.); twenty-eight percent to the Dominions; the remainder to India and the colonies. Figures for the export of human capital (i.e. emigration) would be in the same range. There is some evidence for high imperial profits for 1860-1884, though not for 1885-1912 (179).
7 Davis, Lance, and Robert Huttenback, *Mammon and the Pursuit of Empire: The Political Economy of British Imperialism, 1860-1912* (Cambridge: Cambridge University Press, 1986), pp. 161-165; but see also O'Brien, 189ff. The main costs were for the navy and for stationing about 120,000 troops overseas. Colonial administration was extraordinarily cheap: "the British Empire at the apogee of its existence [i.e. 1892-96] was managed by less than 6,000 souls"

(Davis & Huttenback, p. 14).

8 Schumpeter, *Imperialism. Social Classes* (Cleveland: World Publishing, 1955), p. 65.

9 Schumpeter, pp. 66-69.

10 V.I. Lenin, *Imperialism, the Highest Stage of Capitalism* (Peking: Foreign Languages, 1973); J.A. Hobson, *Imperialism* (London: Allen & Unwin, 1938).

11 O'Brien, pp. 195, 181.

12 Conrad derided the emergent exceptionalism of the U.S. in the Spanish American war; he agreed with his friend Cunninghame Graham that the open imperialism of the Old World was preferable to the hypocrisy (as he saw it) of the New: "The [Americans] may well shout Fiat Lux! It will be only the reflected light of a silver dollar and no sanctimonious pretence will make it resemble the real sunshine" (*Letters II*, p. 60).

13 *Letters II*, p. 230; 25 Dec. 1899. Conrad was writing to Aniela Zagorska who, along with most of Continental educated opinion, favored the Boers. At other times, his own view of the war was more cynical; see Zdzislaw Najder, *Conrad's Polish Background: Letters to and from Polish Friends* (London: Oxford University Press, 1964), pp. 261-62.

14 Quoted in Najder, p. 75.

15 *Letters I*, p. 59; 26 Sept. 1890. "a vulgar ivory-merchant of sordid instincts who thinks of himself as a man of business when in fact he's nothing but a kind of African shopkeeper."

16 D.C.M. Platt, *Finance, Trade and Politics in British Foreign Policy 1815-1914* (Oxford: Clarendon Press, 1968).

17 Parry, *Conrad and Imperialism: Ideological Boundaries and Visionary Frontiers* (London: Macmillan, 1983), p. 15.

18 *Gravity's Rainbow* (New York: Viking, 1973), p. 317.

19 The colony in *Gravity's Rainbow* is not the Congo but the German-held South West Africa, where in 1904-08 a native rebellion was cruelly suppressed.

20 See John McClure, "The Rhetoric of Restraint: *Heart of Darkness*," *Nineteenth Century Fiction* 32, no. 3 (1977): 310-26.

21 *Heart of Darkness*. Ed. Robert Kimbrough (New York: W.W. Norton, 1973), pp. 34, 57.

22 Quoted in J. Stengers, "King Leopold's Imperialism," in Roger Owen & Bob Sutcliffe, eds., *Studies in the Theory of Imperialism* (London: Longman, 1972), p. 263. "The Dutch Indian army, the Indian navy, the Indian administration, are three immense careers open to the activity of Dutch youth. In India, every English family has one or two of their children who live there, and seek and find fortune. These fortunes come back to London and this capital, like a hive where the bees, after having sucked the best flowers, come to deposit their honey, is one of the richest towns in the world."

23 Ricard, quoted in Albert O. Hirschman, "Rival Interpretations of Market Society: Civilizing, Destructive, or Feeble?" *Journal of Economic Literature* 20 (Dec. 1982), 1465.

24 Quoted in Hirschman, 1464.

25 David Ricardo, *On the Principles of Political Economy and Taxation* (Cambridge: Cambridge University Press, 1986. 1st ed. 1817), p. 100. See Regenia Gagnier, "On the Insatiability of Human Wants: Economic and Aesthetic Man," *Victorian Studies* 36:2 (Winter 1993): 125-53.

26 Quoted in Wendy Hinde, *Richard Cobden: A Victorian Outsider* (New Haven: Yale University Press, 1987), p. 208.
27 To proclaim a free-trade colony was unusual for the old imperial powers, and Leopold found it relatively easy to establish himself in the Congo in consequence. See Stengers, pp. 273-274.
28 See Hawkins, 289-291.
29 *Heart of Darkness*, pp. 55-56.
30 *Wealth of Nations*, II, p. 81.
31 *Letters I*, p. 294; 22 July 1896.
32 *Heart of Darkness*, p. 51.
33 Fredric Jameson, *The Political Unconscious* (Ithaca: Cornell University Press, 1981), p. 220.
34 Ibid., p. 227.
35 When Stanley set off from Zanzibar to find Livingstone, he took with him three hundred and fifty pounds of No. 5 and No. 6 brass wire; when he found Livingstone at Ujiji, he had not found any tribes willing to take the wire as currency. James Buchan, *Frozen Desire: An Inquiry into the Meaning of Money* (London: Picador, 1997), p. 284.
36 *Heart of Darkness*, p. 9.

Chapter 6   *Nostromo:* Economism and its Discontents

1 *The Works of Jeremy Bentham*, ed. John Bowring, II (New York: Russell & Russell, 1962), p. 547. Bentham was writing around 1786-89.
2 *The Political Writings. Volume I* (London: William Ridgeway, 1868), pp. 299, 307. Cobden goes on to show that the costs of the navy far outweigh any possible profit from the trade it protects, and that "no class or calling of society can derive permanent benefit from war" (p. 328). Marx and Engels were perhaps echoing Cobden's formula when they spoke in *The Communist Manifesto*, of "cheapness" as the irresistible weapon used by the great trading nations to penetrate less developed societies.
3 See D.C.M. Platt, *Finance, Trade, and Politics in British Foreign Policy 1815-1914* (Oxford: Clarendon Press, 1968), pp. 86ff. The Navigation Acts, which protected British merchant shipping, were repealed in 1849.
4 While Conrad was on his honeymoon in 1896, Unwin sent him the special issue of the *Daily News* celebrating the fiftieth anniversary of the repeal of the Corn Laws, to which Unwin was a contributor. Conrad, however, disliked both Unwin's business practices and his Liberal politics.
5 Conrad, *Notes on Life and Letters* (London: J.M. Dent, 1921), p. 289.
6 The mine's product, silver, follows a similar evolution: first as booty for the Spanish, then as a national treasure that cannot be exploited, finally as the abstract medium of circulation for a global monetary system. *Heart of Darkness* presents a more immediate object of desire in ivory, an organic substance used for adornment.
7 *Nostromo: A Tale of the Seaboard* (London: Penguin, 1990), p. 75.
8 Ibid., p. 100.
9 Ibid., pp. 99, 119-20.

10 Ibid., p. 431.

11 Ibid., pp. 93, 431.

12 Ibid., p. 423.

13 Ibid., p. 417.

14 *The Collected Letters of Joseph Conrad*. Ed. Frederick Karl and Laurence Davies (Cambridge: Cambridge University Press, 1983—), I, p. 425.

15 Said, *Beginnings: Intention and Method* (New York: Basic Books, 1975), p. 133.

16 *Nostromo*, p. 422.

17 Ibid., p. 332. The same opposition, though on different grounds, comes from the reactionary landed interest, "all these Don Ambrosios this and Don Fernandos that, who seemed actually to dislike and distrust the coming of the railway over their lands" (p. 64).

18 *Nostromo*, p. 377.

19 Ibid., p. 417. The miners are Indians, who in the war of secession embraced European universalism: "In a very few years the sense of belonging to a powerful organization had been developed in these harassed, half-wild Indians. They were proud of, and attached to, the mine. It had secured their confidence and belief" (p. 336). Conrad notes their movement into an oppositional economic consciousness, but does not imagine them reverting to a particularist cultural identity.

20 The financiers in these novels are the Duc de Mersch, whose project is a railway across Greenland, and de Barral, whose Sceptre Trust goes bankrupt. For Conrad's involvement with mining as promoter and speculator, see Frederick Karl, *Joseph Conrad: The Three Lives* (London: Faber & Faber, 1979), pp. 355-56, 376.

21 *Nostromo*, p. 275.

22 *Letters II*, p. 25.

23 For Gareth Jenkins, this puts Conrad effectively on the Right: "[he] endorses, quietly but irrefutably, a particular type of class undertaking and a bourgeois-democratic revolution, no matter how fragile and brief the achievements of the society born therefrom." "Conrad's *Nostromo* and History," *Literature and History* 6 (Autumn 1977), 174.

24 See Francis Fukuyama, *The End of History and the Last Man* (New York: Free Press, 1992). However, Fukuyama never mentions Cobden or identifies economism as an ideology.

25 Quoted in Keith Hutchinson,*The Decline and Fall of British Capitalism* (Hamden, Conn.: Archon, 1966), p. 29.

26 See Santiago Colás, "Of Creole Symptoms, Cuban Fantasies, and Other Latin American Postcolonial Ideologies," *PMLA* 110 (May 1995): 382-396.

27 p. 94. The original claim of Manifest Destiny, in the 1840s, was that the United States would expand until it reached the Pacific. Smith Sound is the strait that divides Ellesmere Island, in the Canadian Arctic, from Greenland; so that Holroyd's U.S. would rule the Americas from North to South, as well as East to West.

28 Parry, "Narrating Imperialism: *Nostromo*'s Dystopia," In Keith Ansell-Pearson, Benita Parry and Judith Squires, eds., *The Gravity of History: Reflections on the Work of Edward Said* (London: Lawrence and Wishart, 1996), 230-31.

29 *Letters II*, p. 230.

30 Hutchinson, *British Capitalism*, p. 258.

31 Buell, *National Culture and the New Global System* (Baltimore: Johns Hopkins University Press, 1994).
32 The rubric for this school was "dependency theory," which assumed that economic relations between center and periphery were necessarily exploitive. Immanuel Wallerstein, *The Essential Wallerstein* (New York: New Press, 2000); Raúl Prebisch, *Capitalismo Periférico: Crisis y Transformación* (Mexico: Fondo de Cultura Económica, 1984); André Gunder Frank, *Capitalism and Underdevelopment in Latin America: Historical Studies of Chile and Brazil* (New York: Monthly Review Press, 1960).
33 Buell, p. 116.
34 Quoted in Buell, pp. 115-116.
35 Quoted in Cedric Watts and Laurence Davies, *Cunninghame Graham: A Critical Biography* (Cambridge: Cambridge University Press, 1979), p. 144.
36 Watts, p. 144. The context of Conrad's exchange with Cunninghame Graham was the American campaign to detach Panama from Colombia; this succeeded in November 1903, when Conrad was still writing *Nostromo*.
37 Arif Dirlik posits a similar shift from force to incentive in the rise of "trilateralism" after the U.S. defeat in Vietnam: "A policy of attracting revolutionary or socialist states within the orbit of capitalism rather than containing them militarily." *After the Revolution: Waking to Global Capitalism* (Hanover: Wesleyan University Press, 1994), p. 48.
38 Orwell, *Burmese Days* (Harmondsworth: Penguin, 1967), pp. 37-38.
39 Parry, "Problems in Current Theories of Colonial Discourse," *Oxford Literary Review* 9, nos. 1-2 (1987), 43.
40 *Nostromo* appeared in October 1904; "Autocracy and War," a reflection on Japan's victory over Russia, was published in the *Fortnightly Review* of 1 July 1905.
41 Conrad, "Autocracy and War," in *Notes on Life and Letters* (London: J.M. Dent, 1921), p. 142.
42 Ibid., p. 151.
43 Friedrich Hayek, *The Road to Serfdom* (London: Routledge & Kegan Paul, 1976), p. 170.
44 Britain had, of course, used force in defense of its interests from time to time; but Cobden argued that the existence of mutual commercial advantage would make it less likely that nations would resort to force.
45 Wells, *Experiment in Autobiography* (London: Faber, 1984), pp. 762-63.
46 He saw the only practical solution in the division of the world into "spheres of trade" ("Autocracy" p. 142), so that each of the Great Powers could develop its sphere without coming into conflict with the others.
47 Akin to the Chilean civil war over nitrate, mentioned in *Nostromo*, pp. 93-94. See Michael Montéon, *Chile in the Nitrate Era: The Evolution of Economic Dependence, 1880-1930* (Madison: University of Wisconsin Press, 1982).

Chapter 7   The New Literary Marketplace

1 Wendell R. Smith, "Product Differentiation and Market Segmentation as Alternative Marketing Strategies," in Ben Enis & Keith Cox, eds., *Marketing Classics: A Selection of Influential Articles* (Boston: Allyn & Bacon, 1969), pp. 380-81.

2 Kathleen M. Rassuli, "Evidence of Marketing Strategy in the Early Printed Book Trade," in Terence Nevett & Ronald Fullerton, eds., *Historical Perspectives in Marketing: Essays in Honor of Stanley C. Hollander* (Lexington, Mass.: Lexington Books, 1988), pp. 91-107.

3 Famously, in his decision to "kill" Mrs Proudie during the serialization of *The Last Chronicle of Barset*. Trollope, *An Autobiography* (Berkeley: University of California Press, 1947), pp. 230-231.

4 Trollope, for example, told Thomas Hardy that "I sell everything out and out to my publishers, so that I may have no further bargainings." *The Letters of Anthony Trollope*. 2 vols. Ed. N. John Hall (Stanford: Stanford University Press, 1983), II, p. 715. Hardy, more modern-minded, retained the copyright of his novels where possible.

5 Gagnier, *Idylls of the Marketplace: Oscar Wilde and the Victorian Public* (Stanford: Stanford University Press, 1986), p. 12.

6 In *New Grub Street*, Jasper Mylvain advises his sisters to write prize-books for money; that is, to identify a market segment and exploit it by meeting a specification rather than aiming at originality or intrinsic quality: "Get together half a dozen fair specimens of the Sunday-school prize; study them; discover the essential points of such composition; hit upon new attractions; then go to work methodically, so many pages a day. . . . I don't advocate the propagation of vicious literature; I speak only of good, coarse, marketable stuff for the world's vulgar." Gissing, *New Grub Street* (Harmondsworth: Penguin, 1985), p. 43.

7 James, "The Question of the Opportunities," in *Literary Criticism* (New York: Library of America, 1984), p. 653.

8 Jonathan Freedman, *Professions of Taste: Henry James, British Aestheticism, and Commodity Culture* (Stanford: Stanford University Press, 1990), p. xxvii.

9 McDonald, *British Literary Culture and Publishing Practice 1880-1914* (Cambridge: Cambridge University Press, 1997).

10 Cf. Ian Small: "The diverse nature of these failures [before 1891] is interesting, for it shows Wilde trying his hand (and his luck) at a variety of literary tasks and therefore at a variety of market sectors." Small, "The Economics of Taste: Literary Markets and Literary Value in the Late Nineteenth Century," *English Literature in Transition* 39: 1 (1996), 13.

11 Freedman, p. 47.

12 Pierre Bourdieu, *The Field of Cultural Production: Essays on Art and Literature*. Ed. Randal Johnson (Cambridge: Polity Press, 1993).

13 The creators of the mass market for newspapers in the 1890s realized that papers need not be stratified by class alone. There could be popular papers of the right as well as the left, and any political view would do as the basis for the "brand loyalty" of a large group of readers. For a critical study of this transition see Alan J. Lee, *The Origins of the Popular Press in England, 1855-1914* (London: Croom Helm, 1976).

14 Gedin, *Literature in the Marketplace* (Woodstock, NY: Overlook Press, 1977), pp. 54, 178. Critics of this persuasion have often supported resale price maintenance for books, arguing that it allows for a greater variety of published titles and of bookstores. Gedin also suggests that "serious" novels and poetry should be subsidized by the state, since they cannot survive in the contemporary marketplace.

15 Quoted in Nigel Cross, *The Common Writer: Life in Nineteenth-Century Grub Street* (Cambridge: Cambridge University Press, 1985), p. 216. Buchanan, who attacked the pre-Raphaelites in "The Fleshly School of Poetry," was himself the son of a socialistic tailor.

16 Carey, *The Intellectuals and the Masses: Pride and Prejudice Among the Literary Intelligentsia, 1880-1939* (London: Faber & Faber, 1992), p. 5.

17 Richard Altick, *The English Common Reader: A Social History of the Mass Reading Public, 1800-1900* (Chicago: University of Chicago Press, 1957), p. 171. Overall literacy would be less than these rates, because those marrying would be younger people who had benefited from the steady improvements in literacy through the nineteenth century.

18 Quoted in Altick, p. 171.

19 Altick, pp. 48, 327.

20 Urban areas were allowed to set up public libraries, supported by the rates, by an Act of 1850; county councils were not given this power until 1919.

21 See Tables F6, A8-11, E6 in Simon Eliot, *Some Patterns and Trends in British Publishing 1800-1919* (London: The Bibliographical Society, 1994); Nigel Cross, *The Common Writer: Life in Nineteenth-Century Grub Street* (Cambridge: Cambridge University Press, 1985), p. 206.

22 Altick, pp. 383-386; Michael Anesko, *"Friction With the Market": Henry James and the Profession of Authorship* (New York: Oxford University Press, 1986), p. 46; Walter Besant, *The Pen and the Book* (London: Thomas Burleigh, 1899), p. 29.

23 For sales figures see Altick, pp. 385-86.

24 I am not convinced by the argument of Tuchman and Fortin that the market first welcomed women as writers of popular novels, then moved to exclude them after 1880. Their sample of novels accepted is restricted to a single publisher (Macmillan), and too small to sustain the argument they make. Further, they assume, without evidence, that male authors were "professionals" who could control terms and market access (on the analogy of male doctors moving to exclude midwives). This is not to claim that there was no sexism in the literary world, only that the market was more open to women than almost any other cultural institution—so that, for example, there had been a century of great women novelists in England before the first woman received a university degree. Gaye Tuchman, with Nina Fortin, *Edging Women Out: Victorian Novelists, Publishers, and Social Change* (New Haven: Yale University Press, 1989).

25 *Sunday Times*, 6 April 1997, "Rich List 1997."

26 Say about £120 or more in 2001 prices. However, the circulating libraries who were the predominant buyers of three-deckers insisted on discounts of up to fifty percent; in effect, publishers and libraries conspired to discourage the private purchase of current novels. Details of the three-decker system may be found in Guinevere Griest, *Mudie's Circulating Library and the Victorian Novel* (Newton Abbott: David & Charles, nd [1st ed. 1970]); Norman Feltes, *Literary Capital and the Late Victorian Novel* (Madison: University of Wisconsin Press, 1993).

27 Griest, pp. 17, 145.

28 Sutherland, *Victorian Novelists and Publishers* (London: Athlone Press, 1976), pp. 6, 44.

29 Usually twenty parts at a shilling each—but this was as much as a year's sub-scription to Mudie's. Novels issued in parts included most by Dickens, Thackeray and Trollope, beginning with *The Pickwick Papers* in 1836.

30 Thackeray, Introduction to *Pendennis*.

31 Public libraries were becoming a significant mode of distribution by the end of the century, but they did not have a centralized moral influence of the kind Mudie had exercised.

32 Keating, *The Haunted Study: A Social History of the English Novel 1875-1914* (London: Secker & Warburg, 1989), pp. 245-46.

33 Lawrence Birken, *Consuming Desire: Sexual Science and the Emergence of a Cul-ture of Abundance, 1871-1914* (Ithaca: Cornell University Press, 1988); Regenia Gagnier, "On the Insatiability of Human Wants: Economic and Aesthetic Man," *Victorian Studies* 36:2 (Winter 1993): 125-153.

34 Beginning authors usually were offered a share of profits, with publisher and author sharing the cost of production. See Trollope, *An Autobiography* (Berke-ley: University of California Press, 1947), pp. 62-63.

35 *The Letters of Anthony Trollope*, II, p. 715.

36 Michael Anesko, *"Friction With the Market,"* pp. 54, 209.

37 Royalties did not altogether escape "courtesy of the house," however, because publishers were not supposed to bid against each other by offering a higher royalty than the standard ten percent.

38 For details see Anesko, Appendix.

39 An exception to this prudence was James's (unsuccessful) scheme to make a killing by writing for the stage in the 1890s. Wells, Gissing and Conrad, among others, also used short stories as a source of ready money (Keating, pp. 40-41).

40 After 1892 James also had a private income of at least $1,300 from his father's estate; he had inherited the money in 1882, but assigned it for the support of his sister Alice until her death.

41 Quoted in Feltes, *Literary Capital*, p. 7.

42 Feltes, pp. 8-9. *St. Paul* was also published by Cassell and the controversy died down, presumably because Farrar had come to terms with his publisher.

43 J.M. Keynes went against the tide, much to his own benefit: from *The Eco-nomic Consequences of the Peace* (1919) onwards, he paid the entire costs of printing and gave the publisher a small share of the total profits. He made a profit of 3s on the cover price of 8s 6d—£3,000 on the English edition alone. Keynes never employed a literary agent. Robert Skidelsky, *John Maynard Keynes: Volume I: Hopes Betrayed 1883-1920* (London: Macmillan, 1983), pp. 381, 394.

44 In 1842 the duration of British copyright was set at 42 years after publication or seven years after the author's death, whichever was longer. In 1911 this was extended to fifty years after death, and in 1995 to seventy years after death.

45 In France, visual artists retain an interest in their works—the *droit de suite*—and receive a share of the proceeds on later re-sales.

46 Gissing wrote twenty-odd novels in twenty-three years until his death at age forty-six in 1903. £150 was a typical price; some of his novels brought more, some less.

47 Agents still play a much smaller role in France, where the market for books is restricted by high prices and publishing is more concentrated and paternalistic. Leading French writers tend to remain loyal to one publishing house, which often keeps them on salary in exchange for editorial duties. Bourdieu makes no mention of agents in his discussion of relations between authors and publishers: *The Field of Cultural Production*, p. 134.

48 James Hepburn, *The Author's Empty Purse and the Rise of the Literary Agent* (London: Oxford University Press, 1968), pp. 28, 51; Mary Ann Gillies, "A.P. Watt, Literary Agent," *Publishing Research Quarterly* (Spring 1993): 20-33.

49 Besant, *The Pen and the Book*, pp. 10, vi-vii.

50 Ibid., pp. 20, 23.

51 *The Author* began publication in 1890 and was edited by Walter Besant for its first seven years. It was relentlessly hostile towards publishers.

52 The agent was thus one who reconciled Bourdieu's two domains of economic and cultural capital, and the lack of agents in France makes it easier for critics to think of the domains as formally separate.

53 Hepburn, pp. 1, 80.

54 Ibid., p. 93.

55 Anesko, p. 209.

56 Pinker's other clients included Wilde, Stephen Crane, and Henry James. In general, he was more sympathetic to new or avant-garde writers than A.P. Watt. For Pinker's relations with Lawrence see John Worthen, *D.H. Lawrence: A Literary Life* (Houndmills: Macmillan, 1989).

57 *The Collected Letters of Joseph Conrad*. Ed. Frederick R. Karl and Laurence Davies (Cambridge: Cambridge University Press, 1983—), II, p. 417.

58 Jeffrey Meyers, *Joseph Conrad: A Biography* (New York: Charles Scribner's Sons, 1991), pp. 205, 232.

59 Ibid., pp. 203-205.

60 Conrad, *Letters*, II, pp. 370-371.

61 *Letters*, II, p. 384.

62 *Letters*, II, pp. 375, 368. In 1916 D.H. Lawrence asked Pinker to arrange for him to get a regular stipend of £150 a year from Duckworth; the approach failed (Worthen, p. 60).

63 For the knitting machine, see Chapter Six above.

64 On the earlier development of copyright within England see Mark Rose, *Authors and Owners: The Invention of Copyright* (Cambridge: Harvard University Press, 1993).

65 John Feather, *A History of British Publishing* (London: Croom Helm, 1988), pp. 172-73.

66 Dickens, for example, earned £13,000 from a two-month lecture tour in the U.S. in 1867-68. Between 1854 and 1891, American authors could secure British copyright by being in Canada or the West Indies on the day of publication. Victor Bonham-Carter, *Authors By Profession*. 2 vols. (Los Altos, CA: William Kaufmann Inc., 1978, 1984), I, pp. 70, 77.

67 This condition, a result of trade union pressure, was repealed in 1955 after the U.S. became a signatory to the Universal Copyright Convention of 1952.

68 Anesko, p. 177.

69 The Canadian, Australian and other Empire markets were significant, but not

big enough to induce English writers to significantly modify their works; also, Canada permitted the import of pirated U.S. editions (Bonham-Carter, I, p. 75).

70 *The Collected Letters of D.H. Lawrence* (Cambridge: Cambridge University Press, 1979—), III, pp. 69, 58.

71 *Letters*, IV, p. 278.

72 Anesko, p. 143.

73 The *Guinness Book of Records* estimates Christie's total sales at about two billion copies.

74 Virginia Woolf also found herself making the larger share of her literary income from the American market, despite her entrenched anti-Americanism and her belief that Americans didn't really understand her novels. Of the reviews of *The Waves*, for example, she remarked: "Yes, the plague of half wits from America is already considerable, and one cant even be pleased with their compliments, since they are clearly incapable of adding 2 to 2" (*Letters*, IV, p. 392).

75 Literature in English had in a sense become bi-polar from the time of the "American Renaissance" in the mid-nineteenth century; but my argument is that the single market after 1891 had a specific influence on the relativizing of both literatures.

76 See Frederick Buell, *National Culture and the New Global System* (Baltimore: Johns Hopkins University Press, 1994).

77 George Bernard Shaw told Harmsworth that the *Mail* marked a break between the old journalism and the new. Richard Bourne, *Lords of Fleet Street: The Harmsworth Dynasty* (London: Unwin Hyman, 1990), pp. 27, 29.

78 Carey, p. 58. The price of *The Times* at the time of the *Daily Mail* launch was 3d., of the *Daily Telegraph* 1d.

79 The *Mail* achieved the biggest circulation in Britain (and the world) within three years, nearly a million copies a day. However, Harold Harmsworth bought the *Daily Mirror* from his brother Alfred in 1914 and made it a firm supporter of the Labour Party (which did not interfere with its success in profit or circulation, where it passed the *Mail*).

80 Besant, p. 23.

81 Bennett, *The Truth About an Author* (London: Methuen, 1914), pp. 96, 44, 100.

82 Ezra Pound, *ABC of Reading* (London: Faber, 1951), p. 29.

83 This is the argument of Feltes, though his approach is almost exclusively from the side of production; he sees the capital employed in publishing as "determining in its practices the commodities it produces, down to the last details of text." Feltes announces that his study will try "to avoid the ideologically foreclosing term 'market,' with its residual connotations of free, honest, individual buyers and sellers meeting in a common village space, to exchange simple, straightforward commodities" (pp. 139, 36). This approach begs the question of whether publishers and authors respond to market signals (how could they not?); and it elides the special difficulties of incorporating literary productions into a labor theory of value.

84 This orientation to the past is confirmed by the marginal status of the only future-oriented literary genre, science fiction.

85 Besant, p. 15.

86 Cross, *The Common Writer*, p. 218.

Chapter 8   English Literature and Rentier Culture

1 Walter Bagehot, *Lombard Street: A Description of the Money Market* (Homewood, IL: R.D. Irwin, 1962), p. 2.

2 In 1873 deposits in London public banks amounted to £120 million, as opposed to only £13 million in Paris; if the private banks had been included, the balance in favor of London would have been much greater (Bagehot, p. 2).

3 David Kynaston, *The City of London. Volume I: A World of its Own 1815-1890* (London: Chatto & Windus, 1994), p. 228.

4 Kynaston, p. 166; Eric Hobsbawm, *Industry and Empire: An Economic History of Britain Since 1750* (London: Weidenfeld & Nicolson, 1968), p. 97.

5 Hirschman, Albert O. "Rival Interpretations of Market Society," *Journal of Economic Literature* 20 (December 1982), 1474; Weber, *Economy and Society: An Outline of Interpretive Sociology.* Ed. G. Roth & C. Wittich (New York: Bedminster Press, 1968), p. 186.

6 Robert Foster, *The Nobility of Toulouse in the Eighteenth Century: A Social and Economic Study* (New York: Octagon, 1971).

7 Eliot, *Daniel Deronda* (Oxford: Clarendon Press, 1984), p. 169.

8 Charles Duguid, *The Story of the Stock Exchange* (London: Grant Richards, 1901); E. Victor Morgan and W.A. Thomas, *The Stock Exchange: Its History and Functions* (London: Elek Books, 1969), p. 97. Rentiers often preferred the safer returns from bonds issued to finance infrastructure, again mainly in foreign countries.

9 Kynaston, pp. 7, 30, 88.

10 Quoted in Keith Hutchinson, *The Decline and Fall of British Capitalism* (Hamden, Conn.: Archon, 1966), p. 91.

11 Oxford and Cambridge universities were often intellectually opposed to industry, but the colleges also resisted the building of factories locally because they feared that the wages of their thousands of servants would be driven up.

12 *T.E. Lawrence: The Selected Letters.* Ed. Malcolm Brown (New York: W.W. Norton, 1989), p. 511. Lawrence first enlisted in the R.A.F., though his later service was in the Army.

13 *Letters*, p. 519. His plans became moot when he was killed two and a half months after his retirement.

14 Tanner, *Jane Austen* (Houndmills: Macmillan, 1986), p. 180.

15 Raymond Williams, *Cobbett* (Oxford: Oxford University Press, 1983), pp. 67, 66.

16 Eliot, *The Idea of a Christian Society* (London: Faber & Faber, 1939), pp. 33, 97.

17 George Gissing, *The Odd Women* (New York: Norton, 1977), p. 82.

18 *Cobbett*, p. 68.

19 Quoted in Stephen F. Cohen, *Bukharin and the Bolshevik Revolution: A Political Biography, 1888-1938* (Oxford: Oxford University Press, 1980), p. 20.

20 Bukharin, *Economic Theory of the Leisure Class* (New York: International Publishers, 1927), p. 26. The wine of Tokay belongs here because it is made from late-harvested grapes, covered with the "noble rot" of botrytis.

21 *The Odd Women*, p. 319.

22 Gissing, *The Emancipated* (London: Hogarth Press, 1985), pp. 80-81, 128.

23 Birken, "From Macroeconomics to Microeconomics: The Marginalist Revolu-

tion in Sociocultural Perspective," *History of Political Economy* 20 (1988), 31.

24 Bell, *Civilisation* (New York: Harcourt, Brace, 1928), pp. 209-13..

25 Ibid., p. 246.

26 *The Collected Essays, Journalism and Letters. Volume IV*, (Harmondsworth: Penguin, 1970), p. 205.

27 Quoted in Robert Skidelsky, *John Maynard Keynes: Volume II: The Economist as Saviour 1920-1937* (London: Macmillan, 1992), p. 12.

28 Williams, "The Significance of Bloomsbury as a Social and Cultural Group," in Derek Crabtree and A.P. Thirlwall, eds., *Keynes and the Bloomsbury Group* (London: Macmillan, 1980), p. 63; Wicke, "*Mrs Dalloway* Goes to Market: Woolf, Keynes, and Modern Markets," *Novel*, Fall 1994, 6. Wicke notes, though, how "Bloomsbury" has now been recuperated into the production cycle, as a purchasable "lifestyle" to be delivered to consumers. Laura Ashley in the U.K. and Ralph Lauren in the U.S. typify the commercialization of the Bloomsbury look.

29 Quoted in Jean-Christophe Agnew, "The Consuming Vision of Henry James," in Richard W. Fox and T.J. Jackson Lears, eds., *The Culture of Consumption: Critical Essays in American History, 1880-1980* (New York: Pantheon, 1983), p. 82.

30 Agnew, p. 84.

31 *Henry James Letters*, ed. Leon Edel (Cambridge: Harvard University Press, 1974), II, p. 267.

32 Bourdieu, *The Field of Cultural Production: Essays on Art and Literature* (Cambridge: Polity Press, 1993), p. 68.

33 Orwell, *The Collected Essays, Journalism and Letters. Volume III* (Harmondsworth: Penguin, 1970), p. 239.

34 Cf. Josephine Guy: "by the late 1860s Browning had shown a marked willingness to revise his poetry in acordance with demands for clarity; the 1863 edition of *Sordello*, for example, incorporated some several thousand changes." *The British Avant-Garde: The Theory and Politics of Tradition* (Hemel Hempstead: Harvester Wheatsheaf, 1991), p. 85.

35 Clive Bell, in *Civilisation*, said that no one should have an income of more than £3,000 a year; Virginia Woolf, in her best years, made more than this from her writing alone.

36 Sydney Smith observed, sardonically, that one of their causes should be called "The Society for the Suppression of Vice among those with less than £500 a year." Quoted in Ernest M. Howse, *Saints in Politics: The "Clapham Sect" and the Growth of Freedom* (London: Allen & Unwin, 1953), p. 120.

37 *Essays IV*, p. 347.

38 Forster, *Howards End* (Harmondsworth: Penguin, 1975), p. 134.

39 Ibid., pp. 72-73.

40 In an earlier draft of the novel Forster gave the Schlegel sisters twice as much income, and Tibby £1500—giving the family a total wealth of about £100,000. Mr Wilcox is worth close to £1 million (p. 139).

41 Ibid., p. 112.

42 Forster paid tribute to Gaskell in "The Charm and Strength of Mrs Gaskell," *Sunday Times*, 7 April 1957, p. 10. He mentions having met Gaskell's daughters when he was a boy.

43 Elizabeth Gaskell, *North and South* (Harmondsworth: Penguin 1970), p. 529.

44 "The Challenge of Our Time," in *Two Cheers for Democracy* (Harmondsworth:

Penguin, 1965), p. 65; "Notes On The Way," *Time and Tide*, 2 June 1934, p. 696.

45 *Howards End*, p. 28.

46 P.N. Furbank, *E.M. Forster: A Life* (Oxford: Oxford University Press, 1979), I, p. 159.

47 *Howards End*, p. 28.

48 Matthew Simon, "The Pattern of New British Portfolio Foreign Investment, 1865-1914," in A. R. Hall, ed., *The Export of Capital From Britain 1870-1914* (London: Methuen, 1968), p. 24.

49 *Howards End*, p. 196. The cartoon was "The Plumb-pudding in Danger" (1805).

50 Ibid., pp. 192-93.

51 *Abinger Harvest (London:* Edward Arnold, 1953), p. 399.

52 Hobson, *The Export of Capital* (London: Constable, 1914), p. xxv. See also Perry Anderson, "The Figures of Descent," *New Left Review*, 161 (Jan/Feb 1987).

53 Hobson, p. 236.

54 *Howards End*, p. 176.

55 Ibid., p. 302.

56 *Marianne Thornton* (New York: Harcourt, Brace, 1956), p. 9.

57 The attitude to such rites in *North and South* is quite different. When Margaret Hale goes back to visit her old village in the South, she is shocked to hear that one of the villagers had tried to control the "powers of darkness" by roasting alive her neighbor's cat (pp. 477-78). This "practical paganism" is contrasted to the more progressive attitudes of the industrial North.

58 *Selected Letters of E. M. Forster*, eds. Mary Lago and P. N. Furbank (Cambridge: Harvard University Press, 1985), pp. 11, 107. Compare J. M. Keynes on the "gradual disappearance of a rate of return on accumulated wealth" (the "euthanasia of the rentier"): "A man would still be free to accumulate his earned income with a view to spending it at a later date. But his accumulation would not grow. He would simply be in the position of Pope's father, who, when he retired from business, carried a chest of guineas with him to his villa at Twickenham and met his household expenses from it as required." *The General Theory of Employment, Interest and Money* (London: Macmillan, 1973), p. 221.

59 *Time and Tide*, 23 June 1934, p. 797. The discussion is in the issues of 2 through 23 June.

60 As usual, Forster himself anticipated this criticism: "there is a huge economic movement which has been taking the whole world, Great Britain included, from agriculture towards industrialism. That began about a hundred and fifty years ago, but since 1918 it has accelerated to an enormous speed, bringing all sorts of changes into national and personal life. . . . It has meant the destruction of feudalism and relationship based on the land, it has meant the transference of power from the aristocrat to the bureaucrat and the manager and the technician. Perhaps it will mean democracy, but it has not meant it yet, and personally I hate it. So I imagine do most writers, however loyally they try to sing its praises and to hymn the machine." *Two Cheers for Democracy*, p. 278.

61 *Howards End*, p. 239.

62 *North and South*, pp. 488-89.

63 *Howards End*, p. 324.
64 *Commonplace Book*, ed. P. Gardner, (London: Scolar Press, 1985), p. 37.
65 *Downhill All the Way: An Autobiography of the Years 1919 to 1939* (London: Hogarth Press, 1970), pp. 141-145.
66 *The Journey Not the Arrival Matters* (London: Hogarth Press, 1969), p. 99.
67 Balance Sheet, 11 December 1912, University of Sussex Library.
68 GD/LW, 8 Aug 1912, Sussex.
69 *The Journey Not the Arrival Matters*, p. 99.
70 Suffield House was sold in 1924; Hogarth House was leased for a few years at £150 p.a., then sold. Share purchases of about £2,100 in early 1928 were probably made largely from the proceeds of Hogarth House (Woolf papers, Sussex).
71 *Downhill*, pp. 100-101.
72 *Downhill*, p. 121.
73 *The Letters of Virginia Woolf VI*, pp. 200-201.
74 Richard Kennedy, *A Boy at the Hogarth Press* (1978), p. 100.
75 Investment income accounts for most of the "Other" income listed on the table on p. 142 of *Downhill*; in the early years, there was also income from the leasing of Hogarth House and ground rents from the former Stephen home in Hyde Park Gate.
76 Leonard Woolf, *Empire and Commerce in Africa: A Study in Economic Imperialism* (New York: Howard Fertig, 1968), p. 42.
77 Ibid., p. 109.
78 The latter three were rubber companies based in Malaya, Ceylon, and the Dutch Indies.
79 When making new investments in the thirties Leonard did steer clear of colonial issues (except for £272 put into United Sua Betong in 1934, but soon sold). The stocks he had were all long-term losers, which may have been why he held on to them.
80 *Diary, Volume IV*, p. 326.
81 *Letters, Volume VI*, pp. 107, 353.
82 *Downhill*, pp. 52-63, 129.
83 *The Captain's Death Bed* (London: Hogarth Press, 1950), p. 214.
84 *Letters, Volume V*, p. 312; *Letters, Volume VI*, p. 459.
85 *A Moment's Liberty: The Shorter Diary of Virginia Woolf.* (London: Hogarth Press, 1990), p. 243; *Diary, Volume IV*, p. 3.
86 *Sowing* (1960), p. 38.

Chapter 9   Paying for Modernism

1 These payments are roughly equivalent to £173,000 and £577,000 in 2001 values.
2 Joyce Wexler's *Who Paid for Modernism?* (Fayetteville: University of Arkansas Press, 1997) focuses on the conflict between art and money in the publishing careers of Conrad, Joyce and Lawrence, all of whom were clients of the agent J.B. Pinker. My own approach emphasizes the regime of modernist patronage, but Wexler usefully brings out contradictions in the Flaubertian creed of artistic impersonality and contempt for the market.

3 Qualitative changes in status were associated with quantitative shifts: the census category of "Authors, Editors, Journalists" grew from 6,111 in 1881 to 8272 in 1891, 11,060 in 1901, and 13,786 in 1911. *Census of England and Wales, General Report* (London: HMSO, 1904). This increase of more than double in thirty years is understated, because the figure for 1881 includes "Shorthand Clerks," who in subsequent censuses were moved to another category.

4 Quoted in Guinevere Griest, *Mudie's Circulating Library and the Victorian Novel* (Newton Abbott: David & Charles, nd [1st ed. 1970]), p. 139.

5 Eagleton, "Capitalism, Modernism and Postmodernism," in David Lodge, ed. *Modern Criticism and Theory: A Reader* (London: Longman, 1988), p. 392.

6 The transformation of key modernist works into canonical bestsellers was linked to the arrival of mass higher education after 1945, and is beyond my present scope.

7 Capitalists who encouraged such family links with the arts were likely to be in such tertiary sectors as finance or international trade, rather than in manufacturing.

8 Huyssen, "Mass Culture as Woman: Modernism's Other," in Tania Modleski, ed., *Studies in Entertainment: Critical Approaches to Mass Culture* (Bloomington: Indiana University Press, 1986), p. 189.

9 The landmarks: *Madame Bovary*, the "Nausikaa" chapter of *Ulysses*, Sections II and III of *The Waste Land*, *Lady Chatterley's Lover*.

10 *The Letters of T.S. Eliot. Volume I: 1898-1922* (London: Faber & Faber, 1988), p. 204.

11 *The Selected Letters of Ezra Pound to John Quinn 1915-1924* (Durham: Duke University Press, 1991), p. 41.

12 Sandra M. Gilbert and Elaine Gubar, *No Man's Land: The Place of the Woman Writer in the Twentieth Century. Volume I: The War of the Words* (New Haven: Yale University Press, 1988), pp. 143, 146-47.

13 John Harwood, *Olivia Shakespear and W.B. Yeats: After Long Silence* (Houndmills: Macmillan Press, 1989).

14 Yeats, *Autobiographies* (London: Macmillan, 1955), p. 409.

15 Harwood, pp. 144, 179.

16 Carpenter, *A Serious Character: The Life of Ezra Pound* (London: Faber & Faber, 1988), p. 235.

17 Dorothy's uncle Herbert Leaf gave her £1,000 in 1928 and her mother gave her £5,000 in 1931. All this money seems to have been put into Italian bonds which became worthless during the war, so that Pound relied at that time on the $2,000 a year he was given for his propaganda broadcasts. After the war, Dorothy's inheritances from her mother and her uncle Henry Tucker, which had been blocked in London, were released; they amounted to about £40,000 (Harwood, pp. 179-181, 192).

18 Gilbert & Gubar (p. 147) list the principal female sponsors of modernism.

19 Jane Lidderdale, and Mary Nicholson, *Dear Miss Weaver: Harriet Shaw Weaver 1876-1961* (New York: Viking, 1970).

20 Pound, *A Walking Tour of Southern France* (New York: New Directions, 1992), p. 7. In saying that "Flaubert, Trollope, and towards the last Henry James got through to money," Pound was presumably identifying a novelistic tradition that was more worthy of being taken seriously. Pound, *Selected Prose* (New York: New Directions, 1973), p. 155.

21 Jameson, *The Political Unconscious: Narrative as a Socially Significant Act* (Ithaca: Cornell University Press, 1981), p. 107.
22 Quoted in Carpenter, p. 236.
23 The evolution of the Hogarth Press from the avant-garde to the commercial mainstream – paralleling Virginia's success as a bestselling author from the mid-1920s on – confirms modernism's responsiveness, in the medium-term, to market incentives.
24 Rainey, *Institutions of Modernism: Literary Elites and Public Culture* (New Haven: Yale University Press, 1998), p. 91.
25 Ibid., pp. 98-99.
26 See Grant McCracken, *Culture and Consumption: New Approaches to the Symbolic Character of Consumer Goods and Activities* (Bloomington: Indiana University Press, 1988).
27 Rainey, "Consuming Investments: Joyce's *Ulysses*," *James Joyce Quarterly* 33:4 (Summer 1996), 558-59. It should be noted that Rainey's revision of this essay, in *Institutions of Modernism*, moderates his criticisms.
28 Quinn sold the ms by auction to the book dealer A.S.W. Rosenbach for $1975, much to Joyce's annoyance. Richard Ellmann, *James Joyce: New and Revised Edition* (Oxford: Oxford University Press, 1982), pp. 504, 558-59.
29 "From the Patron to *Il Duce*: Ezra Pound's Odyssey," in *Institutions of Modernism*.
30 Lentricchia, *Modernist Quartet* (Cambridge: Cambridge University Press, 1994), p. 65.
31 Pierre Bourdieu, *Distinction: A Social Critique of the Judgement of Taste* (London: Routledge & Kegan Paul, 1984), p. 1.
32 Horace Liveright wrote to Pound in February 1923: "Just think, Eliot may make about $500 on the book rights of this poem. And Gene Stratton Porter makes $40,000 to $60,000 a year out of her books." Quoted in Rainey, *Institutions*, p. 91.
33 In the event, Quinn's collection was auctioned off after his death at a time of market weakness, and realized less than he had paid for it. B.L. Reid, *The Man From New York: John Quinn and his Friends* (New York: Oxford University Press, 1968), pp. 660-661.
34 On Quinn's Conrad purchases see Jeffrey Meyers, *Joseph Conrad: A Biography* (New York: Scribner's, 1991), pp. 260, 352. The manuscripts were sold in 1923 for $111,000.
35 *The Selected Letters of Ezra Pound to John Quinn 1915-1924*. Ed. Timothy Materer (Durham: Duke University Press, 1991), p. 23.
36 Ibid., p. 26.
37 Ratcliff, "The Marriage of Art and Money," in Howard Smagula, ed., *Re-Visions: New Perspectives of Art Criticism* (Englewood Cliffs, NJ: Prentice-Hall, 1991), p. 147.
38 Pound, *Selected Prose: 1909-1965* (New York: New Directions, 1973), p. 231.

Chapter 10   T.S. Eliot's Personal Finances, 1915-1929

1 *The Pound Era* (Berkeley: University of California Press, 1971), p. 245.
2 *The Letters of T.S. Eliot: Volume I, 1898-1922*. Ed. Valerie Eliot. (London: Faber

& Faber, 1988), p. 107. Hereafter cited as *Letters* (no further volumes have appeared). Various letters to T.S. Eliot are included in this volume. Eliot was no doubt sincere in his dislike of becoming "a professor at some provincial university in America"; but in May he expected to be teaching at Harvard the following year (*Letters*, p. 98), so Vivien probably helped to convince him that he should stay in England.

3 Eliot, *Letters*, p. 104. T.S. Eliot's father will be referred to in this chapter as Henry Ware Eliot, T.S. Eliot's elder brother as Henry Eliot.

4 In 1910, 94.5% of incomes in England were less than £160 a year: Bernard Waites, *A Class Society at War: England 1914-1918* (Leamington Spa: Berg, 1987), p. 87. In general, conversion of prices and incomes across time is more an art than a science. I have used the retail price index at the beginning of Robert Skidelsky, *John Maynard Keynes: Volume II: The Economist as Saviour 1920-1937* (London: Macmillan, 1992), and extended it to April 2000. By this measure, current British prices are 40 times what they were in 1915, 20 times 1920, 28 times 1925 (note that consumer prices doubled from 1915 to 1920, then fell back). An income of £1,000 a year in 1925 would thus be worth £28,000 now. However, £1,000 then was a comfortable upper-middle class income, equivalent to say £55,000 now; the difference between a price conversion and an income conversion reflects the increase in real productivity since the 1920s. Further, people change their purchasing habits in response to relative prices. In 1925 a maid in London might be paid £35 a year, and the Eliots had two of them; but a radio cost as much as it does today. There were more maids than radios then; now there are more radios than maids. Taxes introduce further complications, as do state-supplied medical services and the increase in two-income families. As a rule of thumb – and it can be no more than that – use the price conversion to suggest comparable purchasing power, but double it to get comparable social status. Note also that for the period covered by this article, the US$ was at about $4.90 to the pound; it is currently (February 2001) at $1.45, so that a dollar then was worth only about 30% as much in sterling as it is now.

5 Henry Ware Eliot retired as President of the company at the age of seventy, in 1913. Probate of his will suggests that he owned about four thousand preferred shares, of fifty-two thousand outstanding.

6 The dividend did not resume until 1918.

7 Michael Hastings, *Tom and Viv* (Harmondsworth: Penguin, 1985), p. 87. This information is presented within the imaginative world of Hastings' play, but derives from Hastings' intimacy with Vivien's brother Maurice in the final months of his life. I have supplemented it here from private correspondence with Hastings.

8 In 1916 Eliot moved to the Highgate Junior School at a slightly higher salary; he also did free-lance lecturing.

9 Eliot, *Letters*, p. 132.

10 *The Autobiography of Bertrand Russell: 1914-1944* (New York: Bantam, 1969), p. 9. Russell's remaining private income was about £100 a year (*Autobiography*, p. 127), so he had given nearly two-thirds of his capital to the Eliots; though his notoriety as an opponent of the War enabled him to make money by journalism.

11 Ray Monk, *Bertrand Russell: The Spirit of Solitude* (London: Jonathan Cape, 1996), p. 471.

12 Henry Eliot, Tom's elder by nine years, worked for an advertising agency in Chicago; he was a bachelor. In 1923 he told his mother that his salary had increased from $5,000 to $8,000, most of which he saved.

13 *Letters*, p. 412. The wages are not specified, but probably would have been less than £30 a year.

14 In July 1915, notably, Eliot received eight guineas from *Poetry* for "The Love Song of J. Alfred Prufrock" (*Letters*, p. 106).

15 In 1915, the Woolfs paid over £500 for Virginia's medical expenses. Leonard Woolf, *Beginning Again: An Autobiography of the Years 1911-1918* (London: Hogarth Press, 1972), p. 90.

16 Peter Ackroyd, *T.S. Eliot: A Life* (New York: Simon & Schuster, 1984), p. 77. The letter has not been preserved in the archives of Lloyds Bank.

17 Joint General Manager/Alwyn Parker, 23 November 1923. Lloyds Bank Archives, Book 1382. For this and other details of Eliot's career I am indebted to the archivist of Lloyds Bank, Dr J.M.L. Booker.

18 *Letters of James Joyce: Volume II*, ed. R. Ellmann (New York: Viking, 1966), p. 217.

19 His salary was £475 and his annual bonus £130. This was equivalent to the salary of the manager of a medium-sized branch.

20 Eliot, *Letters*, pp. 177-78. Vivien was writing to Tom's mother, Charlotte.

21 *Letters*, pp. 164, 174-75.

22 Harrison/W.M. Stevenson, 1 July 1921. Correspondence Book 1382, Lloyds Bank. Stevenson's specialist, Mitchell Bruce, recommended a stay abroad (a common remedy for neurasthenia at this time).

23 Also, if Eliot died Vivien would receive a pension from Lloyds, assessed at £60 in October 1920 (*Letters*, pp. 419-20). By March 1923 she would have got a year's salary, followed by a pension (Ackroyd, p. 133). Eliot did not have any health problem that would put his life at risk; it is conceivable that his worries about pre-deceasing Vivien (who was the same age as he was) stemmed from fears that he might commit suicide while depressed. See Ackroyd, p. 51.

24 Ackroyd, p. 133.

25 His first article was a technical note on "Foreign Exchanges." His later contributions, until he left Lloyds in the spring of 1925, were all anonymous, and have not yet been reliably identified.

26 *Letters*, pp. 155, 171, 249, 320.

27 *Letters*, p. 256.

28 The will, with much family correspondence relating to financial affairs, is at the Houghton Library, Harvard. The fourth daughter, Margaret, was mentally infirm. Lyndall Gordon's account of the family finances is inaccurate: *Eliot's Early Years* (Oxford: Oxford University Press, 1977), p. 124.

29 The net value of the estate was equivalent to about £5 million in current UK prices.

30 Apart from "Preludes," which the ms. show to have been set in Boston, there is "Second Caprice in North Cambridge" with its opening stanza on the "charm of vacant lots." *Inventions of the March Hare: Poems 1909-1917* (London: Faber & Faber, 1996), p. 15.

31 H.W. Eliot Jr/Charlotte Eliot: 16 Feb., 3 Nov. 1920; 9 Jan., 3 March 1924. Houghton. These amounts do not include Russell's debentures, or Vivien's capital.

32 *Letters I*, p. 420. Eliot explained that Vivien would not receive anything from her own parents until both were dead; death duties were heavy, and she would have to share the estate with her brother Maurice. When Charles Haigh-Wood did die, in 1927, all his money was put into a family trust controlled by Maurice and Eliot; the income paid for Vivien's expenses and, after 1938, for her support in private mental homes. Hastings, pp. 87-88, Ackroyd, p. 162.
33 CE/HE, 8 April 1922, Houghton.
34 *The Selected Letters of Ezra Pound to John Quinn, 1915-1924*. Ed. Timothy Materer (Durham: Duke University Press, 1991), p. 203. For further details of Bel Esprit see *The Letters of Ezra Pound, 1907-1941*. Ed. D.D. Paige (London: Faber and Faber, 1951), pp. 172-76, and Humphrey Carpenter, *A Serious Character: The Life of Ezra Pound* (London: Faber & Faber, 1988), pp. 409-412.
35 Eliot, *Letters*, p. 514.
36 Eliot met Douglas at Pound's in 1920, and his influence can be traced in Eliot's writing on social issues.
37 Eliot, *Letters*, p. 549. Note that Eliot states his Lloyds income but does not mention his private income or his expectations from his mother. Half of this money was to come from Bel Esprit, firmly guaranteed, and the other half from some not too strenuous literary employment. Seven years before, Pound had spoken of £200 as an adequate income for a serious writer; Eliot was making it clear that he and Vivien were now enjoying an upper-middle class style of life and had no intention of sliding down into bohemia.
38 Aldington, *Stepping Heavenward: A Record* (London: Chatto & Windus, 1931), p. 53.
39 Lawrence Rainey, "The Price of Modernism: Reconsidering the Publication of *The Waste Land*," *Critical Quarterly* 31: 4 (1989), 38. Earnings comprised $150 for the poem in *The Dial*, $2,000 for the award, $580 for American book royalties and perhaps $100 for the Hogarth Press edition.
40 Such as £50 collected for him by Ottoline Morrell and Virginia Woolf in early 1923 (Ackroyd, p. 130).
41 Woolf, *The Letters of Virginia Woolf. Volume III*, pp. 139-40. It was early 1928 before all the money was disposed of.
42 L. Woolf, *Downhill All the Way: An Autobiography of the Years 1919 to 1939* (London: Hogarth Press, 1970), p. 142.
43 Ackroyd, p. 152.
44 Virginia's private response was bitter: *The Diary of Virginia Woolf Volume III: 1925-1930*, p. 41. A full account of relations between Eliot and the Woolfs is in Hermione Lee, *Virginia Woolf* (London: Chatto & Windus, 1996).
45 Michael Hastings, private communication, reporting information received from Maurice Haigh-Wood. Rose Haigh-Wood also came from a moneyed background, and may have had additional private means.
46 Russell, *Autobiography*, pp. 245-46.
47 Eliot/Russell, 22 June 1927. Humanities Research Center, Texas.
48 Henry Eliot/Charlotte Eliot, 5 November 1923. The capital value of Tom's share may have been between $30-40,000.
49 Ackroyd, p. 300.

Chapter 11   The Way We Write Now

1 Bruce Robbins, *Secular Vocations*, p. 182.

2 Sinfield, *Literature, Politics, and Culture in Postwar Britain* (Berkeley: University of California Press, 1989), p. 245.

3 The status of Britain's first such school, at the University of East Anglia, has been validated by the commercial (as well as artistic) success of such graduates as Kazuo Ishiguro and Ian McEwan.

4 Tony Parker, *Russian Voices* (London: Jonathan Cape, 1991), p. 288.

5 Sinfield, pp. 241-50.

6 For the latter argument see John Myerscough, *The Economic Importance of the Arts in Britain* (London: Policy Studies Institute, 1988).

7 Leftists have of course refused or given away financial rewards, notably Sartre with the Nobel Prize for Literature and John Berger for the Booker Award in 1972.

8 Vernon, *Money and Fiction* (Ithaca: Cornell University Press, 1984), pp. 8, 9.

9 Thatcher became leader of the Tory party in 1975, following the resignation of Edward Heath.

10 Drabble, *The Ice Age* (Harmondsworth: Penguin, 1978), p. 20.

11 Ibid., pp. 26-27.

12 Ibid., p. 74.

13 Ibid., pp. 62-65.

14 Edward Heath was also the son of a shopkeeper, but left his origins behind early in his political career.

15 Jonathan Wilson, "A Very English Story," *The New Yorker*, 6 March 1995, 106.

16 "Interview," in Malcolm Bradbury and Judy Cooke, eds., *New Writing* (London: Minerva, 1992), p. 177.

17 Amis, *Money: A Suicide Note* (London: Penguin, 1985), p. 124.

18 Ibid., p. 108.

19 *The Moronic Inferno* (London: Jonathan Cape, 1986) is the title of Amis's collection of essays about his stay in America as a correspondent.

20 Churchill, *Serious Money*. In *Plays: Two* (London: Methuen, 1990), p. 176.

21 Ibid., p. 236.

22 Ibid., pp. 205, 305.

23 Ibid., p. 230.

24 When Nick Leeson bankrupted Baring's in February 1995, having lost over £800 million on the Singapore exchange, many drew the moral that "barrow-boys" like him should never have been allowed to trade on such a scale. But the socially superior management of Baring's gave Leeson a free hand because he was generating for them millions of pounds in bonuses.

25 One might compare J.B. Priestley's play *An Inspector Calls* (first performed in 1945), which assumes that a new Labour regime of planning and self-sacrifice is capable of purging the evils of capitalism.

26 *Serious Money* opened at the Royal Court on 21 March 1987; Thatcher was re-elected on 11 June, and the play transferred to Wyndham's Theater in the West End on 6 July.

27 Talking to Geoff Mulgan, a leading strategist of New Labour, I asked him what

he thought of the criticism that New Labour represented "Thatcherism with a human face." He replied "A human face is always good."

28 *The New Yorker*, 6 March 1995, 106.
29 Random House, for example, is a subsidiary of Bertelsmann; its London branch includes among its imprints Jonathan Cape, Hutchinson and Chatto and Windus (which earlier absorbed The Hogarth Press). Imprints within the same conglomerate may bid against each other for a book, though usually there must also be at least one external bid to justify this.
30 The headquarters of Bertelsmann are in Gutersloh, a small town in central Germany; its 76,000 employees are spread across 300 subsidiaries.
31 On the shifting relations between authors, editors and agents see Richard Curtis, *Beyond the Bestseller: A Literary Agent Takes You Inside the Book Business* (New York: New American Library, 1989), pp. 111-119.
32 Mary Archer, personal communication.
33 Epstein, *Book Business: Publishing Past Present and Future* (New York: W.W. Norton, 2001).
34 *USA Today*, 20 December 2000. In the same year, Rowling sold eleven percent of all U.S. bestsellers.
35 *New Yorker*, 104. Byatt also implied that her earned royalties were higher than Amis's.
36 Curtis, p. 265.
37 Michael Sissons claims that *The Information* earned less than £150,000 of its £500,000 advance: *The Times*, 4 August 1997.
38 *How Hits Happen: Forecasting Predictability in a Chaotic Marketplace* (New York: HarperBusiness, 1998).
39 Amis returned to Cape in December 1996 with a reputed £1 million advance for a four-book package; Cape also paid about £750,000 for Salman Rushdie's next novel (*The Times*, 17 December 1996).
40 *The Bookseller*, 31 May 1996, 16.
41 *The Bookseller*, 10 May 1996.
42 Amis, *The Information* (London: Flamingo, 1996), pp. 130-31.
43 For anecdotal evidence of how an author's looks may affect the fate of his or her book, see Curtis, pp. 148-149.
44 Nicholas Clee, "Final Chapter for the Celebrity Novel?" *The Independent*, 8 Feb. 1996, II: 4.
45 For example, the bestselling title in Dutton's Everyman series is Dylan Thomas's *Under Milk Wood*, with massive sales to Welsh schools. Copyright in this title will now last until 2024.
46 Robert Frank and Philip Cook, *The Winner-Take-All Society* (New York: The Free Press, 1996).
47 The NBA prevented retailers from selling books at less than the publisher's list price; a similar rule is still in effect in France. Since it ended, relatively few titles are being discounted from the publisher's suggested price, but these are bestsellers that account for a significant proportion of total sales. Insofar as bestsellers have become relatively cheaper, and given the high price of books in Britain compared to North America, the end of NBA will reinforce the "winner-take-all" tendency already present for other reasons.
48 Edward N. Wolff, *Top Heavy: A Study of the Increasing Inequality of Wealth in*

America (New York: Twentieth Century Fund Press, 1995). See also Frank and Cook, p. 5.

49 No literary authors figure in the *Sunday Times* "Rich List 1997." The wealthiest writers listed are: Barbara Taylor Bradford, £60 million; Jeffrey Archer, £50m.; Jackie Collins, Ken Follett, £25m.; Joan Collins, Jack Higgins, Terry Pratchett, £20m.; Delia Smith, £17m.

50 In January 2001, Random House offered the first list of "e-books" under the virtual imprint of AtRandom. Hard copies will also be available through bookstores on demand.

51 Jameson, *The Political Unconscious: Narrative as a Socially Significant Act* (Ithaca: Cornell University Press, 1981), p. 140.

52 Ahmad, "Culture, Nationalism, and the Role of Intellectuals: An Interview with Aijaz Ahmad," *Monthly Review,* July-August 1995, 44.

53 The designation "Asian-American," for example, assigns the same identity to Chinese, Korean or Japanese immigrants to the U.S., regardless of historical differences between their national cultures of origin.

54 When the Canada Council was established in 1957 it was given an initial endowment fund, with the mission to foster a culture at arm's length from both the state and the (American-dominated) marketplace. However, the Council has not been able to raise much independent funding, and about ninety percent of its funds come directly from the state.

55 See David Crystal, *English as a Global Language* (Cambridge: Cambridge University Press, 1997), p. 61. A corollary to the rise of English is the rapid extinction of many of the world's approximately 6,700 languages: David Crystal, *Language Death* (Cambridge: Cambridge University Press, 2000).

56 The Kenyan writer Ngugi wa Thiongo decided in the 1970s to write his novels in his native language, as a gesture of resistance against neo-colonialism. However, he also translates his work into English in order to reach a global audience.

57 Frank & Cook, p. 4.

58 Speech to the Publishers' Association, London, 15 March 1996.

Works Cited

Ackroyd, Peter. *T.S. Eliot: A Life.* New York: Simon & Schuster, 1984.

Agnew, Jean-Christophe. "The Consuming Vision of Henry James." In Richard W. Fox and T.J. Jackson Lears, eds, *The Culture of Consumption: Critical Essays in American History, 1880-1980.* New York: Pantheon, 1983. 65-100.

Ahmad, Aijaz. "Culture, Nationalism, and the Role of Intellectuals: An Interview with Aijaz Ahmad." *Monthly Review,* July-August 1995, 41-58.

Aldington, Richard. *Stepping Heavenward: A Record.* London: Chatto & Windus, 1931.

Altick, Richard. *The English Common Reader: A Social History of the Mass Reading Public, 1800-1900.* Chicago: University of Chicago Press, 1957.

Amis, Martin. *The Information.* London: Flamingo, 1996.

____. "Interview." In Malcolm Bradbury and Judy Cooke, eds, *New Writing.* London: Minerva, 1992.

____. *Money: A Suicide Note.* London: Penguin, 1985.

____. *The Moronic Inferno, and Other Visits to America.* London: Jonathan Cape, 1986.

Anderson, Perry. "The Figures of Descent." *New Left Review,* 161 (Jan/Feb 1987): 20-77.

Anesko, Michael. *"Friction With the Market": Henry James and the Profession of Authorship.* New York: Oxford University Press, 1986.

Arnstein, Walter L. "The Survival of the Victorian Aristocracy." In Frederic Cople Jaher, ed., *The Rich, the Well Born, and the Powerful.* Urbana: University of Illinois Press, 1973.

Ashcroft, Bill, Gareth Griffiths, and Helen Tiffin. *The Empire Writes Back: Theory and Practice in Post-colonial Literatures.* London: Routledge, 1989.

Bagehot, Walter. *Lombard Street: A Description of the Money Market.* London: Kegan Paul, 1894.

Barnes, James J. *Free Trade in Books: A Study of the London Book Trade Since 1800.* Oxford: Clarendon Press, 1964.

Barnett, Corelli. *The Audit of War: The Illusion and Reality of Britain as a Great Nation.* London: Macmillan, 1986.

Bell, Clive. *Civilization.* New York: Harcourt, Brace, 1928.

Bennett, Arnold. *The Truth About an Author.* London: Methuen, 1914. [First published serially in *The Academy,* 1900.]

Bentham, Jeremy. *The Works of Jeremy Bentham.* Ed. John Bowring. New York: Russell & Russell, 1962.

Berman, Marshall. *All that is Solid Melts into Air: The Experience of Modernity.* New York: Simon & Schuster, 1982.

Besant, Walter. *The Pen and the Book.* London: Thomas Burleigh, 1899.

Birken, Lawrence. *Consuming Desire: Sexual Science and the Emergence of a Culture of Abundance, 1871-1914.* Ithaca: Cornell University Press, 1988.

____. "From Macroeconomics to Microeconomics: The Marginalist Revolution in Sociocultural Perspective." *History of Political Economy* 20 (1988): 251-64.

Blond, Anthony. *The Publishing Game.* London: Jonathan Cape, 1972.

Bonham-Carter, Victor. *Authors by Profession.* 2 vols. Los Altos: William Kaufmann, 1978, 1984.

Bourdieu, Pierre. *Distinction: A Social Critique of the Judgement of Taste.* Tr.Richard Nice. London: Routledge & Kegan Paul, 1984.

____ . *The Field of Cultural Production: Essays on Art and Literature.* Ed. Randal Johnson. Cambridge: Polity Press, 1993.

____ . "A Reasoned Utopia and Economic Fatalism." *New Left Review* 227 (Jan/Feb 1998): 125-130.

Bourne, Richard. *Lords of Fleet Street: The Harmsworth Dynasty.* London: Unwin Hyman, 1990.

Brantlinger, Patrick. *Fictions of State: Culture and Credit in Britain, 1694-1994.* Ithaca: Cornell University Press, 1996.

Brewer, Anthony. *Marxist Theories of Imperialism: A Critical Survey.* Second edition. London: Routledge, 1990.

Brewer, John, and Roy Porter, eds. *Consumption and the World of Goods.* London: Routledge, 1993.

Buchan, James. *Frozen Desire: An Inquiry into the Meaning of Money.* London: Picador, 1997.

Buell, Frederick. *National Culture and the New Global System.* Baltimore: Johns Hopkins University Press, 1994.

Bukharin, Nikolai. *Economic Theory of the Leisure Class.* New York: International Publishers, 1927.

Burke, Sean. *The Death and Return of the Author: Criticism and Subjectivity in Barthes, Foucault and Derrida.* 2nd ed. Edinburgh: Edinburgh University Press, 1999.

Campbell, Colin. *The Romantic Ethic and the Spirit of Modern Consumerism.* Oxford: Basil Blackwell, 1987.

Cannadine, David. *Class in Britain.* New Haven: Yale University Press, 1998.

____ . *Lords and Landlords: The Aristocracy and the Towns, 1774-1967.* Leicester: Leicester University Press, 1980.

Carey, John. *The Intellectuals and the Masses: Pride and Prejudice Among the Literary Intelligentsia, 1880-1939.* London: Faber & Faber, 1992.

Carpenter, Humphrey. *A Serious Character: The Life of Ezra Pound.* London: Faber & Faber, 1988.

Caute, David. *The Fellow-Travellers: Intellectual Friends of Communism.* New Haven: Yale University Press, 1988.

Census of England and Wales, General Report. London: HMSO, 1904.

Churchill, Caryl. *Serious Money.* In *Plays: Two.* London: Methuen, 1990.

Clee, Nicholas. "Final Chapter for the Celebrity Novel?" *The Independent,* 8 Feb. 1996. II: 4.

Cobbett, William. *Rural Rides.* London: Dent, 1957.

Cobden, Richard. *The Political Writings.* Volume I. London: William Ridgeway, 1868.

Cohen, Derek. "Constructing the Contradiction: Anthony Trollope's *The Way We Live Now.*" In Derek Cohen and Deborah Heller, eds, *Jewish Presences in English Literature.* Montreal: McGill-Queen's University Press, 1990. 61-75.

Cohen, Stephen F. *Bukharin and the Bolshevik Revolution: A Political Biography, 1888-1938.* Oxford: Oxford University Press, 1980.

Colás, Santiago. "Of Creole Symptoms, Cuban Fantasies, and Other Latin American Postcolonial Ideologies." *PMLA* 110 (May 1995): 382-396.

Collins, Bruce, and Keith Robbins, eds. *British Culture and Economic Decline*. London: Weidenfeld & Nicolson, 1990.

Conrad, Joseph. "Autocracy and War." In *Notes on Life and Letters*. London: J.M. Dent, 1921.

_____ . *Chance*. New York: Doubleday Anchor, 1957.

_____ . *The Collected Letters of Joseph Conrad*. Ed. Frederick R. Karl and Laurence Davies. Cambridge: Cambridge University Press, 1983—.

_____ . *Heart of Darkness*. Ed. Robert Kimbrough. New York: W.W. Norton, 1973.

_____ . *Nostromo: A Tale of the Seaboard*. London: Penguin, 1990.

Courtois, Stephane, et al. *The Black Book of Communism: Crimes, Terror, Repression*. Cambridge: Harvard University Press, 1999.

Cowen, Tyler. *In Praise of Commercial Culture*. Cambridge: Harvard University Press, 1998.

Crick, Bernard. *George Orwell: A Life*. Harmondsworth: Penguin, 1982.

Cross, Nigel. *The Common Writer: Life in Nineteenth-Century Grub Street*. Cambridge: Cambridge University Press, 1985.

Crystal, David. *English as a Global Language*. Cambridge: Cambridge University Press, 1997.

_____ . *Language Death*. Cambridge: Cambridge University Press, 2000.

Curtis, Richard. *Beyond the Bestseller: A Literary Agent Takes You Inside the Book Business*. New York: New American Library, 1989.

Darwin, Charles. *The Portable Darwin*. Ed. Duncan Porter and Peter Graham. London: Penguin, 1993.

Davis, Lance, and Robert Huttenback. *Mammon and the Pursuit of Empire: The Political Economy of British Imperialism, 1860-1912*. Cambridge: Cambridge University Press, 1986.

Delany, Paul. "'A Sort of Notch in the Donwell Estate': Intersections of Status and Class in Austen's *Emma*," *Eighteenth-Century Fiction*, vol. 12, no. 4 (July 2000): 533-548.

_____ . "The University in Pieces: Bill Readings and the Fate of the Humanities," *Profession 2000*: 89-96.

Dettmar, Kevin, and Stephen Watt, eds. *Marketing Modernisms: Self-Promotion, Canonization, Rereading*. Ann Arbor: University of Michigan Press, 1996.

Dewald, Jonathan. "The Ruling Class in the Marketplace: Nobles and Money in Early Modern France." In Thomas Haskell and Richard Teichgraeber, eds, *The Culture of the Market: Historical Essays*. Cambridge: Cambridge University Press, 1993. 43-65.

Dickens, Charles. *Great Expectations*. Harmondsworth: Penguin, 1965.

Dirlik, Arif. *After the Revolution: Waking to Global Capitalism*. Hanover: Wesleyan University Press, 1994.

Drabble, Margaret. *The Ice Age*. Harmondsworth: Penguin, 1978.

Duguid, Charles. *The Story of the Stock Exchange*. London: Grant Richards, 1901.

Eagleton, Terry. "Capitalism, Modernism and Postmodernism," in David Lodge, ed. *Modern Criticism and Theory: A Reader*. London: Longman, 1988.

Edel, Leon. *Henry James: A Life*. London: Collins, 1987.

Edsall, N.C. *Richard Cobden: Independent Radical*. Cambridge: Harvard University Press, 1987.

Eliot, George. *Daniel Deronda*. Oxford: Clarendon Press, 1984.

Eliot, Simon. *Some Patterns and Trends in British Publishing 1800-1919*. London:

The Bibliographical Society, 1994.

Eliot, T.S. *The Idea of a Christian Society*. London: Faber & Faber, 1939.

____. *Inventions of the March Hare: Poems 1909-1917*. London: Faber & Faber, 1996.

____. *The Letters of T.S. Eliot. Volume I: 1898-1922*. Edited by Valerie Eliot. London: Faber & Faber, 1988.

Ellmann, Richard. *James Joyce: New and Revised Edition*. Oxford: Oxford University Press, 1982.

Epstein, Joseph. *Book Business: Publishing Past Present and Future*. New York: W.W. Norton, 2001.

Farrell, Winslow. *How Hits Happen: Forecasting Predictability in a Chaotic Marketplace*. New York: HarperBusiness, 1998.

Feather, John. *A History of British Publishing*. London: Croom Helm, 1988.

Feltes, Norman. *Literary Capital and the Late Victorian Novel*. Madison: University of Wisconsin Press, 1993.

Forster, E.M. *Abinger Harvest*. London: Edward Arnold, 1953.

____. *Commonplace Book*. Ed. P. Gardner. London: Scolar Press, 1985.

____. *Howards End*. Ed. Oliver Stallybrass. Harmondsworth: Penguin, 1975.

____. *Marianne Thornton*. New York: Harcourt, Brace, 1956.

____. *Selected Letters of E. M. Forster*. Mary Lago and P. N. Furbank, eds. Cambridge: Harvard University Press, 1985.

____. *Two Cheers for Democracy*. Harmondsworth: Penguin, 1965.

Foster, Robert. *The Nobility of Toulouse in the Eighteenth Century: A Social and Economic Study*. New York: Octagon, 1971.

Frank, André Gunder. *Capitalism and Underdevelopment in Latin America: Historical Studies of Chile and Brazil*. New York: Monthly Review Press, 1960.

Frank, Robert, and Philip Cook. *The Winner-Take-All Society*. New York: The Free Press, 1996.

Freedman, Jonathan. *Professions of Taste: Henry James, British Aestheticism, and Commodity Culture*. Stanford: Stanford University Press, 1990.

Frey, Bruno, and Walter Pommerehne. *Muses and Markets: Explorations in the Economics of the Arts*. Oxford: Basil Blackwell, 1989.

Fukuyama, Francis. *The End of History and the Last Man*. New York: Free Press, 1992.

Furbank, P.N. *E.M. Forster: A Life*. Oxford: Oxford University Press, 1979.

Furet, Francois. *The Passing of an Illusion: The Idea of Communism in the Twentieth Century*. Chicago: University of Chicago Press, 1999.

Gagnier, Regenia. *Idylls of the Marketplace: Oscar Wilde and the Victorian Public*. Stanford: Stanford University Press, 1986.

____. "On the Insatiability of Human Wants: Economic and Aesthetic Man." *Victorian Studies* 36:2 (Winter 1993): 125-153.

Gaskell, Elizabeth. *North and South*. Harmondsworth: Penguin, 1970.

Gedin, Per. *Literature in the Marketplace*. London: Faber & Faber, 1977.

Gilbert, Sandra M., and Elaine Gubar. *No Man's Land: The Place of the Woman Writer in the Twentieth Century. Volume I: The War of the Words*. New Haven: Yale University Press, 1988.

Gillies, Mary Ann. "A.P. Watt, Literary Agent." *Publishing Research Quarterly* (Spring 1993): 20-33.

Gilman, Charlotte Perkins. *Women and Economics: A Study of the Economic Relation Between Men and Women as a Factor in Social Evolution*. Ed. Carl N. Degler. New York: Harper & Row, 1966.

Gissing, George. *The Emancipated*. London: Hogarth Press, 1985.
_____ . *In the Year of Jubilee*. London: J.M. Dent, 1994.
_____ . *New Grub Street*. Harmondsworth: Penguin, 1985.
_____ . *The Odd Women*. New York: New American Library, 1983.
_____ .*The Whirlpool*. London: Hogarth Press, 1984.
Gordon, Lyndall. *Eliot's Early Years*. Oxford: Oxford University Press, 1977.
Goux, Jean-Joseph. *The Coiners of Language*. Norman: University of Oklahoma Press, 1994.
Griest, Guinevere. *Mudie's Circulating Library and the Victorian Novel*. Newton Abbott: David & Charles, nd [1st ed. 1970].
Guy, Josephine. *The British Avant-Garde: The Theory and Politics of Tradition*. Hemel Hempstead: Harvester Wheatsheaf, 1991.
Habakkuk, John. *Marriage, Debt, and the Estates System: English Landownership 1650-1950*. Oxford: Clarendon Press, 1994.
Hall, A.R., ed. *The Export of Capital From Britain 1870-1914*. London: Methuen, 1968.
Hartcup, Adeline. *Love and Marriage in the Great Country Houses*. London: Sidgwick & Jackson, 1984.
Harwood, John. *Olivia Shakespear and W.B. Yeats: After Long Silence*. Houndmills: Macmillan Press, 1989.
Hastings, Michael. *Tom and Viv*. Harmondsworth: Penguin, 1985.
Hawkins, Hunt. "Conrad's Critique of Imperialism in *Heart of Darkness*." *PMLA* 94 (1979): 286-99.
Hayek, Friedrich. *The Road to Serfdom*. Chicago: University of Chicago Press, 1954.
Heinzelman, Kurt. *The Economics of the Imagination*. Amherst: University of Massachusetts Press, 1980.
Hepburn, James. *The Author's Empty Purse and the Rise of the Literary Agent*. London: Oxford University Press, 1968.
Hertz, Bertha Keveson. "Trollope's Racial Bias Against Disraeli." *Midwest Quarterly* 22, 4 (Summer 1981): 372-91.
Hinde, Wendy. *Richard Cobden: A Victorian Outsider*. New Haven: Yale University Press, 1987.
Hirschman, Albert O. *The Passions and the Interests*. Princeton: Princeton University Press, 1997.
_____ . "Rival Interpretations of Market Society: Civilizing, Destructive, or Feeble?" *Journal of Economic Literature* 20 (Dec. 1982): 1463-1484.
Hobsbawm, E.J. *Industry and Empire: An Economic History of Britain Since 1750*. London: Weidenfeld & Nicolson, 1968.
Hobson, C.K. *The Export of Capital*. London: Constable, 1914.
Hobson, J.A. *Imperialism*. London: Allen & Unwin, 1938.
Holcombe, Lee. *Wives and Property: Reform of the Married Women's Property Law in Nineteenth-century England*. Toronto: University of Toronto Press, 1983.
Howse, Ernest M. *Saints in Politics: The "Clapham Sect" and the Growth of Freedom*. London: Allen & Unwin, 1953.
Hutchinson, Keith. *The Decline and Fall of British Capitalism*. Hamden, Conn.: Archon, 1966.
Huyssen, Andreas. "Mass Culture as Woman: Modernism's Other." In Tania Modleski, ed., *Studies in Entertainment: Critical Approaches to Mass Culture*. Bloomington: Indiana University Press, 1986. 188-207.

Ingham, Geoffrey. *Capitalism Divided: The City and Industry in British Social Development*. London: Macmillan, 1984.

James, Henry. *Henry James Letters*. Ed. Leon Edel. Cambridge: Harvard University Press, 1974—.

———. *The House of Fiction: Essays on the Novel by Henry James*. Ed. Leon Edel. London: Mercury Books, 1962.

———. "The Question of the Opportunities." In *Literary Criticism*. New York: Library of America, 1984.

———. *The Wings of the Dove*. Harmondsworth: Penguin, 1965.

Jameson, Fredric. "Reification and Utopia in Mass Culture." *Social Text* 1 (1979): 130-148.

———. *The Political Unconcscious: Narrative as a Socially Significant Act*. Ithaca: Cornell University Press, 1981.

Jenkins, Gareth. "Conrad's *Nostromo* and History." *Literature and History* 6 (Autumn 1977): 138-178.

Joyce, James. *Letters of James Joyce: Volume II*. Ed. R. Ellmann. New York: Viking, 1966.

———. *A Portrait of the Artist as a Young Man*. New York: Viking, 1964.

Karl, Frederick. *Joseph Conrad: The Three Lives*. London: Faber & Faber, 1979.

Keat, Russell. *Cultural Goods and the Limits of the Market*. Houndmills: Macmillan Press, 2000.

Keating, Peter. *The Haunted Study: A Social History of the English Novel 1875-1914*. London: Secker & Warburg, 1989.

Kennedy, Richard. *A Boy at the Hogarth Press*. Harmondsworth: Penguin, 1978.

Kenner, Hugh. *The Pound Era*. Berkeley: University of California Press, 1971.

———. *A Sinking Island: The Modern English Writers*. London: Barrie & Jenkins, 1988.

Keynes, J.M. *The Economic Consequences of the Peace*. New York: Harcourt Brace, 1920.

———. *The General Theory of Employment, Interest and Money*. London: Macmillan, 1973.

Kynaston, David. *The City of London. Volume I: A World of its Own 1815-1890*. London: Chatto & Windus, 1994.

Lawrence, D.H. *The Collected Letters of D.H. Lawrence*. Ed. James T. Boulton. Cambridge: Cambridge University Press, 1979—.

Lawrence, T.E. *T.E. Lawrence: The Selected Letters*. Ed. Malcolm Brown. New York: W.W. Norton, 1989.

Lee, Alan J. *The Origins of the Popular Press in England, 1855-1914*. London: Croom Helm, 1976.

Lee, Hermione. *Virginia Woolf*. London: Chatto & Windus, 1996.

Lenin, V.I. *Imperialism, the Highest Stage of Capitalism*. Peking: Foreign Languages, 1973.

Lentricchia, Frank. *Modernist Quartet*. Cambridge: Cambridge University Press, 1994.

Lewis, Thomas J. "Persuasion, Domination and Exchange: Adam Smith on the Political Consequences of Markets," *Canadian Journal of Political Science* XXXIII: 2 (June 2000): 273-89.

Lidderdale, Jane, and Mary Nicholson. *Dear Miss Weaver: Harriet Shaw Weaver 1876-1961*. New York: Viking, 1970.

Macherey, Pierre. *A Theory of Literary Production*. London: Routledge & Kegan Paul,

1978.

Marx, Karl. *Early Writings*. Harmondsworth: Penguin, 1975.

McClure, John. "The Rhetoric of Restraint: *Heart of Darkness.*" *Nineteenth Century Fiction* 32, no. 3 (1977): 310-26.

McCracken, Grant. *Culture and Consumption: New Approaches to the Symbolic Character of Consumer Goods and Activities*. Bloomington: Indiana University Press, 1988.

McDonald, Peter. *British Literary Culture and Publishing Practice 1880-1914*. Cambridge: Cambridge University Press, 1997.

McMaster, Juliet. "Trollope's Country Estates." In John Halperin, ed., *Trollope Centenary Essays*. London and Basingstoke: The Macmillan Press, 1982. 70-85.

Mehta, Ved. *Remembering Mr Shawn's* New Yorker. Woodstock, NY: Overlook Press, 1998.

Meyers, Jeffrey. *Joseph Conrad: A Biography*. New York: Scribner's, 1991.

Michaels, Walter Benn. *The Gold Standard and the Logic of Naturalism: American Literature at the Turn of the Century*. Berkeley: University of California Press, 1987.

Mingay, G.E. *Land and Society in England 1750-1980*. London: Longman, 1994.

Monk, Ray. *Bertrand Russell: The Spirit of Solitude*. London: Jonathan Cape, 1996.

Montéon, Michael. *Chile in the Nitrate Era: The Evolution of Economic Dependence, 1880-1930*. Madison: University of Wisconsin Press, 1982.

Moore, Stanley. *Marx Versus Markets*. University Park: Pennsylvania State University Press, 1993.

Morgan, E. Victor & Thomas, W.A. *The Stock Exchange: Its History and Functions*. London: Elek Books, 1969.

Myerscough, John. *The Economic Importance of the Arts in Britain*. London: Policy Studies Institute, 1988.

Najder, Zdzislaw. *Conrad's Polish Background: Letters to and from Polish Friends*. Tr. Halina Carroll. London: Oxford University Press, 1964.

Netzer, Dick. *The Subsidized Muse: Public Support for the Arts in the United States*. Cambridge: Cambridge University Press, 1978.

O'Brien, Patrick K. "The Costs and Benefits of British Imperialism 1846-1914." *Past and Present* 120 (August 1988): 163-200.

O'Dair, Sharon K. "The Status of Class in Shakespeare; or, Why Critics Love to Hate Capitalism." In Viviana Comensoli and Paul Stevens, eds, *Discontinuities: New Essays on Renaissance Literature and Criticism*. Toronto: University of Toronto Press, 1998. 201-23.

Orwell, George. *Burmese Days*. Harmondsworth: Penguin, 1967.

____ . *The Collected Essays, Journalism and Letters. Volume III: As I Please 1940-43*. Harmondsworth: Penguin, 1970.

____ . *The Collected Essays, Journalism and Letters. Volume IV: In Front of Your Nose 1945-1950*. Ed. Sonia Orwell and Ian Angus. Harmondsworth: Penguin, 1970.

____ . *Down and Out in Paris and London*. London: Secker & Warburg, 1986.

Parker, Tony. *Russian Voices*. London: Jonathan Cape, 1991.

Parry, Benita. *Conrad and Imperialism: Ideological Boundaries and Visionary Frontiers*. London: Macmillan, 1983.

____ . "Narrating Imperialism: *Nostromo's* Dystopia." In Keith Ansell-Pearson, Benita Parry and Judith Squires, eds, *The Gravity of History: Reflections on the Work of Edward Said*. London: Lawrence and Wishart, 1997. 227-246.

____ . "Problems in Current Theories of Colonial Discourse." *Oxford Literary Review*

9, nos. 1-2 (1987): 27-58.

Peacock, T.L. "A Mood Of My Own Mind." (1825; pub. 1837) In *The Works of Thomas Love Peacock*, 10 vols. (New York: AMS Press, 1967), VII, p. 115.

Platt, D.C.M. *Finance, Trade, and Politics in British Foreign Policy 1815-1914*. Oxford: Clarendon Press, 1968.

Pound, Ezra. *ABC of Reading*. London: Faber, 1951.

_____ . *The Letters of Ezra Pound, 1907-1941*. Ed. D.D. Paige. London: Faber and Faber, 1951.

_____ . *Pound/Joyce: The Letters of Ezra Pound to James Joyce*. Ed. Forrest Read. London: Faber & Faber, 1967.

_____ . *The Selected Letters of Ezra Pound to John Quinn 1915-1924*. Ed. Timothy Materer. Durham: Duke University Press, 1991.

_____ . *Selected Prose: 1909-1965*. New York: New Directions, 1973.

_____ . *A Walking Tour of Southern France*. Ed. Richard Sieburth. New York: New Directions, 1992.

Prebisch, Raúl. *Capitalismo Periférico: Crisis y Transformación*. Mexico: Fondo de Cultura Económica, 1984.

Pynchon, Thomas. *Gravity's Rainbow*. New York: Viking, 1973.

Rackham, Oliver. *The History of the Countryside*. London: Weidenfeld and Nicolson, 1995.

Rainey, Lawrence. "Consuming Investments: Joyce's *Ulysses*." *James Joyce Quarterly* 33:4 (Summer 1996): 531-67.

_____ . *Institutions of Modernism: Literary Elites and Public Culture*. New Haven: Yale University Press, 1998.

_____ . "The Price of Modernism: Reconsidering the Publication of *The Waste Land*." *Critical Quarterly* 31: 4 (1989): 21-47.

Rassuli, Kathleen M. "Evidence of Marketing Strategy in th Early Printed Book Trade." In Nevett, Terence & Ronald Fullerton, eds, *Historical Perspectives in Marketing: Essays in Honor of Stanley C. Hollander*. Lexington, Mass.: Lexington Books, 1988. 91-107.

Ratcliff, Carter. "The Marriage of Art and Money." In Howard Smagula, ed., *Re-Visions: New Perspectives of Art Criticism*. Englewood Cliffs, NJ: Prentice-Hall, 1991.

Reid, B.L. *The Man From New York: John Quinn and his Friends*. New York: Oxford University Press, 1968.

Ricardo, David. *On the Principles of Political Economy and Taxation*. Cambridge: Cambridge University Press, 1986. 1st ed. 1817.

Robbins, Bruce. *Secular Vocations: Intellectuals, Professionalism, Culture*. London: Verso, 1993.

Rose, Mark. *Authors and Owners: The Invention of Copyright*. Cambridge: Harvard University Press, 1993.

Rosenberg, Edgar. *From Shylock to Svengali: Jewish Stereotypes in English Fiction*. Stanford: Stanford University Press, 1960.

Rubin, Gayle. "The Traffic of Women: Notes on the Political Economy of Sex." In Rayna R. Reiter, ed., *Toward an Anthropology of Women*. New York: Monthly Review Press, 1975. 157-210.

Rubinstein, W.D. *Wealth and Inequality in Britain*. London: Faber & Faber, 1986.

Russell, Bertrand. *The Autobiography of Bertrand Russell: 1914-1944*. New York: Bantam, 1969.

Ryan, Kiernan, ed. *New Historicism and Cultural Materialism: A Reader*. London: Arnold, 1996.

Said, Edward. *Beginnings: Intention and Method*. New York: Basic Books, 1975.

_____ . *Culture and Imperialism*. New York: Viking, 1994.

_____ . *Orientalism*. New York: Vintage, 1994. First published 1978.

Schreiner, Olive. *Women and Labor*. New York: Frederick A. Stokes, 1911.

Schumpeter, Joseph. *Imperialism. Social Classes*. Cleveland: World Publishing, 1955.

Shanley, Mary Lyndon. *Feminism, Marriage and the Law in Victorian England, 1850-1895*. Princeton: Princeton University Press, 1989.

Shell, Marc. *Money, Language, and Thought: Literary and Philosophical Economies from the Medieval to the Modern Era*. Berkeley: University of California Press, 1982.

Shumway, David. "The Star System in Literary Studies." *PMLA* vol. 112, no. 1 (January 1997): 85-100.

Simmel, Georg. *The Philosophy of Money*. Translated by Tom Bottomore and David Frisby. London: Routledge & Kegan Paul, 1978.

Simon, Matthew. "The Pattern of New British Portfolio Foreign Investment, 1865-1914." In A. R. Hall, ed., *The Export of Capital From Britain 1870-1914*. London: Methuen, 1968. 15-44.

Sinfield, Alan. *Literature, Politics, and Culture in Postwar Britain*. Berkeley: University of California Press, 1989.

Skidelsky, Robert. *John Maynard Keynes: Volume I: Hopes Betrayed 1883-1920*. London: Macmillan, 1983.

_____ . *John Maynard Keynes: Volume II: The Economist as Saviour 1920-1937*. London: Macmillan, 1992.

Small, Ian. *Conditions for Criticism: Authority, Knowledge, and Literature in the Late Nineteenth Century*. Oxford: Clarendon Press, 1991.

_____ . "The Economics of Taste: Literary Markets and Literary Value in the Late Nineteenth Century." *English Literature in Transition* 39: 1 (1996): 7-18.

Smith, Adam. *An Inquiry into the Nature and Causes of the Wealth of Nations*. Ed. Edwin Cannan. 2 vols. Chicago: University of Chicago Press, 1976.

_____ . *Lectures on Jurisprudence*. Ed. R.L. Meek, D.D. Raphael and P.G. Stein. Oxford: Oxford University Press, 1978.

Smith, Wendell R. "Product Differentiation and Market Segmentation as Alternative Marketing Strategies." In Enis, Ben & Keith Cox, eds, *Marketing Classics: A Selection of Influential Articles*. Boston: Allyn & Bacon, 1969. 377-384.

Stengers, J. "King Leopold's Imperialism." In Roger Owen & Bob Sutcliffe, eds, *Studies in the Theory of Imperialism*. London: Longman, 1972. 248-275.

Stone, Lawrence, and Jeanne C. Fawtier Stone. *An Open Elite: England, 1540-1880*. Oxford: Clarendon Press, 1984.

Super, R.H. *The Chronicler of Barsetshire: A Life of Anthony Trollope*. Ann Arbor: University of Michigan Press, 1988.

Sutherland, John. *Bestsellers: Popular Fiction of the 1970s*. London: Routledge & Kegan Paul, 1981.

_____ . "Trollope at Work on The Way We Live Now." *Nineteenth Century Fiction* 37, 3 (December 1982): 472-93.

_____ . *Victorian Novelists and Publishers*. London: Athlone Press, 1976.

Swift, Jonathan. *The Correspondence of Jonathan Swift*, Volume II, ed. Harold Wil-

232 *Literature, Money and the Market*

liams. Oxford: Clarendon Press, 1963.

Tanner, Tony. *Jane Austen*. Houndmills: Macmillan, 1986.

_____ . "Trollope's *The Way We Live Now*: Its Modern Significance," *Critical Quarterly* 9, 3 (Autumn 1967): 256-71.

Tawney, R.H. *The Acquisitive Society*. Brighton: Wheatsheaf, 1982. (1st. ed. 1921).

Thicknesse, Ralph. "The New Legal Position of Married Women." *Blackwood's Edinburgh Magazine* 133 (1883): 207-220.

Thomas, Brinley. "The Historical Record of International Capital Movements to 1913." In John H. Dunning, ed., *International Investment: Selected Readings*. Harmondsworth: Penguin, 1972. 27-58.

Thompson, E.P. "The Peculiarities of the English." In *The Poverty of Theory and Other Essays*. London: Merlin Press, 1978. 35-91.

Trollope, Anthony. *An Autobiography*. Berkeley: University of California Press, 1947.

_____ . *The Claverings*. Oxford: Oxford University Press, 1986.

_____ . *Dr Thorne*. London: J.M. Dent, 1908.

_____ . *The Eustace Diamonds*. New York: The Modern Library, n.d.

_____ . *Framley Parsonage*. Oxford: Oxford University Press, 1980.

_____ . *Is He Popenjoy?* London: Oxford University Press, 1944.

_____ . *The Last Chronicle of Barset*. London: Penguin, 1986.

_____ . *The Letters of Anthony Trollope*. 2 vols. Ed. N. John Hall. Stanford: Stanford University Press, 1983.

_____ . *Mr Scarborough's Family*. Oxford: Oxford University Press, 1989.

_____ . *Phineas Finn*. London: Oxford University Press, 1937.

_____ . *Phineas Redux*. St Albans: Panther Books, 1973.

_____ . *The Prime Minister*. London: Oxford University Press, 1938.

_____ . *The Way We Live Now*. Oxford: Oxford University Press, 1982.

Tuchman, Gaye and Nina Fortin. *Edging Women Out Victorian Novelists, Publishers, and Social Change*. New Haven: Yale University Press, 1989.

Veeser, Aram, ed., *The New Historicism*. New York: Routledge, 1989.

Vernon, John. *Money and Fiction: Literary Realism in the Nineteenth and Early Twentieth Centuries*. Ithaca: Cornell University Press, 1984.

Waites, Bernard. *A Class Society at War: England 1914-1918*. Leamington Spa: Berg, 1987.

Wallerstein, Immanuel. *The Essential Wallerstein*. New York: New Press, 2000.

Watts, Cedric, and Laurence Davies. *Cunninghame-Graham: A Critical Biography*. Cambridge: Cambridge University Press, 1979.

Weber, Max. *Economy and Society: An Outline of Interpretive Sociology*. Ed. G. Roth & C. Wittich. New York: Bedminster Press, 1968.

Wells, H.G. *Experiment in Autobiography*. 2 vols. London: Faber, 1984.

Wexler, Joyce. *Who Paid for Modernism?: Art, Money, and the Fiction of Conrad, Joyce, and Lawrence*. Fayetteville: University of Arkansas Press, 1997.

Wicke, Jennifer. "*Mrs Dalloway* Goes to Market: Woolf, Keynes, and Modern Markets." *Novel* (Fall 1994): 5-23.

Wiener, Martin. *English Culture and the Decline of the Industrial Spirit 1850-1980*. Cambridge: Cambridge University Press, 1981.

Williams, Raymond. *Cobbett*. Oxford: Oxford University Press, 1983.

_____ . *Marxism and Literature*. Oxford: Oxford University Press, 1977.

_____ . "The Significance of Bloomsbury as a Social and Cultural Group." In Derek

Crabtree and A.P. Thirlwall, eds, *Keynes and the Bloomsbury Group*. London: Macmillan, 1980. 40-67.

Wilson, Derek. *Rothschild: A Story of Wealth and Power*. London: André Deutsch, 1988.

Wilson, Jonathan. "A Very English Story." *The New Yorker*, 6 March 1995. 106.

Wolff, Edward N. *Top Heavy: A Study of the Increasing Inequality of Wealth in America*. New York: Twentieth Century Fund Press, 1995.

Woolf, Leonard. *Sowing: An Autobiography of the Years 1880 to 1904*. London: Hogarth Press, 1960.

____ . *Beginning Again: An Autobiography of the Years 1911-1918*. London: Hogarth Press, 1972.

____ . *Downhill All the Way: An Autobiography of the Years 1919 to 1939*. London: Hogarth Press, 1970.

____ . *The Journey Not the Arrival Matters*. London: Hogarth Press, 1969.

____ . *Empire and Commerce in Africa: A Study in Economic Imperialism*. New York: Howard Fertig, 1968. 1st. ed. 1920.

Woolf, Virginia. *The Diary of Virginia Woolf*. Ed. Anne Olivier Bell. London: Hogarth Press, 1977—.

____ . *The Essays of Virginia Woolf. Volume I: 1904-1912*. Ed. Andrew McNeillie. London: Hogarth Press, 1986.

____ . "George Gissing." In *The Second Common Reader*. New York: Harcourt Brace, 1960.

____ . *The Letters of Virginia Woolf*. Ed. Nigel Nicolson. London: Hogarth Press, 1975—.

____ . *A Moment's Liberty: The Shorter Diary of Virginia Woolf*. Ed. Ann Olivier Bell. London: HogarthPress, 1990.

____ . "Mr Bennett and Mrs Brown." In *The Captain's Death Bed*. London: Hogarth Press, 1950.

____ . *A Room of One's Own*. New York: Harcourt, Brace, 1929.

____ . *Three Guineas*. London: Hogarth Press, 1938.

Worthen, John. *D.H. Lawrence: A Literary Life*. Houndmills: Macmillan, 1989.

Yeats, William Butler. *Autobiographies*. London: Macmillan, 1955.

Ziegler, Philip. *The Sixth Great Power: Barings, 1762-1929*. London: Collins, 1988.

Zwerdling, Alex. *Virginia Woolf and the Real World*. Berkeley: University of California Press, 1986.

Acknowledgements

In the Preface to his 1986 biography of Richard Cobden, Nicholas Edsall remarked that "Cobden himself and the particular mix of ideas and policies that went under the label Cobdenism . . . have long ceased to be an influence." My Keynesian and Marxist professors, when I was a student of economics in the 1950s, would have agreed; but one of the purposes of this book is to revisit what I was then taught, before I changed fields and became a teacher of English literature. Instead of Freud and Marx, Darwin and Cobden now seem to me the Victorian intellectuals who count for most in our contemporary debates about globalization and the nature of human nature.

My ideas on this subject began to crystallize at the conference on New Economic Criticism, sponsored by the Society for Critical Exchange at Case Western Reserve University in 1994. I am indebted in several ways to its organizers, Martha Woodmansee and Peter Jaszi; to Mark Osteen; and to Regenia Gagnier for the follow-up conference at Exeter in 1998. Above all, conversations with Sharon O'Dair and Deirdre McCloskey helped me immeasurably in staking out my somewhat eccentric position within the new economic criticism. Benita Parry shaped my thoughts on Conrad and imperialism, if to a different end from her work. Crucial ideas about finance and British culture came to me from Elspeth McVeigh.

For support during a long period of incubation I am indebted, first, to a Killam Fellowship from the Canada Council and to research grants from the Social Sciences and Humanities Research Council. Bob Brown, as Dean of Arts at Simon Fraser University, was helpful on several occasions, as was Kathy Mezei as Chair of the English Department. For their hospitality to a visiting fellow in 1995-96 I thank Sir Tony Wrigley, then Master of Corpus Christi College, Cambridge, and the present Master, Professor Haroon Ahmed. Stefan Collini provided valuable comments on

English literary culture. Information on the current literary marketplace was provided by Georges Borchardt, by Bruce Hunter of David Higham Associates, and by Judith Murray of Greene and Heaton. Students in English 803 at Simon Fraser University helped me develop my ideas in the autumn of 2000.

Parts of this book have appeared, in different form, in *SEL, The Charleston Magazine, English Literature in Transition, The New Economic Criticism* (edited by Martha Woodmansee and Mark Osteen) and in *Seeing Double: Revisioning Edwardian and Modernist Literature* (edited by Carola Kaplan and Anne Simpson).

Index

Campbell, Roy, 171
Canada, 189, 210 n. 69
canonicity, 117–19, 121, 185
Cantos, 151, 158
Carey, John, 101
Carlyle, Thomas, 23–24
Carpenter, Humphrey, 151
Cassell's, 108
Catholic Church, 28, 127
Caxton, William, 98
Chamberlain, Joseph, 93
Chance, 113
Christie, Agatha, 118
Church of England, 8, 29, 36–37, 104, 127; *see also* Anglican Church
Churchill, Caryl, 174, 178–80
Civilisation, 130–31
Clarissa, 9, 63
class, 9–12, 28, 85, 98, 100, 117, 118, 119, 133, 134, 178, 206 n. 13; *see also* aristocracy; bourgeoisie; gentry; middle class; proletariat; rentier culture; social mobility; yeomen
Claverings, The, 35–37, 38, 39, 40, 41–42
Clodd, Edward, 126
Cobbett, William, 22, 25–26, 126, 128, 178, 179
Cobdenism, 2, 8, 9, 15, 74, 79–81, 84, 86, 88, 89–92, 102, 203 n. 2
Cocktail Party, The, 171
Coleridge, Samuel Taylor, 122, 175
Collins, Joan, 184
commerce, 2, 9, 11, 21, 22, 58, 61, 66, 70–71, 74–75, 77, 80, 138, 172, 173, 181; *see also* free trade
commodification of culture, 5, 14–15, 32–48, 112, 119, 121–22, 124, 148–49, 153–55, 156, 161, 173, 186–88, 189, 212 n. 28
Common Reader, The, 142
communism, 8, 88, 193 n. 27
conglomerates; *see* multinational corporations
Congo; *see Heart of Darkness*
Conrad, Joseph, 15, 65–77, 78–93, 112–15, 160, 203 n. 4
Conservative Party, 89
consumer culture, 13, 15, 47, 97, 99,

102, 103, 119, 129–30, 174, 175, 178, 189, 194 n. 41
Cook, Philip, 185, 190
copyright, 112, 115–19, 208 n. 44, 209 n. 66
Corelli, Marie, 103
Corn Laws, 79, 91, 138
corruption, 73, 86
Cowen, Tyler, 6
Cravens, Margaret, 151
Cross, Nigel, 123
cultural materialism; *see* new historicism
Culture and Imperialism, 90
Cunninghame Graham, Robert, 85–86, 89
Curtis, Richard, 183

Davis, Lance, 67
De Medicis; *see* Medicis
De Witts, 15
Defoe, Daniel, 125
Delcommune, Camille, 70
Dettmar, Kevin, 5
Dewald, Jonathan, 3
Dial, The, 154–55, 169–70
Dickens, Charles, 10, 99, 102, 103, 109, 115, 120, 121, 191, 209 n. 66
Disraeli, Benjamin, 29, 103, 147
Domesday, 21
domination, 3–4, 65; *see also* imperialism
Douglas, Major C.H., 168
Down and Out in Paris and London, 50
Doyle, Arthur Conan, 118
Dr Thorne, 9, 33–34
Drabble, Margaret, 175–77
Duckworth, George, 142
Duke's Children, The, 19

Eagleton, Terry, 149
economic liberalism; *see* neo-liberal economics
economic rationality, 77, 87
Economic Theory of the Leisure Class, 129
economism, 1, 4, 79, 93, 159
Education Acts (1870-71), 55, 101, 119

Heinzelman, Kurt, 5
Hemingway, Ernest, 150–51, 156
Hirschman, Albert, 1, 126
historicism; *see* new historicism
Hobson, C.K., 138
Hobson, J.A., 127
Hogarth Press, 60, 142, 143, 170
Hoggart, Richard, 173
Holland; *see* Netherlands
homo economicus, 8, 77, 93; *see also* Smith, Adam
Hong Kong, 89
Hopkins, G.M., 127
Howards End, 15, 64, 133–42, 175, 177
Huttenback, Robert, 67
Huxley, Aldous, 150
Huyssen, Andreas, 149–50

Ice Age, The, 175–77
Idea of a Christian Society, The, 128
imperialism, 65–77, 137, 138
In the Year of Jubilee, 54–55, 64, 155
income, authors', 14, 19, 49–64,
    107–10, 110–15, 120, 121–24, 128,
    134, 140, 142–46, 147, 153, 159,
    162–71, 174, 180–86, 188, 189, 212
    n. 35; *see also* patronage; private
    income; publishing industry;
    royalties
individualism, 85
Industrial Revolution, 10, 11, 68, 83
"industrial spirit," 12
Information, The, 180–81, 182–84
information industries, 12, 14
Ingham, Geoffrey, 12
international rights agreements, 112
internationalist liberalism, 86
internet, 186
investment, 24, 30, 125, 128, 135,
    136, 140, 142–46, 156, 178, 214 nn.
    75, 79; *see also* banking and finance;
    foreign investment; money
Ireland, 28, 74
Italy, 11

Jacob's Room, 60
James, Henry, 15, 34, 38, 41–48, 63,
    64, 99, 107–8, 109, 112, 115–16, 123,
    131, 132, 148, 155, 158, 163, 188

Jameson, Fredric, 14–15, 76, 153,
    186–88
Jane Eyre, 61
Japan, 2, 11–12, 189
Jews, 20, 25–30, 179, 196 n. 29
Johnson, Samuel, 93
Joseph, Michael, 112
Journal of Cultural Economics, The, 6
journalism, 51, 59–60, 111, 119–21,
    123, 124, 142, 145, 147, 164, 166,
    168; *see also* magazines; newspapers
Joyce, James, 61, 148, 150–52, 153,
    154, 156–57, 158, 160, 165
Joyce, Nora (Barnacle), 150, 165
Jude the Obscure, 106

Kangaroo, 116
Kant, Immanuel, 92
Kavanaugh, Pat, 182
Keating, Peter, 106
Keynes, John Maynard, 8, 71–72, 131,
    208 n. 43
Kipling, Rudyard, 65, 86, 157
knitting machine, 83, 114
Knopf, 181
Korea, 89
Korzeniowski, Apollo, 70, 114

Labour Party, 7, 102, 142, 145, 172,
    174, 177, 180
land ownership, 20–22, 26, 30–31,
    32–33; *see also* aristocracy
"landed interest," 11
Larkin, Philip, 172
Latin America, 89
Lawrence, D.H., 61, 106, 112, 116,
    152, 156
Lawrence, Frieda, 116, 150
Lawrence, T.E., 127–28
Leavis, Q.D., 100
Lehmann, John, 143
Lenin, Vladimir, 90, 180
Lentricchia, Frank, 158
Leopold, King, 73, 74
Lewis, Thomas, 4
Lewis, Wyndham, 61, 160, 171
Liberal Party, 79
liberalism; *see* neo-liberal economics
libraries, 102